DOROTHY L. SAYERS

A Careless Rage for Life

Published by
Lion Publishing
1705 Hubbard Avenue, Batavia, Illinois 60510, USA
ISBN 0 7459 1922 7

First edition 1992
All rights reserved

Acknowledgments for photographs
Page 1: top, © Bodleian Library, Oxford, UK;
bottom © Mrs Eileen Bushell
Page 2: both pictures © Bodleian Library, Oxford, UK
Page 3: top, supplied by the The Dorothy Sayers Society,
Witham, Essex, UK; bottom © Guinness plc
Page 4: both pictures © Popperfoto
Page 5: Associated Press photograph
Pages 6 and 7: inset, loaned by Dr K. Pickering;
The Zeal of Thy House photos loaned by Miss N. Lambourne
Page 8: top, Glasgow Herald and Evening News;
bottom, © Dee Conway, courtsey of the Lyric Theatre

Library of Congress Cataloging-in-Publication Data

Coomes, David
    Dorothy L. Sayers : a careless rage for life / David Coomes—1st ed.
    Includes bibliographical references and index
    ISBN 0-7459-1922-7
    1. Sayers, Dorothy L. (Dorothy Leigh), 1893–1957—Biography. 2. Authors,
English—20th century—Biography. 3. Translators—Great Britain—Biography. 4.
Christian biography—England. I. Title.
PR6037.A952627 1992
823'.912–dc20 92-19347 CIP

Printed and bound in the United States of America

DOROTHY L. SAYERS
A Careless Rage for Life

David Coomes

A LION BOOK

Oxford · Batavia · Sydney

Contents

Preface

Dorothy Leigh Sayers (1893–1957) is known to millions as a writer of detective fiction, the creator of Lord Peter Wimsey whose infallible (some might say infuriating) intelligence bestrides the pages of a dozen novels.

Not so many know her as a controversial apologist for the Christian faith in closely-argued books like *The Mind of the Maker* and epic-proportioned plays like *The Zeal of Thy House*, nor as the imaginative translator of Dante's *The Divine Comedy* (for Sayers, her most gratifying achievement). And very few appreciate just what a complex personality she was: witty, bawdy, good company, intolerant of fools (many of whom indulged their foolishness in long letters to her), and often downright rude to them; yet someone who kept the existence of an illegitimate son secret from even her closest friends, who 'cried every night for three years'[1] following a broken love affair, and whose latter years were not immune to self-doubt, guilt and loneliness. She was kind, generous, enthusiastic, robust, opinionated, self-deprecating, contradictory—and extremely likeable.

It is this *complex* Sayers—a woman moved, she said, by 'a careless rage for life'[2]—whom I hope to reveal with what Tennyson called 'discriminating love'. It will be done principally but not exclusively through her letters, many thousands of which form part of the invaluable Marion E. Wade Collection at Wheaton College, Illinois. My wife and I were privileged during the icy months of February and March 1989 to spend many happy and profitable hours studying them—and I should like to acknowledge with grateful thanks the assistance of a kindly and informed staff, headed by the then curator Professor Lyle W. Dorsett, and their gift of a Clyde S. Kilby research grant.

Christianity, it is fair to say, dominated most of Sayers' life.

Other biographers, notably James Brabazon,[3] have concluded that her faith owed more to the head than the heart, that she merely exulted in the stimulus of an intellectual godgame. I believe her letters prove otherwise. Admittedly, her faith was expressed primarily in intellectual terms, but this was because she was determined to prove that Christianity does not have to be intellectually disreputable. It does not crumble under interrogation.

For Sayers, the Christian faith was 'the most exciting drama that ever staggered the imagination of man'.[4] Christ himself was no 'household pet for pale curates and pious old ladies', but God made flesh, 'a shattering personality... a dangerous firebrand... hero and victim':[5]

> True, He was tender to the unfortunate, patient with honest inquirers, and humble before Heaven; but He insulted respectable clergymen by calling them hypocrites... He went to parties in disreputable company... He drove a coach-and-horses through a number of sacrosanct and hoary regulations; He cured diseases by any means that came handy, with a shocking casualness in the matter of other people's pigs and property; He showed no proper deference for wealth or social position; when confronted with neat dialectical traps, He displayed a paradoxical humour that affronted serious-minded people, and He retorted by asking disagreeably searching questions that could not be answered by rule of thumb.[6]

She enjoyed herself enormously as she engaged in extravagant banter with, as she saw them, humanists who ignored the facts and churchmen who had watered them down. She laid about her with gusto on such issues as the role of women in society (about which she was ahead of her time), socialism and tyranny, heaven and hell, advertising and journalism.

Lord Peter Wimsey was no Wexford, Morse or Dalgliesh; he was not given to introspective agonizing, nor did he see criminals or criminal activity in anything other than black and white terms.

But the distinguished crime novelist P. D. James, not without cause, has referred to Sayers' treatment (in the novels) of the themes of 'justice, guilt, punishment and the imperatives of personal responsibility . . . the unifying theme in all her work of the almost sacramental importance of man's creative activity'.[7] Some devotees have gone too far, of course, sifting out every religious morsel—Wimsey saying he was 'brought up religious', Chief Detective Inspector Parker brushing up on his New Testament hermeneutics, and Wimsey and Bunter parsing the same passage in the Vulgate, Revised and King James versions until they discover a vital clue.

Also to be found in the later detective novels is a mirror image of Sayers herself, in the form of Wimsey's lover, Harriet Vane. A thinly-disguised autobiographical figure, Vane recalls her 'bitter years' when she had gone to London to write fiction, 'to live with a man who was not married to her'. She had 'broken all her old ties and half the commandments'.[8] And she reflects upon her face in the mirror:

> Rather pale, with black brows fronting squarely either side of a strong nose, a little too broad for beauty. Her own eyes looked back at her—rather tired, rather defiant—eyes that had looked upon fear and were still wary. The mouth was the mouth of one who has been generous and repented of her generosity; its wide corners were tucked back to give nothing away.[9]

Harriet Vane is also highly educated and exceptionally bright; she often out-sleuths Wimsey, and delights—as did her creator—in showing off her powers.

In 1943 letters were exchanged between Dr James Welch, Director of Religious Broadcasting at the BBC, and the Archbishop of Canterbury, William Temple. Dr Welch suggested that Sayers' series of plays just broadcast—*The Man Born to be King*—'have done more for the preaching of the Gospel to the unconverted than any single effort of the churches, or religious broadcasting, since the last war'.[10] Would it not be possible, therefore, to offer her a Lambeth Degree? The Archbishop needed no further persuading. A devoted fan of Lord Peter Wimsey, he believed that *The Man Born to be King* was 'one of the most powerful instruments in evangelism which the Church has had put into its hands for a long time past'.[11] The Archbishop, anticipating no difficulty, wrote to Sayers, offering the Degree.

Now Sayers was by no means averse to honours and dignities. She revelled in pomp and ceremony. Also, she would have been the first woman to receive the Lambeth Degree. Yet, despite pressure from Archbishop Temple, she refused it. Her reasons reveal much of the complex Sayers—uncertain of her own worthiness, uncomfortably aware of personal sinfulness, and fearful of journalists probing into her personal life.

Seduced by letters as honest as these,[12] I set out to discover the story of Dorothy L. Sayers who, as crime novelist, religious playwright, broadcaster, theologian and scholar, pursued truth and excellence; who, as a private person moved by 'a careless rage for life', was loved by friends who still miss her, decades after her death; who was dogmatic about everything, yet—sharing the frailties of human nature—strangely vulnerable in personal relationships. To know *all* about a person is usually to understand and forgive *all*—and Sayers, I believe, proves no exception to the rule.

1

The Battle of the Scripts

When, in February 1940, Dr James Welch, Director of Religious Broadcasting at the BBC, asked Dorothy L. Sayers to 'write a series of plays on the life of Our Lord for broadcasting in the Sunday Children's Hour',[1] he could not have envisaged the outcome of such an innocuous request: a bitter exchange of letters between Sayers and the BBC staff, controversy fuelled by Protestant pressure groups, stirring newspaper headlines, even a question raised in Parliament.

In the midst of it all, Sayers—now free of Lord Peter Wimsey, and winning acclaim as a scholar, dramatist and theologian—strutted and fumed, demanding her own way and insensitive to the feelings of lesser mortals, but also revelling in verbal battle, and pugnacious in defence of principle. The battle of the scripts, as the episode might be called, lays bare some of the strengths and weaknesses of a woman now in her late forties—and at a critical point in her life.

Sayers' initial reaction gave no hint of the crises to come. As long as she wasn't expected to write 'down' to children, whom she believed understood and absorbed much more than adults gave them credit for, she would be happy to put pen to paper.

> When you are writing for children of all ages it is difficult
> to hit on the highest common factor of their combined
> intelligence, but I always think it is far better to write a
> little over the heads of the youngest rather than insult the
> older ones with something they think babyish.[2]

In due course, her first script landed on the desk of Miss May Jenkin, assistant to Derek McCulloch, who was away in

Scotland, and herself an experienced producer of children's plays. So she was within her rights to suggest to Sayers that certain speeches would go 'right over the heads of children'.[3] One such speech was: 'Jove himself, the imperial star, was smitten and afflicted between the sun and moon in the constellation of the Virgin.' Such criticisms—'spots in the sun'[4]—formed part of a letter generally full of praise. Certainly Miss Jenkin could not have been prepared for Sayers' response, which didn't waste space with niceties: 'I shall now proceed to be autocratic...'

> I don't think you need trouble yourselves too much about certain passages being 'over the heads of the audience'. They will be over the heads of the adults, and the adults will write and complain. Pay no attention. You are supposed to be playing to children—the only audience perhaps in the country whose minds are still open and sensitive to the spell of poetic speech... The thing *they* react to and remember is not logical argument, but mystery and the queer drama of melodious words... I know how *you* would react to those passages. It is my business to know. But it is also my business to know how my *real* audience will react, and yours to trust me to know it...[5]

McCulloch, returning to find a shell-shocked assistant, wrote to Sayers suggesting that she come to Bristol, where Children's Hour was based during the war years, to discuss the matter. Sayers sent off another missive:

> Dear Mr McCulloch, Oh no you don't, my poppet! You won't get me to do three days of exhausting travel to Bristol in order to argue about my plays with the committee. What goes into the play, and the language in which it is written, is the author's business. If the management don't like it, they reject the play, and there is an end of the contract...[6]

Sayers proceeded to write of Miss Jenkin's 'blazing impertinence': 'If I am asked to write a play for you it is because

I have the reputation of being able to write.'[7] She now rounded on the hapless McCulloch himself:

> I must also make it plain to you that I am concerned with you as producer for my play. In that capacity you are not called upon to mirror other aspects of your work at the BBC; you are called upon to mirror me. If you prefer to act as the director of a committee of management, well and good; but in that case you cannot also exercise the functions of a producer. You can reject the play, in which case the matter is closed; or you can accept it, in which case you must find me another producer . . . I am sorry to speak so bluntly, but I am a professional playwright and I must deal with professional people who understand where their proper spheres of action begin and end . . .[8]

'Another producer'. Here we reach the heart of the matter. Sayers, far less self-confident than her shrill belligerence would indicate, needed the security of someone known to her; namely, Val Gielgud—brother of the actor, John Gielgud—who had produced her nativity radio play, *He That Should Come*, but who had since been promoted to Head of Radio Drama. At the very start she had pleaded with Dr Welch:

> I am still obstinately set upon Val Gielgud's production. Very likely it is impossible. I do not care if it is. If the cursing of the barren fig-tree means anything, it means that one must do the impossible or perish, so it is useless to tell me it is not the time of figs.[9]

Now she tries again:

> Get me Val, and I will go to Bristol or Manchester or anywhere . . . The brutal fact is this, that I consented to do these plays, representing about a hundred pounds' worth of my work apiece, for a derisory sum, merely because I so much liked the idea that I felt it would be a pleasure to do them. If I cannot do them in my own way, it will no longer be a pleasure . . . My reply to Miss Jenkin was not

conciliatory, I admit, but I knew that I had come to the point where to cede an inch was to cede the whole territory.[10]

Dr Welch, committed heart and soul to the project, decided to tread gently. He had spoken to McCulloch, who offered to step down as producer if that would pacify Sayers. But, before anything so drastic, would she contemplate a meeting in London to clear the air and begin again? Sayers would. And in a further letter to Dr Welch she laid all the blame on McCulloch's 'tactless... misguided' assistant: 'By all means let us pretend that Miss Jenkin never happened, and return to the starting point.'[11] All seemed set fair; but the abused Miss Jenkin chose that moment—understandably but unwisely—to defend her professional reputation against Sayers' charges of 'impertinence, tactlessness and literary ignorance'. With some asperity she pointed out to Sayers that she had produced fifty or sixty radio plays: 'I therefore can claim to know something of radio drama and something of children's taste in it.'[12]

Sayers' furious scrawls in the margins of the letter are clear indications of her mood on receiving it. For example, Miss Jenkin writes: 'Had your play been written for the stage, I should never have suggested altering any lines on the score of difficulty. But a play over a loudspeaker is an entirely different pair of shoes.' Sayers scribbles: 'BALLS!—How would a stage set make the passage easier?' More seriously, beside Miss Jenkin's comment that no author, however distinguished, has 'the right to say what shall or shall not be broadcast in a Children's Hour play', Sayers comments: 'But the author can refuse to write.' And with that she tore up her contract and told Dr Welch that the project was off.

Surprisingly, perhaps, he was reluctant to leave it at that, calling instead for a cooling-off period. He did feel, however, that Sayers was being 'unnecessarily fierce'. He had hoped that 'in the writing of these plays the Spirit of God would be working through you'.[13] That was a red rag to a bull for Sayers, who didn't take kindly to what she saw as spiritual blackmail: 'Dear

Dr Welch, I do not greatly care about arguing a business contract on a religious basis...'[14]

She maintained that the BBC was in breach of contract. Hers contained clauses which allowed approval of the producer and disapproval of anyone tampering with her work. As Miss Jenkin had 'instructed' her to make changes, the agreement was clearly null and void. A single scenario would persuade her to carry on: '*One* management, *one* producer who is not a secondary management and *one* responsible contracting party who understands the nature of contractual obligation.'[15]

The BBC gave in, removing the plays from the control of the Children's Hour team and giving them to Val Gielgud to produce. Sayers, uncouth and arrogant in her fight, had won an outright victory; McCulloch and Jenkin, with right on their side from first to last, had suffered a morale-sapping defeat. But Sayers was a distinguished personality, a household name, a literary heroine of the masses—and, because of that, rudeness was allowed to reap its own reward. That there was more to it than undiluted rudeness—Sayers *needing* Val Gielgud—is borne out by a letter Gielgud had written after working with Sayers on *He That Should Come*:

> As far as anything connected with her work is concerned Miss Sayers is professional of the professionals. She can tolerate anything but the shoddy or slapdash. *Of all the authors I have known she had the clearest and the most justifiable view of the proper respective spheres of author and producer, and of their respective limitations.* [Itals mine.] She is authoritative, brisk and positive.[16]

Sayers at last got her head down, completing five of a total of twelve plays by December 1941, the date of the first monthly broadcast. She provided comprehensive character studies for the actors, and generally helpful notes for the production staff.

But if James Welch had hoped for an uncontroversial series and a quiet, approving reception, he was to be a disappointed man—and, bearing in mind that this was Britain in the forties, it was clear from the outset why this should be so. In *The Man Born to be King*, Sayers set out to bring dramatic realism to the Gospel story, to avoid sanctimoniousness, to use 'the kind of language we use nowadays'. The very name of Jesus, she warned, 'seems to call for that wheedling and unctuous brightness in voice and manner which makes so many irritated citizens switch their wireless off'.[17] She had no sympathy, either, with a soft-centred faith:

> I believe it to be a grave mistake to present Christianity as
> something charming and popular with no offence in it ...
> we cannot blink the fact that gentle Jesus meek and mild
> was so stiff in His opinions and so inflammatory in His
> language that He was thrown out of church, stoned,
> hunted from place to place, and finally gibbeted as a
> firebrand and a public danger. Whatever His peace was, it
> was not the peace of an amiable indifference.[18]

As she toiled to translate the Greek faithfully into a modern equivalent, and studied the wisdom of the sages in her desire to be both theologically and psychologically acceptable, Sayers agonized over the background of the disciples, whom she felt sure were just like the rest of us—even Judas:

> What *did* the man imagine he was doing? He is an absolute
> riddle. He can't have been awful from the start, or Christ
> would never have called him; I mean one can't suppose
> that He deliberately chose a traitor in order to get Himself
> betrayed—that savours too much of the agent
> provocateur, and isn't the kind of thing one would expect
> any decent man, let alone any decent God, to do ...[19]

The Judas Sayers finally portrayed was an impatient man, who wanted revolution overnight; a man aware of injustice and corruption but who couldn't wait for changed hearts to lead to changed circumstances. He felt betrayed by Christ long before he himself dealt in betrayal. 'Jesus ... was hard as nails about the lofty-minded sins ... If He spoke of Judas with almost un-exampled sternness, it is likely that the sin of Judas was of a peculiarly over-weening loftiness ... an intellectual devil of a very insidious kind.'[20] It was a subtle idea, possibly true, and one that many dramatists since Sayers have promoted as their own interpretation.

Christ 'impersonated' on radio, a controversial Judas, updated language—indeed, *additions* to the language by a former crime novelist... a storm could be anticipated and, at a press conference given by Welch and Sayers at the Berners Hotel on 10 December 1941, it duly broke. Sayers read a statement outlining some of the dramatic difficulties involved in writing the plays; she also read, at the request of the Press, chunks of her dialogue.

Away went the journalists to headline just those points likely to arouse objections: the representation of Christ and the use of modern speech. No paper could match the *Daily Mail*'s misleading headline: 'BBC "Life of Christ" play in US slang.'[21] In fact, this referred to a single line in the script, where former tax-collector Matthew admonishes another disciple, Philip, for being naive in the market-place: 'Fact is, Philip my boy, you've been had for a sucker.' Even then the charge of 'US slang' was dubious; Sayers wanted a Matthew with 'a frank cockney accent' and cockney slang would have included Americanisms. (She also described her Matthew thus: 'As vulgar a little commercial Jew as ever walked Whitechapel.' Which, while allowing for the context of the times, still says something about Sayers' unappealing snobbishness.)

Taking up the newspaper reports, and not having read or heard a single script, the Protestant Truth Society and the Lord's Day Observance Society ventured into battle, defending their narrow definitions of the truth which time would expose (as time so often does) as no more than culture tainted by prejudice. The secretary of the LDOS, Mr H. H. Martin, launched an expensive advertising campaign in the national and religious press:

> Christian people have been shocked at the announcement
> of the proposed impersonation of our Lord Jesus Christ in
> a Sunday play on the wireless... The play is also to

---

include the use of many modern slang terms in its presentation of New Testament history—which means in effect a spoliation of the beautiful language of the Holy Scriptures which have been given by inspiration of the Holy Spirit.[22]

Mr Martin pleaded with 'thousands' to write to the Director-General of the BBC. He led the way, making clear that this was not the *first* time the Corporation had offended his Society:

My Council desire to inform the BBC that this proposed theatrical exhibition will cause much pain to devout people, who feel deeply that to impersonate the Divine Son of God in this way is an act of irreverence bordering on the blasphemous. It is a contemplated violation of the Third Commandment which forbids taking the Name of God in vain. The BBC, by its recent continentalising of Sunday broadcasts with Music Hall and Jazz programmes, has already distressed multitudes of good citizens. We therefore make an earnest appeal to the BBC Authorities to respect what remains of the hallowed hours of the Lord's Day, and to refrain from staging on the wireless this revolting imitation of the voice of our Divine Saviour and Redeemer.[23]

Petitions were posted to the Prime Minister, Winston Churchill, and the Archbishop of Canterbury, William Temple urging them to use their power to ban the broadcasts. Correspondence columns in the national newspapers carried little else:

No actor, however eminent, can, without blasphemy, represent the voice of Christ. 'He spake as never man spake.' The BBC is not capable of reversing that truth. To place imaginary words on His lips is perilously near sacrilege.

In the medieval miracle and mystery plays, from which our serious drama traces its direct descent, the Voice of God was heard and none were offended . . . They were accepted as a form of worship by the good Christians of an age more deeply religious than ours.

It seems to me an outrage. The narrative as presented in the authorised version is a literary treasure, and should be so regarded.

The Lord's Day Observance Society cannot be allowed to believe they represent the majority of Christians in this land... Those who would confine us to the Authorised Version I would accuse of being idolators.[24]

A question was even raised in Parliament two days before the first play was due to be broadcast: Sir Percy Hurd, MP—supported by the Council of the Church Association, an ex-Lady Mayoress of London, and, of course, the Lord's Day Observance Society—asked the Minister of Information if he was 'taking steps to revise the script of the series of plays on the life of Jesus, which are announced to be broadcast by the British Broadcasting Corporation from 21st December, in the Children's Hour, so as to avoid offence to Christian feeling?'[25] The Parliamentary Secretary to the Ministry, Ernest Thurtle, MP, replied that it was not the business of Parliament to tell the BBC how to do its job. (Fifty years on, this is a sentiment likely to be greeted with hollow laughter. Progress is a fickle thing.) He might also have pointed out that Britain was currently at war with Germany, and there were more important matters pressing for attention. As Sayers herself realized: 'It's distressing that all this should have boiled up just when Hitler was making all other considerations seem so petty.'[26]

Sayers, in fact, was enjoying herself hugely, and entered the verbal knockabout with gusto. For Messrs Kensit and Martin she entertained mixed emotions. These 'doughty opponents' were securing a larger audience for her plays: 'Their beneficence is none the less real for having been unintentional... The irony of the situation is, however, not of my making—it is part of the universal comedy.'[27] On their specific quarrel with her putting words into the mouth of Christ, she was swift to show their historical shortsightedness:

> This is hard hearing for Protestants, who have hitherto
> supposed that John Milton was a not wholly irreverent or
> irreligious poet. Yet, in *Paradise Regained*, the Son of God
> is made to conduct, at great length, and in a style singularly
> unlike that of His recorded utterances, an argument with
> Satan . . . When Mr Kensit makes a public holocaust of the
> medieval Mystery Plays, together with the works of all the
> mystics, Catholic and Protestant, who have recorded the
> dialogue of Christ with the soul, he must not forget to heat
> the furnace seven times hotter for the great Puritan . . .[28]

Sayers believed that the likes of Messrs Kensit and Martin
suffered from what she called 'the Manichee prejudice'. This
afflicted Protestants rather than Catholics: Protestants were
taught to fear the human body and to loathe the stage; Catholics
had the benefit of being instructed both in a well-rounded doctrine of the Incarnation and in the high drama of the Mass.[29]
Sayers objected fiercely to the newspaper campaign, which re-
putedly cost the Lord's Day Observance Society twelve hundred
pounds—a small fortune in those days: she saw it as a threat to
both religious and civil liberty, and insisted that a stand shoud be
made. The Sabbatarians, she said, had been appeased enough in
the last four hundred years.[30]

The stand was made, the first play duly broadcast, and immediately much of the opposition, perceiving it was on thin
ground after all, reduced its splutterings to a whimper. Dr
Welch recalled much later that even among the whimperers
there lurked a few halfwits:

> One opponent went to the length of accusing Robert
> Speaight (the voice of Christ) of 'personifying the
> Godhead'!—a blasphemy beyond all the blasphemies of
> which Miss Sayers was accused. Others said that
> Singapore fell because these plays were broadcast, and
> appealed for them to be taken off before a like fate came to
> Australia! They were answered by the supporter who

thanked us for the plays which (ending in October) 'made possible the November victories in Libya and Russia'.[31]

More common were letters like these: 'Your play is quite changing the atmosphere in our home, and where there has been resentment and criticism, we can feel it all dying away in the presence of Christ' . . . 'I have long felt that the archaic though beautiful English of the Bible and church services constitutes a barrier to the understanding of religion. I think you have torn that barrier down' . . . 'The very language you use "shocks" us out of worn conventional terms, and I know that the thousands of people who never dream of reading their Bibles, let alone try to understand it, will be led to see the way of Christ as most necessary for our times.'[32]

First play out of the way, the second, which would introduce Speaight as Christ, was delayed for a meeting of the BBC's Central Religious Advisory Committee, which represented every major Christian denomination in the country. James Welch was to call it 'an unforgettable meeting': the members 'boldly urged the Corporation to broadcast the whole series of plays and unanimously pledged their public support of the venture. Why? Because they had *read* the plays.'[33] The Chairman of CRAC and Bishop of Winchester, Dr Cyril Forster Garbett, went further: *The Man Born to be King* was, he asserted, 'one of the greatest evangelistic appeals made in this century'.

That was more or less that. The plays went out live, which meant the cast found themselves speaking faster and faster to finish before the Six o'Clock News. Shortly after the final transmission, the Controller of Programmes for the BBC, Mr B. E. Nichols, offered a delighted Sayers a complete set of processed recordings of the dozen plays—seventy-five double-sided records—and told her that the King himself had 'taken a great interest in the recent broadcasts and asked for particulars of the casts'.[34]

The series was broadcast again in 1943, with only mild protest from the General Association of the Free Church of Scotland (who complained of the 'vast irreverence in the conception'), and new versions were broadcast in 1947 and 1975—the latter produced by Raymond Raikes, who commented: 'If the characters were not to "talk Bible", Sayers' difficulty was, in her own words, "steering between slang on the one hand and Wardour Street on the other". In the event, her break with convention did exactly what she anticipated, and today it's hard to see what all the fuss was about.'

Sayers heard the original broadcasts sitting at home with her husband—and was well satisfied: 'He said it was a "good show" and added that we'd got a good Christ—he's not strong on religion.' But just *how* good was *The Man Born to be King*, which, surrounded by so much fuss, filled the news columns and largely escaped critical attention?

It was, of course, a breakthrough in religious broadcasting. The plays succeeded in bringing Christ, man or God or both, into millions of homes, and making his message comprehensible to those who couldn't understand the Bible. But there was little spark or crackle in the production, no fresh innovative use of radio as *sound*, and there seems little doubt that Sayers' triumph owed as much to the Lord's Day Observance Society as to her own undeniable skills. Incidentally, the Society, decades later, by professing to know how *every* true Christian must feel, still sought to justify its stand:

> The objection which the Society felt . . . was that the play was irreverent and treated our Lord in a manner which to those who have a personal knowledge of Him as Saviour was most objectionable and hurtful. We must confess that the offence now seems mild compared with the excesses to which modern playwrights have gone in relation to our Lord Jesus Christ, but probably the milder incidents, such as that of Miss Sayers' play, were the beginning of the outrageous exhibitions in this field which we witness today.[35]

The Man Born to be King was a triumph for Sayers. Gollancz published it in book form and since then it has been translated into almost every language, including Swahili and Persian. In the fifties there was a plan to put it on television but Sayers refused permission on the grounds that it would be interrupted by advertisements...

> Though, of course, it offers scope: the episode of the feeding of the five thousand presented by Hovis Bread and Mac Fisheries, for instance, would be very suitable.[36]

Val Gielgud's skills, expressed over many years, merited an OBE in 1942; Sayers wrote to congratulate him, expressing good-natured surprise at the decoration 'when you're living in the temple of blasphemy and working hand in glove with me who has, according to my kind correspondents, emulated Judas and committed the unforgivable sin'.[37] Gielgud replied that OBE must stand for the Order of Blasphemous Enterprise.

Sayers, looking back on the battle of the scripts, wondered whether people had been 'shocked by the hanging of God, or merely shocked by the language'.[38] She feared she knew the answer only too well:

> He was executed by a corrupt church, a timid politician and a fickle proletariat... His executioners made vulgar jokes about Him... flogged Him with the cat, and hanged Him on the common gibbet... If you show people that, they are shocked. So they should be... If the mere representation of it has an air of irreverence, what is to be said about the deed? It is curious that people who are filled with horrified indignation whenever a cat kills a sparrow can hear that story of the killing of God... and not experience any shock at all.[39]

No more battles, then, but one skirmish. Sayers had long been irritated with descriptions of *The Man Born to be King* as 'one of the greatest evangelistic appeals'—but, basking in the glow of work well done, she maintained an uncharacteristic silence. Until, that is, Lady Lees, in a *Report on Evangelisation Through Religious Drama*, referred to 'the most notable example of evangelistic broadcasts' which 'achieved the author's purpose in wakening her public's heart and mind to Christ'.

Had Lady Lees left it at that, Sayers might have pursed her lips and let it go. But the Report went on: ' . . . Her object was to demonstrate that a number of quite commonplace human beings . . . killed and murdered God almighty.'

Sayers took up her pen and rather icily informed Lady Lees that she should alter the reference . . . 'her object was to demonstrate'. She had made very clear on numerous occasions that 'demonstration' was no object of hers, and ought not to be the object of any writer on this subject. It was not properly the object of a work of art to preach, teach, convince, convert, evangelize; her sole legitimate object had been to tell the story—nothing more and nothing less. Quality was all important: piety and a prayerful spirit would not turn a bad play into a good one, and all too often sloppy books, amateurish plays and syrupy music provided intelligent people with powerful arguments against the Church. The corruption of intellectual integrity had to be guarded against. Religion might be superior to Art, but Religion should resist the temptation to order Art about; the artist's task was not to do good, but to express truth according to his or her own experience.[40]

Lady Lees kept her reply brief: she would immediately alter the wording as Sayers had suggested. Wise lady.

The story behind the broadcasts of *The Man Born to be King* reveals Sayers as publicly combative, although entertainingly so; brave and gritty; romantically nostalgic in her cherished opinions, and aggressive to the point of rudeness. Yet it is difficult not to believe that, from start to finish, Sayers positively revelled in the controversy, cheerfully stoking up the flames, assuming outrage and aggression while largely unaware of the finer feelings of more sensitive souls.

The story is also of a woman to whom work and the worth of work was an obsession, a creed. Everything else was subservient to it.

People are always imagining that if they get hold of the writer . . . shake him long enough . . . something exciting and illuminating will drop out . . . But it doesn't. What's due to come out has come out in the only form in which it can ever come out... What we make is more important than what we are, particularly if 'making' is our profession.[41]

'What we make is more important than what we are.' It is the comment of someone who obsessively guarded her private life. Most people would say: What we make is *because* of what we are... *because* of what we have experienced, endured, wept and laughed over, been defeated by, despaired of, embraced, rejected, come through. For Sayers, that means turning back the pages of time to the end of the last century, where we find her a privileged yet lonely child who survived, as she was to survive so much else in later years, through escape into fantasy.

2

'Suppose sometime I sinned a great sin . . .'

'Katherine Lammas was born, very characteristically, at Oxford. All her life she remained exceedingly proud of this achievement, which was due to no exertion of her own, but merely to the fact that her father was headmaster of the Choir School at Wolsey College.'[1]

Dorothy Leigh Sayers *was* Katherine Lammas. Sayers wrote barely-disguised autobiography in two hundred pages of unpublished manuscript called *Cat o' Mary*. This, as might be expected, provides fascinating insights into her *true* feelings as she grew up; such a document is invaluable because Sayers spent so much of her life *hiding* what she really felt—and as a result often suffered a bad and misleading press. People who met her and simply wished to chat about the writer rather than the work she had no time for at all.

Cat o' Mary is helpful to Sayers' cause, revealing as it does a sensitive young woman, only too well aware of her failings, and with a disarming ability to mock them. She knew herself well. Without this manuscript it would be forgivable, but wrong, to judge her solely on the level of an arrogant, somewhat brash personality, given to displays of monumental insensitivity.

There came a time, unfortunately, when she abandoned *Cat o' Mary*, possibly as an essentially shy woman realized that it was too risky admitting to increasingly complex feelings and circumstances, even in fictional guise. She also penned thirty-three pages of undated (and unpublished) manuscript called *My Edwardian Childhood*, which describes her first four years of life in Oxford.

That was where Dorothy L. Sayers, like Katherine Lammas, was born: on 13 June, 1893, in the old Choir House, 1 Brewer Street, off St Aldate's. Her father was the Rev. Henry Sayers, MA, chaplain to the college as well as headmaster; her mother Helen Mary Sayers, née Leigh. He was almost forty, she over thirty—at that time quite elderly for parenthood, so they called their only child Dorothy, which means 'a gift from God'.

Time had yet to catch up with Oxford. The town itself had changed little in a hundred years, with horse-drawn trams and cobbled streets. Sayers was to say later that anyone who grumbled about the noise of twentieth-century traffic should have had to endure metal-shod tram wheels rolling over cobble-stones. As for the university, the ideas of Marx and Freud, sweeping through universities in Europe, had received short shrift.

But some changes *were* underway. In 1879, for example, two halls of residence had been set up for young ladies to study. The pace of change was slow, of course; how slow can be gauged from the fact that these young ladies could not consider themselves part of the university proper, and their learning, however profound, would never find reward in actual degrees.

The Rev. Henry Sayers, besides being a classical scholar, was a musician of some repute. Previously he had been headmaster at both St Michael's College, Tenbury, and the Cathedral Choir School, Hereford, and chaplain of New College, Oxford. A high churchman who adored his daughter, his books and his music—not necessarily in that order—dullness seemed his only failing. Mrs Cross, his long-serving organist, remembered him as 'a severe master' who seldom smiled.[2] Sayers was to write after her father's death: 'He bored [mother] to death for nearly forty years, and she always grumbled that he was no companion for her—and now she misses him dreadfully.'[3]

Helen Sayers was much more lively, but also a patient and loyal wife and mother. A self-taught woman, she was the daughter of a solicitor, a great-niece of Percival Leigh, one of the founders of *Punch*, and one of the Leighs whose pedigree was traceable—or so they claimed—to 'Jacobi Ley or de Lygh, who held his lands in Landford, Wiltshire, by Knight's service of Aldrela de Boterell, in the reign of Henry III'. All that could be said of the Sayers' side of the family was that they hailed from County Tipperary in Ireland, and Sayers' great-grandfather was 'agent to one or two large properties' and 'a man of singular piety and virtue'.

Sayers, in *My Edwardian Childhood*, described her father thus:

> ... a tall man ... with a fine nose and forehead, the latter being the more noticeable because he was almost entirely bald at a very early age. The lower part of the face was less powerful than the upper, and his mouth I never really saw at any time, for he wore the rather full and drooping moustache of the period. His eyes, like those of all the Sayers family, were blue.[4]

Sayers' portrait of her mother perceptively went deeper than mere physical characteristics:

> ... a very vivacious and attractive woman. I suppose her long upper lip, strong nose and wide mouth made her face too decided for actual beauty, in a day when regularity of feature was more highly esteemed than it is now; but her broad, intelligent forehead, speaking eyes and liveliness of expression must have made her admired in any period. She was a woman of exceptional intellect, which unfortunately never got the education which it deserved.[5]

In 1897, when Sayers was four, the family decided to move from Oxford to the living of Bluntisham-cum-Earith in Huntingdonshire. Bluntisham Rectory, in the bleak heart of Fen country, where the countryside's monotonous flatness can seem so oppressive, was to be Sayers' home for the next twenty years. She would return to Oxford and write of:

> *The moonlight over Radcliffe Square,*
> *Small sunset spires that drowse and dream,*
> *Thin bells that ring to evening prayer,*
> *Red willow roots along the stream ...*[6]

Several reasons lay behind the move: Henry Sayers was growing tired of schoolmastering; more space was needed to house not only father, mother and daughter, but also Granny Sayers, Aunt Mabel, the servants, and a parrot; and the living of Bluntisham-cum-Earith happened to be one of the richest of the period, worth £1500 a year. Mr Sayers required that kind of money, being a High Tory of generous disposition: any appeal for money, from society or individual, always found a ready response. Sayers, many years later, recalled first impressions:

> I recollect very well my first arrival at the Rectory, wearing a brown pelisse and bonnet trimmed with feathers, and accompanied by my nurse and my maiden aunt, who carried a parrot in a cage . . . The winter must have been mild that year, for the drive near the gate was already bright yellow with winter aconites—a plant which is said never to grow except where the soil has been watered by Roman blood.[7]

Bluntisham Rectory, despite its two acres of garden, towering beech trees, paddock and stable, compared badly with 1 Brewer Street: only oil lamps and candles to see by, only a tin bath in front of the nursery fire to wash in. But there was room now for Henry Sayers' library, and plenty of gloomy space for entertaining the parishioners. Indeed, village life suited the dour Henry rather more than it did the sociable Helen. The nearest neighbours of their own class (and this was a class-ridden area in a class-ridden age) were the rectors and vicars of neighbouring parishes.

The Sayers were traditionalist by nature and traditionalist in their politics; God, they never doubted, had ordered their privileged estate, and they saw no reason for change. Nonetheless, judged by knowledge of the times, not by hindsight, they were kindly and dedicated folk. In a community like Bluntisham, Henry Sayers would have been legal expert, political spokesman and handyman, as well as spiritual comforter and adviser. He fulfilled his duties faithfully, if not amiably. Parish visiting was looked after by Helen Sayers, who also cooked hot dinners for the aged and the housebound. The couple provided all the social services expected by the villagers—nine hundred of them—and no voice of complaint was ever heard.

Bluntisham rests on the southern edge of the Fens —until the seventeenth century an uninhabitable swamp of waterlogged peat. Then the land was drained and made suitable for agriculture by a drainage system of long straight dykes. Such a system continues to this day—safely, apart from one major disaster in 1713, and severe flooding in 1937 and 1947. (Sayers' fictional flood in *The Nine Tailors*, published in 1934, was based on accounts from 1713.) Winter in the Fens was one of Sayers' abiding memories:

> Year after year, someone would regularly observe at
> breakfast: 'We've been having a lot of rain; they'll be
> letting the water out.' Year after year, we could see from
> our front window the overflowing of the Upper Ouse, that
> turned plough and pasture into standing water . . . Year by
> year, Earith parishioners from outlying places excused
> lateness at church by the natural explanation that the
> water was over the causey and they had to wait for the
> ferry. Year by year, a journey by train in almost any
> direction found us looking from the carriage-window over
> a sheet of sullen water, broken only by the lines of sunken
> hedges and the tops of willow and poplar trees . . . When
> we first came to the parish . . . the memory of the ancient
> marsh agues was still vivid, and old women still smoked
> opium in clay pipes as a prophylactic.[8]

Life improved at Bluntisham. The Rectory was decorated throughout. The family, quite well off, dressed for dinner, and dined well. The staff of cook, nurse, three maids and a man-servant doted on Sayers. 'Nice' village children were allowed in to play with her. The amusing antics of Aunts Mabel and Gertrude persuaded her that the companionship of women was every bit as much fun as that of men. Mabel apparently had 'an almost supernatural power of self-detachment from all forms of responsibility'.[9] Granny Sayers was not so popular; her idea of amusing Sayers was to show off her gold tooth at close quarters. When a teenage Sayers fell ill at school, Katherine Lammas felt 'that she must be well again if she could only get back to the cool green garden, with its ancient ivy-hung trees, to the seemly beauty of crystal and silver and fine starched linen'.[10] It was an ordered, conventional, protected, but not unhappy childhood.

Her real friends existed in books. She had 'a robust taste for literary horrors, pleading for the most murderous tales of ogres and the bloodiest parts of Robinson Crusoe'.[11] But her mother always insisted that the terrible events in books could not possibly happen to her:

> Consequently, I was always readily able to distinguish
> between fact and fiction, and to thrill pleasantly with a
> purely literary horror . . . I dramatised myself, and have at
> all periods of my life continued to dramatise myself, into a
> great number of egotistical impersonations of a very
> common type, making myself the heroine (or more often
> the hero) of countless dramatic situations—but at all times
> with a perfect realisation that I was the creator, not the
> subject, of these fantasies.[12]

Sayers, all her life, was no self-deceiver; she knew what she was about, and could be remarkably objective about her deeds and motivations: 'To me, a tree was a tree, a stone a stone, and I myself a child in a white pinafore with a big frill round the neck; nor had any creative fancy the least influence to disturb facts, so solidly and obviously concrete . . . my imagination is purely literary . . .'[13] As Katherine Lammas, she could be mercilessly self-deprecating:

> When Katherine in later years looked back on the childish
> figure that had been herself, it was with a hatred of
> anything so lacking in those common human virtues which
> were to be attained in after years at so much cost and with
> such desperate difficulty . . . Strangers rightly considered
> her a prig.[14]

'The Biography of a Prig' is Sayers' sub-title for *Cat o' Mary*, whose title is explained by accompanying lines of verse:

The cats o' Mary seldom bother; they have inherited
that good part;
But the cats o' Martha favour their mother of the anxious
brow and the troubled heart.[15]

This is 'Kipling, as adapted by Somebody', the adaptation comprising 'cats' for 'sons', and 'anxious brow' for 'careful soul'. In the manuscript children are described as being 'secretive as cats'. In the Bible it is Mary who stopped to listen to Jesus while Martha worried about work to be done. Is a 'cat o' Mary', therefore, someone who ponders quietly and learns quickly, who has her priorities right, and who puts intellect above all else? If so, that is certainly a picture of Sayers.

One story from *Cat o' Mary* will suffice. Each evening, just before bed, Sayers sang a song to the family:

Goodnight, Mamma, goodnight, Papa
Goodnight to all the rest
Goodnight, Mamma, goodnight, Papa
I must love dolly best.

She soon learned of the emotional power to be wielded by substituting for 'dolly' the name of someone currently in her good books. Mamma, Papa, and the rest waited each night to hear who was loved the best—or who was out of favour.

It became an extremely embarrassing business to Katherine, and very wearisome. It was however expected of her. Tedious as the duty became, it never occurred to Katherine to shirk it unless the evening had been a stormy one, and even then the rite would eventually be performed amid hiccups of distress, after suitable pressure had been applied.[16]

For education, Sayers relied on her parents and a series of governesses. By the age of four she could read, and well before her teens was fluent in Latin, French and German. She was just six years old when her father entered the nursery one day, carrying a copy of Dr William Smith's *Principia*. 'I think, my dear, that you are now old enough to learn Latin,' he said.

> I was by no means unwilling, because it seemed to me that it would be a very fine thing to learn Latin, and would place me in a position of superiority to my mother, my aunt and my nurse—though not to my paternal grandmother, who was an old lady of parts, and had at least a nodding acquaintance with the language.[17]

Sayers, no less objective about her talents than about her failings, grew up believing herself intellectually superior to those who loved her and taught her. She had no competition, of course. 'She had a great opinion of her own cleverness, and to be proved wrong was humiliating.'[18]

Being so aware of her own precocious skills, it was inevitable that she would turn to writing. The earliest effort that survives—written when she was about seven—could, if one is charitable, be called mildly promising:

> *The spider with eight long legs was there*
> *The cricket and grasshopper fought for the chair*
> *The beetle and ladybird each took their seat*
> *The dragonflies came with the butterflies fleet*
> *The small tortoiseshell came with puss-moth his bride*
> *The clearwings also, their larvae beside.*
> *And then there swam in all the fish of the sea*
> *In company with the wasp, hornet and bee.*
> *When all was prepared they had nothing to say,*
> *So sullen and moody they all went away.*

About ten years elapsed between that poem and the next, and during that time Sayers conquered the language and found her style:

> *The Gargoyle takes his giddy perch*
> *On a cathedral or a church.*
> *There, mid ecclesiastic style*
> *He smiles an early Gothic smile*

And while the parson, full of pride,
Spouts at his weary flock inside,
The Gargoyle, from his lofty seat,
Spouts at the people in the street;
And like the parson, seems to say,
In accents doleful, 'Let us pray'.
I like the Gargoyle best. He plays
So cheerfully on rainy days—
While parsons, no-one can deny,
Are awful dampers when they're dry.

Offspring of devout parents—raised under a loving but chastising eye, maturing confused with sinfulness, experiment with wilfulness—often grow into adults rebellious towards all things spiritual, or neurotic slaves to a harsh taskmaster of a God. Sayers was among the lucky ones; in later years she had acquired her fair share of neuroses, but faith or the lack of it was not one of them. Her parents, though devout, were not overtly pious; they were middle-of-the-road Anglicans, part of a breed undiminished by the passing of a century:

> For a daughter of the parsonage Katherine was oddly
> uninstructed in Christian dogma. Mrs Lammas . . . shrank
> instinctively from doctrinal argument . . . Mr Lammas,
> actuated by God knows what sense of personal inadequacy
> or nervous dread of intimate personal contact, had
> sedulously refrained from giving any religious instruction
> to his daughter . . .[19]

'Mr Lammas' would have considered daily prayers—at 8.15 each morning, with family and servants present—quite sufficient to instil in 'Katherine' a life-enhancing devotion to matters eternal. Should there be any doubts, however, his further encouragement of Sayers' fondness for hymns would have banished them. Not that his daughter was undiscerning in her affection; as always, she knew what she liked and why:

> When I was a kid, did I like singing 'The King of Love my
> Shepherd is'? or 'We are but little children weak'? or 'Jesus

meek and gentle'? Not on your life. I liked 'Christian, dost thou hear them?'—especially the bit about 'prowl and prowl around,' 'The Church's one foundation'—good swinging, thick stuff, with a grand line or two about heresies and schisms—quite unintelligible, but gloriously rending and distressful; and 'Lo! He comes with clouds descending'—that was *fine*, with all the sinners deeply wailing . . . And all the Good Friday hymns, wallowing in a voluptuous gloom.[20]

'Christian, dost thou hear them?' . . . 'The Church's one foundation' . . . 'Lo, He comes with clouds descending' . . . Sayers was in love with language, with words and phrases that tripped ecstatically off her tongue, or rolled merrily around in her mind. It was at this time also that she became convinced that children are able to benefit from language their years prevent them from fully understanding. (Miss May Jenkin was to feel the force of her argument forty years later.) For example, she was overwhelmed by the wonders of the very un-juvenile Athanasian Creed:

I know I should never have dared to confess to any of the grown-ups the over-mastering fascination exercised on me by the Athanasian Creed. They were kind . . . and I felt instinctively that they would be surprised and amused, and say, 'Surely you can't understand that,' and tell each other about it as a quaint thing I had said. So I hugged it as a secret delight.[21]

'Secret delight' it may have been, but even at that tender age Sayers was passionate for correctness in all things, and wasn't reluctant to comment on what she saw as a 'serious blot' in the Creed:

It was, I felt, quite unnecessary to warn anybody that there was 'one Father, not three Fathers; one Son, not three sons; one Holy Ghost, not three holy ghosts'. The suggestion seemed quite foolish. It was difficult enough to imagine a God who was Three and yet One; did anybody exist so demented as to conceive of a ninefold deity? . . . I found myself blushing faintly at the recitation of words so wildly unrelated to anything that the queerest heathen in his blindness was likely to fancy for himself.[22]

If Sayers revelled in language, she also basked in the glow of the order of things. Having discovered one day in the Rectory garden the post-holes of the tennis court hitherto buried beneath shrubbery, Sayers (or Katherine) could feel she had been

> . . .brought face to face with beauty. It had risen up before her again—the lovely satisfying unity of things—the wedding of the thing learnt and the thing done—the great intellectual fulfilment. Nothing would ever quite wipe out the memory of that magnificent moment when the intersecting circles marched out of the Euclid book and met on the green grass in the sun-flecked shadow of the mulberry tree. [23]

A photograph of Sayers at the age of eight shows a fresh-faced, dark-haired child, wicked wit in the eye, knowing obstinacy in the mouth. It was at this time that two other children were invited to stay at the Rectory to share her education. It was not a happy meeting of minds. Called Charles and Gertrude in *Cat o' Mary*, they only 'confirmed her in the belief that she was cleverer and more interesting than other people'.[24] But five years later, her cousin Ivy Shrimpton—Katherine's friend, Myrtle—entered her life, and was not dismissed so casually. Not only was she to steer Sayers through an exacting adolescence, but she was to play a critical role sixteen years later when Sayers found herself in desperate trouble. Ivy was eight years older than Dorothy, which made her 'old enough to seem like a grown-up person'.[25] Her father had been unsuccessful as a farmer in America, and now the family was settled in Oxford. This experience had given Ivy (or Myrtle)

> . . . more wisdom of the rough and ready kind than any other person in Katherine's circle . . . Her great merit was that she would discuss any question seriously and

thoughtfully, and that if she did not know the answer, she said so . . .[26]

Ivy, at twenty-one, was probably amused—affectionately so—by the thirteen-year-old Sayers' letters, invariably superior and preachy, and without the saving graces of *Cat o' Mary*'s self-awareness and self-mockery. She made sure Ivy knew of her own burgeoning skills, like reading French novels in the original: 'Why don't you work up your French a bit? You'd find it such a help . . .'[27] And she swept aside the complexities of religion with simple exposition, Ivy's attention being drawn to Romans 2 where the apostle Paul had answered the hard question of whether 'savages' would be given another chance 'because of course God wouldn't punish them for disobeying laws they had never heard of'.[28]

Ivy, in her own letters, was content to list modest achievements and share a handful of stories and poems which Sayers airily dismissed. The friendship stuck, however, and a year later—during one of Ivy's holidays at the Rectory—the two of them enveloped the household in daily dramatizations of *The Three Musketeers*. So much so that Sayers subsequently headed her letters 'le Château de Bragelonne' and signed them 'Athos'. Such passionate devotion lasted for over a year, and at its height saw Sayers as Athos addressing Ivy as 'My love' and 'Belle Cousine'. On one occasion she sent a love poem in French: 'If I love you, it is because I have no choice, and because, in the happy days of contentment and love, your heart has taken hold of mine . . .' On another she signed a pledge of lasting devotion: '. . . though ages should sever and oceans divide us; though the tongue of one or both were forever made motionless in the grave, I should still be true, dear heart'.

A sexual preference is not being expressed here. Sayers, it is true, possessed masculine tastes: as a girl, she emulated heroes rather than heroines; as a woman, she dressed increasingly mannishly. But, as events and correspondence amply confirm, her sexual instincts were strictly heterosexual—often passionately so. Sayers was simply indulging, as she often did, in fantasy rather than reality. On the whole she preferred it and, whenever possible, escaped to its comforting regions. She was not to remain an escapist; on the contrary, she was ruthless in demanding, and facing up to, the facts. But she never lost the unfulfillable longing for reality to order itself like fiction.

The adult Sayers would be hailed as one of the great letter-writers.[29] Occasionally, the adolescent Sayers penned letters which linked fascinatingly with those written decades later, and provided just a glimpse of the greatness to come. For example, she wrote to Ivy:

> I suppose you know that I have got a Fräulein here for the holidays. It really is perfectly *loathsome*. It isn't that she isn't nice... But you see I *can not* get away from her... And I hate not being able to get away from a person.[30]

Sayers, who was to point to her work as the sole legitimate concern of others, and to dismiss any interest in herself as a person, wrote in 1940:

> I can't altogether explain my violent dislike of personal interest except that I connect it with the atmosphere of solicitude which surrounded me in childhood and of which I have been trying to rid myself ever since. So much so that I can't be civil if I am told that I am missed when I am away or welcomed when I return.[31]

Another letter to Ivy—a fifteen-year-old addressing a twenty-three-year-old—is twenty pages long and her most important to date. Here we see the first signs of her finding in the New Testament a morality, an ethic, she could submit to willingly. Here, too, as she parades and extols the virtues of tolerance and acceptance, is proof that the head didn't always stifle the heart. Her intellect—which she hoped would be her salvation—was in fact to be her constant temptation. But at her best as a person and as a writer she desired to give head and heart equal credence. That someone fails to live up to an ideal does not invalidate either the ideal or the desire.

The letter opens quietly, with a description of a village con-
cert held on a platform so rickety that 'at every stroke of the bow
the platform shook and danced and swung and sprang and
jumped and rolled and tossed like a ship at sea'.[32] Halfway
through, it shifts up a gear. Apparently Ivy's cousin, Freda,
was thinking of leaving the Anglican fold and becoming a
Roman Catholic. Don't mock her, Sayers warns her friend:

> I should never sneer at anyone or think the worse of him
> because he had changed his ideas . . . In the majority of
> cases . . . it probably requires a lot more courage to
> renounce one's faith and embrace another publicly than to
> march up to the cannon's mouth.[33]

Now Sayers is motoring, and she reaches the destination
planned ever since the modest opening:

> I think, old girl, that you are just a bit inclined to form a
> harsh judgement—or perhaps I ought to say a hard
> judgement of other people . . . I think you are a little apt to
> say, in effect, 'What this man did was an offence against
> morality. It was therefore wrong and inexcusable. I do not
> care what excuse this person had—he did wrong.
> Therefore he is a wicked person and there is an end of it!'
> Dear old girl, get out of the way of thinking that. It is
> terribly closely allied to Pharisaism, which, you know, is
> the one thing our Lord was always so down upon. And I
> think that this attitude towards other people will make you
> have fewer friends, because they will be afraid of you. I
> shouldn't like to feel, Ivy, that suppose sometime I sinned
> a great sin, I should be afraid to come to you for help. Only,
> unless you would try to make allowances for me, I'm afraid
> I should. St Paul says . . . 'Though I speak with tongues of
> men and of angels, and have not charity, I am become as
> sounding brass or as a tinkling cymbal.' And I think one
> phase of charity is making allowances for other people's
> mistakes . . .[34]

'Suppose sometime I sinned a great sin.' Sixteen years later,

Sayers, by her own standards of morality, did just that. And she wasn't afraid to turn for help and consolation to Ivy, who—as far as we know—cared for Sayers' illegitimate son without complaint, without judgment, and without any reference to a sixteen-year-old letter . . .

Life was about to change dramatically for the teenage Sayers. Introspective and self-centred from too secluded and pampered a childhood, academically superior to parents and governesses but with her knowledge untried in competition, she now needed something to satisfy her 'eagerness to know and to do some one thing in preference to all others'.[35] Mr and Mrs Sayers believed that eagerness would be satisfied if she became a boarding student at Godolphin School in Salisbury, Wiltshire. Their daughter breezily imparted the news to Ivy:

'Twill out, I am leaving the Court and going far away. I am going to School! But alas and alas! for our noble company, the grand bond will be broken forever after Christmas! for ever and for ever, and now no more shall the four Musketeers walk side by side in the garden or fight together for the King.[36]

In fact, two mostly miserable years lay ahead. The start itself could hardly have been more daunting: as if it wasn't unsettling enough to be transferred overnight from a comfortable home, where she was used to being the centre of attention, to a boarding school shared with two hundred girls, Sayers also arrived one term late, in January, 1909, having been laid low by a bout of chicken-pox. This put her in the unenviable position of outsider, as the other girls had already settled in and formed friendships. Worse, an administrative error placed Sayers—aged nearly sixteen—in a class of girls several years younger. Sayers, true to form, although feeling it deeply, skated over the humiliation in a letter to Ivy:

. . . my sky has been troubled, my beloved, very troubled by storms, wherefore I know not, save that such things come—whence no man knows, borne by some homeless wind, to stay a little while and then to depart towards their own place.[37]

She now found herself the odd one out among girls whose small talk consisted of clothes, parties and boys, and whose leisure hours were devoted to perfecting their skills on the hockey pitch. A sense of isolation was heightened by self-consciousness over her need of spectacles, and an unusually long and slender neck, which earned her the nickname of 'Swanny'. As Katherine Lammas, however, she concentrated on her good points:

> A commanding height . . . Blue eyes—but they might have
> been bigger. A snub nose—dear, dear! A high forehead—
> very unfashionable. Dark hair, rather thin and soft. A long
> upper lip—and she had read somewhere that this was
> reckoned a defect. A wide but rather well-shaped mouth,
> with dimples at the corner. A good skin—when it wasn't
> afflicted with spots. And, of course, pretty hands. Not a
> very good list of charms, but you never knew. The face
> must surely have character. It could not help being an
> interesting face—could it?—when it belonged to such an
> interesting person.[38]

Academically, Sayers could more than hold her own, but she was rather tactless in showing off the fact. During her first French lesson there came the teacher's question she had been waiting for. Who could tell the story of Molière? Sayers, alone among the girls, could—and in infallible French, too:

> This brought every head round with a jerk to stare at the
> strange phenomenon in the back row. Miss Larotte, who
> had never before in her life heard the subjunctive
> accurately and readily placed within the walls of the lower
> fifth, reeled slightly from the shock.[39]

Miss Larotte was impressed; the girls less so. 'She could never be comfortably and ordinarily part of the herd. She would be either the school star or the school butt. Which? She had not imagined that it was perfectly possible to be both.'[40] This was the secretive but self-aware Sayers of *Cat o' Mary*; her actual letters home at the time told only of a contented teenager. She knew just how much her happiness meant to Mr and Mrs Sayers.

Sayers had grown up embraced by the comforts of religion—but even these eluded her at Godolphin. Salisbury itself, as Sayers would write in one of her novels, was a little stuffy: 'the atmosphere of the Close pervades every nook and corner ... and no food in that city but seems faintly flavoured with prayer-books'.[41] The school was child to the parent, with annual obeisance to its Cornish foundress, Elizabeth Godolphin; a Mark Reading Day each term to announce girls' achievements; and full-blooded celebrations of Empire Day.

It follows that the same charge could be levelled at its brand of Christianity: low church, pietistic, dull, enough to put her off it for life, she said, had it not been for the influence of G. K. Chesterton to whom Christianity was 'one whirling adventure'.[42] Her parents didn't help by insisting on her confirmation at Salisbury Cathedral. Her conflicting responses speak volumes. To Ivy and to her parents she wrote only about 'the lovely day' which 'went off beautifully'. To her private treasure, *Cat o' Mary*, she was ever true:

> The awkward stutter and hush that accompanied the word 'Gawd' was even more indissolubly attached to the words 'communion' and 'sacrament' ... To these rites, which were held in secret, a strong flavour of the indecent seemed to cling.[43]

And in a letter written years later to Ivy, concerning her own son's religious upbringing, Sayers complained that confirmation against her will

> ... gave me a resentment against religion which lasted a long time ... the cultivation of religious emotion without philosophic basis is thoroughly pernicious.[44]

'Lasted a long time'—but before she left Godolphin, Sayers came to appreciate that abuse of a truth does not invalidate the truth itself. That her argument was not with the Christian faith but with its distortions, she made clear in a sonnet sent to her parents:

> A hundred years and yet a hundred years
> Pass, and no change. How long, O Lord, how long?
> We grow weary of the shame and wrong.
> Over our painted cheeks run bitter tears.
> Oh stainless Christians, how your Christ appears!
> What shall we call him who did sit among
> The publicans and sinners—wise, kind, strong?—
> Him whom his Christendom nor heeds nor hears?
> Nor have we sinned. We are thy servants still,
> And they would take our service from us—yea,
> God, they would take our very God away.
> Hard is belief when Christians use so ill
> Christ's prodigals. Just heaven, is this thy will?
> We watch the dark. How slowly breaks the day![45]

The adolescent Sayers 'passionately wanted friends. And still more passionately wanted approval. Most passionately of all she wanted to attract attention.'[46] What made adolescence so much harder for Sayers was her ability to be analytically objective about such an uncomfortable mix: 'In this last object she succeeded only too well, and probably lost thereby both approval and friends.'[47] There was no comfort in such searing self-analysis: 'She [Katherine] would wake in the morning with the heavy certainty that she could not get through the day.'[48] *Cat o' Mary*, an honest tale of insecurity and despair, ends during the Godolphin years; perhaps Sayers could no longer face the constant reminder that what she longed to be bore so little resemblance to what she was.

It was not all doom and gloom for Sayers, however. Moments of elation, glimpses of joy, the occasional healing influence—these too, she experienced. To begin with, she fell in love with words, and was intoxicated by the pictures she could paint:

Le Roi Soleil, small, bewigged, superb, and with him all

the people from the Viscomte de Bragelonne, rustling through the sun-drenched parterre to view the latest triumph of their court poet, that wandering player with his melancholy eyes, worn lung and broken heart . . . the darkening room and two nuns only to help him as he coughs out his soul. Black night and glimmering torches . . .[49]

Also shedding light rather than shade was her schoolgirl crush on a French teacher, Miss White. Such one-sided flirtations in adolescence can be extremely painful, but this was a crush with a difference—Sayers *knew* she was playing a part, and was able to step back and revel in the melodrama, even while suffering the pangs of unrequited affection:

Katherine's pash ran its course with no more deviation from traditional lines than an L.C.C. tram. She suffered exquisite pangs and enjoyed herself enormously. Here she could dramatise life to her heart's content. The ridicule that she inevitably encountered she did not resent, for she was playing a chosen part, and the laughter of the audience was the world's tribute to the accomplished comedienne.[50]

Elation, joy, perhaps healing, Sayers found in the piano playing of Fräulein Fehmer, whose music room was called Chopin, after her favourite composer. Sayers, in later years, did her best to forget Godolphin, but she always retained a soft spot for Fehmer and in 1944, as British planes bombed German cities, she published a poem in her memory.

Fräulein Fehmer was also colourful material for another word picture: '. . . stiffly built, with a strong square face, lionish, slightly blunted, as though the hand of the potter had given a gentle push to the damp clay'.[51]

Sayers continued to shine academically. It was announced in 1909 that 'six full certificates have been gained, and six distinctions, three by one girl, D. Sayers'. In 1911 there was 'the delightful news' that Sayers had passed Group B in the Cambridge Higher Local Examination, and gained distinction for written French, spoken French and spoken German. She had done 'better than any other candidate in England who had taken both languages'.

Almost the final entry in *Cat o' Mary* shows Sayers' own competitive streak—none too attractive, perhaps, but written in the context of social and sporting, though not academic, failure:

> One day I will show them. I will set my feet on their heads, put the world in my hand like clay and I will build, build, build—something enormous—something they never even dreamed of. It is in me. It is not in them and I know it.[52]

Disaster struck just as Sayers was preparing to work for her scholarship and qualification to Oxford. A few Godolphin girls contracted measles, but instead of isolating them the staff advocated a cure of fresh air and exercise, with the predictable result that practically everybody went down with measles, in Sayers' case with the complication of pneumonia. So ill was she that her mother was allowed to nurse her, and her life was probably saved only by a school doctor's late-hour decision to administer a saline injection.

Following six months' convalescence in a nursing home, Sayers had to endure one further humiliation: as a result of her illness, she lost all her hair and was forced to wear a wig. It was a devastating blow for a sensitive eighteen-year-old, who for the rest of her life would lose her hair at times of stress. Commendably brave as ever, she not only returned to Godolphin, in the autumn of 1911, but defiantly joined the school orchestra and choir, playing violin and singing alto. But as if all that wasn't enough, she now fell victim to a psychological error on the part of the headmistress.

Miss Mary Alice Douglas—whose initials caused mirth among the girls, though never in her presence—thought highly of her charge. But she didn't endear herself to Sayers, who despised her bland religiosity. 'The blade is not made in the fight, but in the forge' was one of her favourite maxims. 'Fight the good fight' was another. The season of Lent brought forth

'He that overcometh shall inherit all things' and 'Help us to further fruitfulness'.

The error—an unwitting one, motivated only by kindness—was to appoint Sayers House Prefect. Such swift promotion distanced her still further from her contemporaries, who were not prepared to put up with her bossiness and sarcastic wit. Sayers, the vision of Oxford radiant before her, clung on at Godolphin for as long as possible, but the strain was too much and she ended her association with the school.

Back home at the end of the year and content at last, as she always was when on her own, she put everything aside to concentrate on her studies. Her just reward was to win the coveted Gilchrist Scholarship in Modern Languages to Somerville College in Oxford.

3

Oxford—'The Holy City'

Post-Oxford, Sayers was to summarize the strengths and weaknesses of university life. The strengths were to be found in 'the fruits of scholarship':

> The integrity of mind that money cannot buy; the humility in face of the facts that self-esteem cannot corrupt; these are the fruits of scholarship, without which all statement is propaganda, and all argument special pleading.[1]

The weaknesses had more to do with the protected environment, the rarefied atmosphere; inexperienced in the art of living, staff were ill-equipped to cope with 'social difficulties' among the girls:

> When I lived in Academe I should never have thought of going to one of its guardians for advice in any social difficulty. I should have feared, not unkindness or unwillingness to help, but just blank want of knowledge. 'This kind of thing never happened to me,' says the guide, philosopher and friend; 'to a nice girl social difficulties do not occur.' That is a cowardly lie. Things do happen; it is monstrous to pretend that they do not or ought not.[2]

For Sayers, to whom 'things' did happen, the advantages nonetheless far outweighed the disadvantages. Somerville was to provide her with exclusively happy memories, despite the irksome restrictions, born of convention rather than conviction, put upon the hundred or so students.

Daily prayer was compulsory. Everyone was addressed as

47

Miss. No student could attend dances in the city during term, or even go to a tennis party on foot because it was thought unlady-like to carry a racquet through the streets. Male visitors to the girls' quarters were restricted to their relations and spiritual advisers. Whenever the sexes met elsewhere, a chaperon had to be present. (Once upon a time, no girl had been allowed to attend a lecture without a chaperon.) It is unclear just how rigidly these rules were obeyed. Suffice it to say that the girls, concerned no doubt about the state of their souls, rapidly acquired a remark-able number of spiritual advisers.

Sayers came to Somerville in 1912, when female students qualified for degrees without actually being able to receive them. The ruling changed in 1920, and Sayers was one of the first women to be awarded a degree from Oxford University. In 1912 women still had to prove themselves intellectually the equals of men, and although that battle was nearly won, another—that women could find satisfaction outside a home environment—was only just beginning. Sayers didn't make an auspicious start in a college committed to winning such battles. She was her loud and boisterous self, unashamedly talking in the Bodleian, cutting lectures, none too surreptitiously smoking cigars, wearing a badly fitted wig, and proclaiming to all who would listen (and those who wouldn't) that she was an agnostic and proud of it. Her dress sense, too, was nothing if not eccentric. Fellow-student Vera Farnell recalled that she appeared at break-fast one morning

> ... wearing a three-inch-wide scarlet riband round her head and in her ears a really remarkable pair of ear-rings: a scarlet and green parrot in a gilt cage pendant almost to each shoulder and visible right across the hall. [The Principal] Miss Penrose, shocked, but ever mindful of the rights and liberties of the individual student, was loth to abuse her authority by direct interference, but deputed to me, as a fellow student of D.L.S., the delicate task of effecting the removal of the offending bedizenment by gentle persuasion.[3]

This was Sayers taking the fight to the enemy, or the supposed enemy; over-compensating for her natural instinct to hide her shortcomings from public view. But Somerville was not Godolphin, and perhaps to her astonishment she made a host of acquaintances and not a few genuine friends who were thoroughly entertained in her company. One of these friends, Dorothy Rowe, said of her: 'Whenever she found anyone enjoying anything, she couldn't not join in.'[4] Vera Brittain, an acquaintance rather than a friend, and of the opinion that she dominated her group at college, admitted to taking

an immediate liking to Dorothy Sayers, who was affable to freshers and belonged to the 'examine-every-atom-of-you' type. A bouncing, exuberant young female who always seemed to be preparing for tea-parties, she could be seen at almost any hour of the day or night scuttling about . . . with a kettle in her hand and a little checked apron fastened over her skirt.[5]

Dorothy Rowe, together with Charis Barnett, formed the Mutual Admiration Society with the motto: 'The best of what we are and do, just God forgive.' The motto was Barnett's, the name of the Society Sayers'—on the grounds that if they didn't call themselves that, others undoubtedly would.

Qualification for membership was a piece of original writing, judged by the current membership. Sayers penned a conversation between the Three Wise Men, and was accepted. Perhaps, thirty years later, she recycled some of the material for *The Man Born to be King*. Students may have sneered at this precocious clique, but that didn't prevent them attempting to join it—an attempt doomed to failure if the Society didn't happen to like them.

Clique it may have been, but girls from that Society invariably went on to greater things—although Sayers was not only the most brilliant among them but also the most durable.

Sayers' closest friend was Muriel Jaeger, who therefore quite naturally belonged to the MAS. One vacation, Sayers wrote to her, complaining that she missed 'our loud-voiced arguments . . .

hang it all, what were tongues made for?'[6] Clearly, Sayers enjoyed Muriel's willingness to stand up to her and trade verbal punches. So much so that she would dedicate her first novel, *Whose Body?*, to her: 'To M.J.—Dear Jim, This book is your fault. If it had not been for your brutal insistence, Lord Peter would never have staggered through to the end of this inquiry. Pray consider that he thanks you with his accustomed suavity.' Another knot in the tie between them was a natural interest in religion. Sayers, as a clergyman's daughter, enjoyed shocking people with her profession of agnosticism—but it was not just a case of being mischievous. The adolescent experience of certainties being overturned was uncomfortable. She wrote home:

> It is difficult to make people see that what you have been taught counts for nothing, and that the only things worth having are things that you found out for yourself . . . It isn't a case of 'here is the Christian religion—the one respectable and authoritative rule of life, take it or leave it'. It's, 'here is a muddling affair called Life, and here are nineteen or twenty different explanations of it, all supported by people whose opinions are not to be sneezed at. Among them is the Christian religion in which you happen to have been brought up. Your friend so and so has been brought up in quite a different way of thinking. He is a perfectly splendid person and thoroughly happy. What are you going to do about it?' I am worrying it out quietly, and whatever I get hold of will be valuable because I will have found it for myself.[7]

Valuable indeed, as history would prove. In less serious vein, she described in another letter her thoughts about Christ's disciples: ' . . . I came to the conclusion that such a set of stupid, literal, pig-headed people never existed as Christ had to do with.'[8]

If Oxford raised a dismissive eyebrow to Sayers' social shortcomings, it positively winked at her prowess as a scholar, which was no less assured here than at Godolphin. In the early months, her tutors were unsure. She was not attentive in subjects, like mathematics, that didn't interest her. She should resist the temptation to be 'smart', said Miss Bruce, who also commented on Sayers' debating style: 'Miss Sayers took a lively part in the discussion, was always to the point and often suggestive' (*sic*). More pertinently, Miss Jourdain felt that 'at worst, she runs off with rhetoric or journalistic slang, or a pulpit manner and spoils her style'. But Sayers' natural brilliance, especially in Medieval French, won them over. Their own role should not be ignored, either; dedicated to their task, they were responsible for teaching Sayers how to work. Somerville was where she developed the methodical way of working which stood her in such good stead for the rest of her life. Miss Pope, in a college report of 1913, delivered this verdict:

> She combines with a strong literary appreciation and
> considerable insight, a real, and rather rare, liking for
> thoroughness. She has tackled the linguistic side of her
> work with real competence, shirks no difficulties, and so
> laid the foundations of a scholarly knowledge of her subject.

Sayers, lacking confidence despite the bravado, warned her parents not to expect too much: 'Even if I come out with a fourth, I have learnt an enormous amount about people and things at Oxford ...'[9] She must have worked hard, but could never remember doing so:

> It must ... be a trick of memory that presents to me an
> Oxford day made up as follows. 9.30, breakfast—no later
> than 10, anyway because the scouts started clearing away
> at that hour. 10, clean a pair of tennis-shoes and set them to
> dry in the quad. 10.30, gather with a party of friends in the
> lodge to await the arrival of the post: read letters. 11, coffee
> with friends. 12, cut a lecture, and write a sonnet for the
> literary society. Discuss Rupert Brooke—(it was in those
> days). Borrow a thermos, and go into the matter of the 2nd
> year play with the lender. 1.15, lunch. 2.15, punt on the
> Cher; the college expert harsh with me for failing to get the
> pole up in three. 4, tea with large and argumentative circle.
> 6.30, canoe and dinner on the river. Early return to attend

Bach Choir (very strenuous). 9.30, recruit nature with
coffee and cakes in friend's room. 10.45, bath; reproved by
Don for singing Bach in the bath-room. Midnight, bed
(unless anybody happened to drop in).[10]

Sayers, a not unattractive young woman despite alopecia and
an eccentric taste in clothes—'How *very* kind of *dear* Mrs Wilde
to say that I was good looking!!!! ... It's only that when I am
properly dressed I give a sort of spurious impression of good
looks—it's more a kind of smartness than anything else'[11]—
now fell hopelessly in love. A member of the Bach Choir, she
had an unconcealed passion for its Director, and New College
organist, Dr Hugh Percy Allen. So unconcealed, in fact, that it
became a standing joke in college. Vera Brittain recalled that
during the practices for the Verdi *Requiem* 'she sat among the
mezzo-contraltos and gazed at him with wide, adoring eyes as
though she were in church worshipping her only God'.[12]

Although the feelings were of greater depth and intensity
than she had had for Miss White, Sayers again exploited her
emotions to the full, determined to squeeze maximum pleasure
even from personal pain and public embarrassment. Very much
the observer, she had yet to learn that an essential part of an
observer's armoury is the gift of discrimination.

She delighted in Allen's quips at rehearsals which could well
have come from her own lips: for example, a note held by sopra-
nos should have sounded like a single star on a clear night, but
'you make it sound like a damp firework'. On his death, in 1946,
Sayers wrote:

In my Oxford days I rejoiced in H.P.'s eccentricities,
exulted when he threw his baton at the tenors and
performed his well-known striptease act, beginning with
his hat and scarf and ending, with miraculous timing, just
at the end of the movement, when there seemed nothing
but his trousers that he could take off.[13]

It was not an uncritical infatuation, however. Of Allen's
appearance on the podium, for example, she commented: 'He

really does look terrible in a frock coat, with his hair plastered down.'[14]

Sayers holidayed in France during the summer of 1914, and it might have been expected that she would return to college with passion dimmed. Not a bit of it. She caught Allen's attention by verbally giving as good as she got, and was rewarded with a singing role at one of his lectures.

Interest was no longer one-sided, either, and Allen began issuing invitations to his organ loft. She accepted them, afterwards referring to him as 'a pet', and 'a big spoilt baby'.[15]

Sayers' feelings eventually cooled—to the point where, years later, she could describe someone who for so long had dominated her emotions as 'a strange man . . . the statue of a god, flawed in the smelting, poor dear'[16]—but she maintained the relationship, partly for pleasure, principally for what she could get out of it. After all, when Allen agreed to lecture to the Literary and Philosophical Society, of which Sayers was secretary, she could legitimately call it 'an awful achievement':[17]

> I should rather like to make a good job of H.P. while I am about it—finish him off neatly, and not hurry or spoil him with careless workmanship, so to speak. He is worth taking trouble for, both in himself and on the low ground that he is a useful person to know. (There is a mercenary streak in me somewhere. Where does it come from?)[18]

Somerville students lived a sheltered existence, barely aware that the world outside was growing dark with forebodings of war. Sayers' first volume of verse, despite a post-Oxford publication in 1916, deals only in nostalgia and introspection. One student, Vera Brittain, it is true, seemed wide awake to the impending drama—but that owed something to having a brother and a boyfriend in army training. (Both were to perish in the trenches.)

Sayers' holiday in France, with two friends, was ill-timed and risky: Tours was in a state of siege, trains were packed with people escaping to the countryside. But Sayers, not yet entirely free of the fantasy world of childhood, sensed only the excitement, none of the fear: 'This thing is like a novel by H.G. Wells.

The whole world is going to war.'[19] For a twenty-one-year-old she was also remarkably unperceptive about events outside her narrow world, doubting on this occasion that the Germans were as hellbent on wickedness as rumours suggested.

Back in Oxford, it was to discover that half the male under-graduates had volunteered for service in the Forces—many of them to die in battle—and filling the gaps left were Belgian refugees. Within a year Somerville had been commandeered as a military hospital, and students were shifted into the almost empty Oriel College. Charis Barnett heard of her brother's death and left Oxford, unable to raise enthusiasm for her studies; she found greater purpose serving in France with the Quakers. Nursing or relief work was the choice confronting a frustrated Sayers, who seemed on the whole to prefer the former:

> Of course in one way I should hate nursing, hard labours and horrors, but I should be frightfully glad to have done it, and to have done something *real* for the first time in my life. And it's better than peasants and babies and local administration and inspecting drains, which is what one does in the other job.[20]

Sayers, in fact, asked for Dr Allen's advice on whether or not she should nurse in France. You're ideal for it, he said, because you don't get excited. But I do, she replied. In that case, Dr Allen insisted, you certainly know how to control yourself. Sayers wrote gleefully: 'As a testimony to character, I value it highly, because it shows, doesn't it, that at least I have never made a fool of myself before him.'[21] Sayers, it seems, always knew what she was doing; she had the gift, or curse, of the only child—and, indeed, the budding writer—in being able to indulge in melodrama, or melancholy, or downright tomfoolery, and at the same time observe it dispassionately and know just how far she could go.

Nothing came of nursing *or* relief work, so she knuckled down to her studies. Academic work may have been dis-rupted—'The war does make a great difference, it's no good saying it doesn't'[22]—but that didn't prevent Sayers from achieving the equivalent of a First Class Degree with Honours in Modern Languages. So impressed were the examiners that they took the unusual step of adding a written blessing to their marking: her French Prose Composition was unsurpassed, they said, for elegance and style.

Between final exams and the end of term Sayers paid her last tribute to Dr Hugh Percy Allen. (Vera Brittain didn't see it as a tribute at all. She believed that Sayers 'caricatured her idol with triumphant accuracy and zest'.[23]) As co-writer and musical director, she threw herself whole-heartedly into the Going-Down Play called *Pied Pipings or The Innocents Abroad*. She even acted in it—in the role of Dr H. P. Rallentando—dressing up as 'the strange man', and caricaturing to cruel perfection his style and his pose:

My good woman, what kind of a noise do you call that? I want a beautiful, round, golden sound, like a poached egg for Schools People, and you make it exactly like College coffee at nine o' clock in the morning.

The play, put on in Oriel's Skimmery Quad, was constructed ingeniously, so that the audience moved their position between acts to save having to change the settings. This sad tale of students who, unable to catch up on the facts about famous people ('It has just been proved that the *Chanson de Roland* is of Icelandic origin'), are led to Never-Never Land where they meet the famous face to face, was produced by Dorothy Rowe, in later years the creator of Bournemouth's outstandingly successful Palace Court Theatre.

Sayers penned three songs for the play, the best of them in the style of a song from Gilbert and Sullivan's *The Mikado*. One stanza referred to her post as Bicycle Secretary—or Bicycle Tyrant, as the students labelled her. Apparently, she impounded any cycles not returned to their proper place, and only released them on payment of a donation to the Red Cross.

It's well to be methodical where culprits are concerned,
So I've made a little list, I've made a little list

Of members of this commonwealth who ought to be interned,
And who never would be missed, who never would be missed.
The brutes who borrow bicycles without the owners' leave,
Who get their own in pound and come and ask for reprieve.
Who take their breakfast on the Cher at half past six a.m.
And say they thought the general rule did not apply to them,
The people with excuses that you really can't resist,
I'm sure they won't be missed, I'm sure they won't be missed.

In another stanza, Sayers wisely wielded the satirical pen against herself:

But these are not the only pests who poison College life,
And I've made a little list, I've made a little list
Of those who wake the midnight air with dialectic strife
And who never would be missed, who never would be missed.
The nymphs who stroll at breakfast time in nightgowns
*   made of silk,*
The people who remove your books, your matches
*   and your milk,*
The blighters who drop catalogues and whisper in the Bod.,
Or whistle Bach and Verdi as they walk across the Quad,
The superficial sceptic and the keen philanthropist,
They'll none of them be missed, they'll none of them be missed.

The term drew to a close, and it was a depressed young woman of twenty-two who trudged back to Bluntisham. Sayers, like so many other university students, suffered immediately from homesickness for Oxford. She tried to postpone the final break by inviting home for the weekend members of the Mutual Admiration Society. She envied Muriel Jaeger, who had another year to look forward to: 'I wish I could be there, to have your company on my bed when you were in the dumps, and bring you a hot water bottle occasionally.'[24]

She composed a poem, and sent handwritten copies to her friends.

Now that we have gone down—have all gone down,
*   I would not hold too closely to the past,*

56

Till it become my staff, or even at last
My crutch, and I be made a helpless clown.

All men must walk alone, not drowse, nor drown
Their wits, with spells of dead things overcast,
Now that we have gone down, have all gone down,
I would not hold too closely to the past.

Therefore, God love thee, thou enchanted town,
God love thee, leave me, clutch me not so fast;
Lest, clinging blindly we but grope aghast,
Sweet friends, go hence and seek your own renown,
Now that we have all gone down—have all gone down.[25]

Twenty years later, Sayers' novel *Gaudy Night*, set in a fictional women's college based on Somerville, drew heavily on her Oxford experiences, with characters late at night discussing 'love and art, religion and citizenship'. However, Muriel St Clare Byrne, a member of the MAS and a lifelong friend, believed she failed to portray the dons' essential eccentricity. Why, for example, could she not have worked in her description of principal Miss Penrose at a garden party: 'frightfully nervous... making the silliest remarks in a very high nervy tone of voice. As for the famous grin, she never took it off...'[26] *Gaudy Night* remains the most personal of Sayers' novels, although it is only fair to quote from her preface: '... however realistic the background, the novelist's only native country is Cloud Cuckooland...'

Life at Bluntisham Rectory was not calculated to lift Sayers' spirits. Back in the world of her childhood, parents, aunts and servants, however doting, no longer held the same attraction for her. Visitors tended to be sick relatives home from the front. And Mrs Sayers herself was suffering acute anxiety over the war. There was little to do except join sewing and knitting parties and help out at Red Cross fetes. So it was a miserable young woman who took herself by the scruff of the neck, collected poems she had written at Somerville, added a fresh handful, and sent them off to Basil Blackwell in Oxford.

Blackwell, having inherited his father's publishing company, was in the process of catching new poets early—among them, Aldous Huxley—in the hope that they would make their reputations with him. The scheme was to backfire when those who *did* make their reputation were seduced away by bigger firms and bigger cheques. All went well at first, however, and Sayers' initiative was rewarded: within a year, she saw her collection published as Number 9 in Blackwell's 'Series of Young Poets Unknown to Fame'. She called the collection, rather grandly, *Op 1*.

Technically stunning, brazenly nostalgic, overtly sentimental, most of the poems are drenched in the spirit of the world she loved best—that of French medieval romance. (At Oxford, she had produced a verse translation of *The Song of Roland*. Pure knights on quests for holy objects, an ordered social structure where one's place is known and kept, a battle between good and evil, heroism and cowardice: such values, superficially attractive and inherently contradictory, were very much the young Sayers' own. 'Paynims are wrong, Christians are in the right; courage and loyalty are all that matters; a noble death is the crown of a noble life.'[27])

Quotes from four of the poems take the veil from Sayers at twenty-two, in much the same way *Cat o' Mary* does for the maturing youngster. 'The Gates of Paradise' tells the story of Judas Iscariot, but with no sign of the sympathetic and subtle insight into character of *The Man Born to be King*:

> *I cast shame on King Jesus then,*
> *Wearing His painful crown,*
> *And scorn upon His Royal Head,*
> *Whence the pale sweat dripped down.*
>
> *O rudd-red were the five blest wounds*
> *Where nails and spear went in,*
> *A thousand, thousand years of Purgatory fire*
> *Never can cleanse my sin.*[28]

In a batch of nine poems, called 'The Last Castle', Sayers

experiments with various stylistic schools—among them, 'School of Sentiment', 'Pastoral School' and 'School of Strong Simplicity'. Her one outright success is the latter, whose example shows a Sayers only too aware that hell can be oneself, or hell can be other people:

> I said to the devil one day,
> 'What is the price that a man must pay?
> What is the end of shameful desire?'
>   He answered: 'Hell-fire.'

> 'You sell sin for a song,' I said,
> 'And the day of reckoning is far ahead';
> Nor knew that, even when he threatens hell-fire,
>   The devil is a liar.

> For the bitter end of shame
> Is not any sort of fire or flame,
> But the chill of a scorn too sick for laughter,
>   Here, not hereafter.[29]

Sayers' 'Hymn in Contemplation of Sudden Death' is, as the title suggests, somewhat pretentious—yet here is the maturing of Katherine Lammas, the beginning of wisdom, the private depths of a public fool:

> Lord, if this night my journey end,
> I thank Thee first for many a friend,
> The sturdy and unquestioned piers
> That run beneath my bridge of years.

> And next, for all the love I gave
> To things and men this side the grave,
> Wisely or not, since I can prove
> There always is much good in love.

> Next, for the power thou gavest me
> To view the whole world mirthfully,
> For laughter, paraclete of pain,
> Like April suns across the rain.

Also that, being not too wise
To do things foolish in men's eyes,
I gained experience by this,
And saw life somewhat as it is.[30]

Arguably the most persuasive poem is Sayers' heartfelt valediction to 'the holy city'. Called simply 'Last Morning in Oxford' it represents a regretful passing and letting go; only a chapter in her life, of course, but at such times endings seem eternal:

I do not think that very much was said
Of solemn requiem for the good years dead.

Like Homer, with no thunderous rhapsody,
I close the volume of my Odyssey.

The thing that I remember most of all
Is the white hemlock by the garden wall.[31]

4

'Let's pretend—the only game worth playing'

Teaching offered Sayers the one chance to escape the stifling atmosphere of Bluntisham. It was not what she wanted, indeed she knew well just how unsuited temperamentally for its rigours she was, but in desperation she applied for the post of teacher of Modern Languages at Hull High School for Girls and, when accepted, didn't know whether to laugh or cry. She started in the autumn of 1916, and made the best of it for almost a year. As she was to reason in a lecture thirty years later, lack of aptitude for a job is not necessarily a disqualification:

> Bishops air their opinions about economics; biologists, about metaphysics; celibates, about matrimony; inorganic chemists, about theology; the most irrelevant people are appointed to highly-technical ministries; and plain, blunt men write to the paper to say that Epstein and Picasso do not know how to draw.[1]

In one sense all that Sayers feared came to pass. The standard of learning at the school was embarrassingly low, with girls expected to absorb knowledge parrot-fashion without any opportunity to dissect and discuss. She was overheard on one occasion confiding that she 'would rather sweep the streets than teach children'. Allowing for exaggeration, it's a statement supported by part of an article written years later in the *Sunday Times*:

> For some reason, nearly all school murder stories are good ones—probably because it is so easy to believe that murder

could be committed in such a place. I do not mean this
statement to be funny or sarcastic; nobody who has not
taught in a school can possibly realise the state of nervous
tension and mutual irritation that can glow up among the
members of the staff at the end of a trying term, or the
utter spiritual misery that a bad head can inflict upon his
or her subordinates.[2]

Sayers also learned the true meaning of fear—as distinct
from the mythical kind propagated by *The Three Musketeers*.
Zeppelins, long the scourge of Britain's cities, now sought to
bomb the port of Hull, and Sayers, through long tense nights,
huddled for safety with hundreds of others in underground
shelters. It wasn't Athos who wrote to Muriel Jaeger about
fear: 'Believe me, it is brutal, bestial and utterly degrading. I
should say it was the one experience that is good for neither
man nor beast.'[3]

But there was also a sense in which Sayers unexpectedly
thrived. Schoolgirls thought of her as 'gay and attractive' as
she stimulated them to independent thought. Her hair grew,
and she celebrated by flirting mildly with the local curate: in
his company she could be 'sprightly' or 'rather religious'
because 'variety is the spice of wife'.[4] Her lodging quarters—
80 Westbourne Avenue—were comfortable, and, having lived
with a caricature impression of the north of England, it was a
pleasant surprise to discover shops and cafés actually worth
frequenting.

Poetry was her constant companion: she wrote for the *Ox-
ford Magazine* and won a poetry competition in the *Saturday
Westminster Review*. She also knocked off seven stanzas to
'Members of the Bach Choir on Active Service'.

> *... stuck waist deep in a slimy trench*
> *Your nostrils filled with the battle stench*
> *The reek of powder and smoke of shell*
> *And poison fumes blowing straight from hell—*
> *Do your senses ache for another smell?*

For the smell of fossils and sticks and stones,
Camphor and mummies and old dry bones,
Of strenuous singers, and gas and heat—
While you strove for a tone that was pure and sweet
In air you could cut with a baton's beat?[5]

Hull and teaching may not have proved as bad as she feared, but her heart and mind remained firmly in Oxford. It was probably at her own bidding that the Rev. Henry Sayers suggested to Basil Blackwell—who had just published *Op 1*—that his company might prosper if it employed one Dorothy L. Sayers. Blackwell agreed and, in January 1917, terms were finalized: Mr Sayers was to give Blackwell's £100 out of which—at £2 a week—his daughter's living expenses would be paid. Coincidentally, the Sayers' family was on the move, to a still more remote parish deep in the heart of Fen country. Sayers was to use Christchurch as the setting for her most famous novel, *The Nine Tailors*, but that fact didn't blind her to its faults: she described it as 'the last place God made, and when He finished it He found He'd forgotten the staircase'.[6]

In April Sayers settled at 17 Long Wall Street, at a rent of twelve shillings and sixpence a week. Pricey for those days, perhaps, but what did she care? She was back in her 'enchanted town'. And, at first, the enchantment worked its magic, as she met again Muriel Jaeger, Muriel St Clare Byrne, and a suitably chastened Hugh Percy Allen, rejoined the Bach Choir which sang regularly to the wounded troops in the Infirmary, made a close friend of Doreen Wallace, in her second year at Somerville, taught herself to play a wind instrument, and at Blackwell's began 'the learning of the whole business, from discount to the three-colour process'.[7]

She must have been happy; otherwise, not even Sayers would have marched imperiously down the High, singing 'Fling wide the gates, for the Saviour waits.' Doreen Wallace, an agnostic who argued theology with her friend long into many nights, never forgot her: 'I have never known anyone so brimful of the energy of a well-stocked mind . . . Nothing would content her but fact ... Everything she said was a statement, almost an edict.'

Sayers was not an unattractive woman, and it probably came as no surprise to her friends when she received her first proposal of marriage. Much impressed by the sentiments behind the poetry of *Op 1*, Leonard Hodgson, Vice-Principal of St Edmund Hall, went out of his way to meet Sayers at parties and outings. Smitten apparently by the personality of the poet, he suddenly declared his love and popped the question. Caught unawares, she stammered out the appropriate clichés: 'good friend ... deeply honoured ... never thought of you in that way'. Unfortunately, Hodgson wouldn't leave it at that, but dogged her footsteps and advertised his undying love. He even joined the Bach Choir to be near her. Sayers was not amused:

> To have somebody devoted to me arouses all my worst feelings. I *loathe* being deferred to. I ABOMINATE being waited on. It INFURIATES me to feel that my words are numbered and my actions watched. I want somebody to fight with![8]

She was much more at home with the flirtatious Mr Whitelock who, as surgeon at Aclands Nursing Home, removed her troublesome appendix and paid unusually close attention to her recovery:

> I love having someone to fool with ... The moment either person begins to be even a trifle in earnest, the whole thing is spoilt. You remember Alice? Her favourite game was 'Nurse, let's pretend'. The only game worth playing![9]

Her morale lifted by such easy conquests, Sayers now flirted outrageously. The number of eligible young men was strictly limited, of course: Oxford, since the introduction of conscription, was a ghost town, haunted by groups of pale young soldiers who, unlike Sayers, had long since lost faith in enchantment. Before the war there had been 3,500 male university students; now there were a couple of hundred.

The flirtatious Sayers did not neglect her writing. Another collection of poems—twenty-five in all—was ready for publication. *Catholic Tales and Christian Songs* demonstrates an advance in style, experience and scholarship as Sayers portrays the figure of Christ in a multitude of guises. A burst of satirical energy resulted in the verse drama 'The Mocking of Christ', in which all sorts and conditions of men offer advice and gifts to the crucified Christ: the Pope . . . 'The key of heaven, the key of hell,/ And the world's treasure-house as well'; the preacher . . . 'a better crown,/ Here's a better gown,/ pull the old ones down'; the bishop . . . 'In respectable gaiters which button up tight / He might walk in the precincts on Sunday, / While his innate good taste will remind Him it's quite/ Shocking form to be found there on Monday'; and the sentimentalist . . . 'Gentle Jesus mild and meek / Smooth your hair down neat and sleek; / I am sure you did not say: / "Tasteless salt is cast away" . . .'[10]

Sentimentality is dominant in poems like 'Christ the Companion'. The public Sayers fought shy of any hint of sentimentality; the private, poetic Sayers acknowledged a streak of it in herself. Sentimentality can easily be the soft option for true feeling, certainly for action, and the young Sayers, who took care not to get her hands dirty in the war, cannot be absolved from the charge:

> *When I've thrown my books aside, being petulant*
>   *and weary,*
> *And have turned down the gas, and the firelight*
>   *has sufficed,*
> *When my brain's too stiff for prayer, and too*
>   *indolent for theory,*
> *Will you come and play with me, big Brother Christ?*
>
> *Will you slip behind the book-case? Will you stir*
>   *the window-curtain,*
> *Peeping from the shadow with Your eyes like flame?*
> *Set me staring at the alcove where the flicker's so*
>   *uncertain,*
> *Then, suddenly, at my elbow, leap up, catch me, call*
>   *my name? . . .*

*And when we say good-night, and You kiss me on the
    landing,
Will you promise faithfully and make a solemn tryst:
You'll be just at hand if wanted, close by here where
    we are standing,
And be down in time for breakfast, big Brother Christ?[11]*

The most personal poem is the long 'The House of the Soul:
Lay', whose introspective opening lays bare the soul of a young
woman coping with the loss of make-believe. She was coming to
terms with reality late in life—a case of delayed adolescence—but
that owed much to the cloistered and privileged nature of her
upbringing and was no fault of hers:

*I have forgotten my name and the name of my nation . . . yea,
I know alone I have lost myself, and have wandered far astray
From the land where the magic fir-trees grow, farther than
    far Cathay,
Farther than fair Atlantis or the hills of Tir-fa-tonn,
Or the isles of Bran and Mailduin, or the isle of Avalon . . .*

*. . . And I know that I am lonely, and the night and the sea
    and the spray,
Unrestingly, unhastingly, march on with no delay,
And the sheer height of the cliffs white stands like the
    base of the great white throne,
And I seem to be left with God, bereft any wisdom to
    plead or pray.[12]*

Sayers, of course, could not omit 'the holy city' or 'enchanted
town'. But at least she kept her 'Carol for Oxford' brief.

*When all the Saints that are in Heaven keep Christmas
    at the board,
Our Lady Mary calls a health before her Son our Lord,
Says: 'Let us sing the fairest town that is in all Your
    earthly crown;
Nowell, Nowell, Nowell, Nowell
To the Bells of Oxenford!'[13]*

Blackwell again was the publisher; an attempt to persuade G.K. Chesterton to publish the poems in *New Witness* failed. Sayers and Muriel Jaeger now concocted a plan to stir up theological controversy over the book, and thereby stimulate sales. Jaeger, about to review the collection for the *Church Times*, received this missive from her friend:

> Don't slate it, because the C.T. is the organ of the High Church party, and I would as soon have them with me as against me. But having got it nicely reviewed there, you couldn't do better than send a furious letter from 'Pewholder' or 'Via Media', wondering how they could possibly allow even the name of the vile publication to sully their pages.[14]

The joke spread from the *Church Times* to *New Witness*, as (non-existent) readers expressed their holy outrage. Jaeger wrote the letters; Sayers supplied the arguments. An Anglican all her life, Sayers nonetheless respected the steadfastness of Catholic dogma: 'What I feel is this, there is a real truth about everything, which (I believe) Catholicism has got hold of (as far as it is possible for us to grasp the truth about everything; we really couldn't grasp all of it unless we were omnipotent and eternal. That's how God sees it. Catholicism only gives us the whole truth as far as man is concerned).'[15]

Sayers' official biographer, James Brabazon, suspects the poems of insincerity: 'So many views of Christ are on show, but which of them is *hers*...?'[16] Perhaps all, perhaps none, but why should that denote insincerity? Sayers is enjoying playing with words and images, but she is also seeking for the historically reliable, emotionally satisfying and intellectually respectable Christ—and the older Sayers was to believe that it is possible to discover all three. It is true that Sayers agonized over *questions* of sincerity and emotion. Which self should she be true to? Could emotion be trusted?

> A man's fundamental beliefs are to be found, not in his expressed opinion, for to express an opinion is to admit

that a contrary opinion may exist—but in his expressed assumptions. A thing really believed has passed beyond possibility of discussion and to say 'I believe' is to say 'I doubt'.[17]

But this was Sayers' personal inner journey, asking questions pertinent to her taste and temperament and in the context of her upbringing and education. Such questions would shift with the passing of years and the accumulation of experience. In this life winds blow from every direction, storms burst through shuttered doors, peaks of elation beckon, valleys of disillusionment mock, memories haunt early idealism, influences flicker in and out of consciousness. Sayers was not immune to the common lot of humanity. And, of course, it changed her. No single act, no scattering of quotes, can fairly define once and for all any human being.

'Let's pretend—the only game worth playing!' Sayers played it with utmost enthusiasm, as we have seen, and it was to cost her dear in personal relationships; but all the evidence is that her Christian faith at this stage was no mere pretence; on the contrary, Doreen Wallace regretted that she was 'so bloody religious'.

Soon, battered by poverty, lost love, the weakness of the flesh and an unhappy marriage, she was to grow weary of the faith and allow it to lie dormant for nearly twenty years. During this period she was to play the game of 'let's pretend' much less often. Life grew too serious, too dark, for such indulgence. It was used only sparingly now, to escape inside herself from pain and anxiety. Instead, she turned to satire and mockery, the twin havens of disillusioned idealists. It is worth remembering that the satirist does not mock the valueless; only that which is recognized as essentially important in the vain hope that it might live up to its original claim or promise.

Sayers' other work, outside proof-reading and judging manuscripts at Blackwell's, included a translation of the *Tristan* of Thomas (a poet who wrote in *France* in the twelfth century), a short story for a magazine devoted to the Mutual Admiration Society (aptly named *Blue Moon*, as it folded after a single issue), and the submission of poems to the annual *Oxford Poetry*. One of these expresses deep emotions about a real, possibly lost, relationship—one which put in the shade anything on offer from Mr Hodgson or Mr Whitelock.

The hawthorn brave upon the green
She hath a drooping smell and sad,
But God put scent into the bean
To drive each lass unto her lad.

And woe betide the weary hour,
For my love is in Normandy,
And oh! the scent of the bean-flower
Is like a burning fire in me.

Fair fall the lusty thorn,
She hath no curses at my hand,
But would the man were never born
That sowed the bean along his land![18]

'My love' was Eric Whelpton. With the ending of the war, undergraduates began to return in droves to Oxford, all of them seeking accommodation. Sayers had to move—and a rise of five shillings a week from Blackwell's enabled her to rent rooms on the first floor of a house in Bath Place. Eric Whelpton, invalided out of the Berkshire Territorials after suffering from polio, moved in on the ground floor. Pale, thin and weak, with Byronic good looks, he needed mothering; Sayers was immediately on hand.

Strictly speaking, she was far from beautiful, but her grey eyes radiated intelligence, her mobile features vividly expressed her thoughts and her emotions ... She usually wore black, but was given to large pendulous earrings and exotic strings of beads. From the first, her manner to me was protective and almost maternal.[19]

According to Whelpton, a ladies' man if ever there was one, they 'seldom visited each other', although they did meet at coffee parties which he found 'fairly entertaining' because of the talk about books which he had not yet read.[20] 'Seldom visited' doesn't quite tally with Sayers' describing his use of her as a 'pillow'. She sympathized with his sad stories of disillusionment and loss. Some women—and Sayers was fated to be among them—fall for that line every time.

He was right about the coffee parties, however—most of them dedicated to games in which those present, one after the other, built up the wildest narrative they could muster. Years later, Sayers told a newspaper reporter that the basic plot of *Whose Body?*, which begins with the discovery in a bath of a naked male corpse, grew out of one such narrative. Sayers and friends also dabbled in amateur dramatics, and ran something called the Rhyme Club, in which a member had to offer a line of verse and the next was given a minute to produce the rhyming line.

Doreen Wallace, herself gregarious and known as a breaker of men's hearts, believed Sayers to be 'a passionate woman', quite fixated on sex, concerned that in her mid-twenties she was still a virgin. But whereas Wallace flirted easily and outrageously, the insecure Sayers covered her embarrassment with sharp rebuttal or adolescent antics. In an article in *Oxford Outlook* she quoted with approval a contemporary of hers:

> I am twenty-six, and I see now that I do not want an
> independent career; but I am unfit for marriage because I
> have been taught to demand too much, and I do not know
> how to give men what they want.[21]

Sayers had lost all sense of contentment. Frustration, both sexual and spiritual, was her constant companion. And when Whelpton, unable to face the hardships of an Oxford winter, set sail to work in one of the finest schools in Europe, the Ecole des Roches near Verneuil in Normandy, she penned those tell-tale lines: 'Woe betide the weary hour,/ For my love is in Normandy...'[22]

As Whelpton departed, Blackwell's heaped misery on misery by dispensing with her services. It was a sacking, although Basil Blackwell softened the blow with a promise of freelance work. It wasn't that she was incompetent—far from it; Blackwell thought of her as a 'racehorse harnessed to a cart'—but a purely commercial decision meant that the company was abandoning the risky promotion of young poets to concentrate on the safer publication of school books. Sayers filled the days by coaching in French and contributing to the *Oxford Chronicle*. With any real sense of purpose missing, her future looked bleak. She had, she wrote, 'come to a blank wall . . . and lost grip'.[23]

Then, in what seems to have been no more than a coincidence, Whelpton invited her to France where he required a French-speaking assistant. Sayers' letters to Muriel Jaeger and her parents took on a note of scarcely repressed excitement: 'Look here, should you mind awfully if I went to France for a bit?'[24] . . . 'Last night I had to decide several things in a great hurry, and lost my head, France has materialized very suddenly. After our conversations of last Easter, you will be amused to know that I am going out to be Mr Whelpton's secretary . . .'[25]

A dubious Mr and Mrs Sayers were visited by Eric Whelpton to assure them of his honourable intentions—which, charm in the presence of innocence, he had no trouble doing:

> Needless to say, we dressed for an excellent dinner of five courses and Dorothy wore an evening frock to display her bare arms which were slim and well-shaped. Mr Sayers looked at me with suspicion at first, but calmed down when I told him that his daughter would not be in the same house as myself, and that we were not likely to meet very often out of office hours . . .[26]

Sayers was raring to go—and a letter to Leonard Green, an author who had requested a contribution to a proposed book on friendship, although a digression, is not unrevealing of her curiosity about sexual relationships, her self-image as an observer with a heart of iron (false, of course), and a picture of someone who, in Whelpton's company, plans to be devoted but discreet:

> . . . As regards 'Friendship', I must confess to being one of those cynically-minded people who consider that the least

said on the subject the soonest mended. Few friendships among women will stand the strain of being romantically considered—all those I've ever watched have ended in dead-sea apples (the romantic ones, I mean), and I avoid them like the plague. Men manage better, I think, because most of them spend half their lives in Cloud cuckoo-land in any case! Of course there is the amusing cock-and-hen friendship—but it is so very like a game of chess, & one can't make literature out of KB to QR4—at least, not the sort of literature you would care about: This is to explain why I'm very unlikely to write much about the subject. If I ever do, of course, I will send it to you with pleasure, but it would probably be in the strain of my contribution to this year's *Oxford Poetry* (q.v. when published)—Now scold me for blasphemies! . . .[27]

Certainly once Sayers arrived in France the relationship was cool enough. At table, she and Whelpton addressed each other as 'Monsieur' and 'Mademoiselle', and in the office she was on hand simply to make sure he was never without pen, ink, newspaper, and hot coffee. Les Roches, as Whelpton explained, was a rich man's school with a board of governors chosen from the elite of the universities, the army, and men of letters. Sayers was not part of the teaching staff, but secretary to the scholastic bureau responsible for organizing the exchange of British and French schoolboys. She found Whelpton amusing company, and the mother touch was often called upon by one who endured 'faints, agues, and heart attacks of all sorts'.[28] Whelpton was not ungrateful:

She ran the office with great efficiency and she did a great deal to complete my literary education, for my correspondence was not heavy, and so in our spare time we read the more obscure 17th-century poets and we discoursed about French literature where I could hold my own.[29]

Not that all Sayers' literary interests were so high-minded:

When I came upon her unexpectedly I would find her reading the cheap crime books which were known as penny dreadfuls, the novels of Maurice Le Blanc and Barbey d'Aurevillers' *Les Diaboliques*. One day, when I teased her for reading such rubbish, she told me that she was part of a team . . . who were deliberately preparing to create a vogue in detective novels; she suggested that I should join them. I replied rather sourly that I did not imagine for a moment that the public would fall for such rubbish and that I would have nothing to do with it.[30]

There is no evidence for the formal existence of any such 'team', but plenty for the newfound urge to write detective stories. While in France Sayers engaged in elaborate correspondence with Muriel Jaeger, subjecting Sexton Blake's preposterous activities to serious critical analysis:

I may state, in short, that I do not hesitate to connect the legend of Sexton Blake not only with the Osiris mysteries and possibly with the Mithraic solar ritual, but also with the oriental Jesus cults whose solar origins have been so indisputably established by Drews and Robertson . . .[31]

Money was scarce, and Sayers was realist enough to study the crime novel genre, for that was where the money was. As Harriet Vane was to tell Miss de Vine in *Gaudy Night*: ' . . . Writers can't pick and choose until they've made money . . . I know what you're thinking—that anybody with a proper sensitive feeling would rather scrub floors for a living. But I should scrub floors very badly, and I write detective stories rather well. I don't see why proper feeling should prevent me from doing my proper job.'

The catalyst for the relationship between Sayers and Whelpton was the pregnancy of a member of staff following a casual affair with a soldier. Sayers counselled her against having an abortion. That would be a sin, she said. In the sorting out of the mess, the two were thrown carelessly together, and true feelings emerged. Whelpton acted unfairly towards the impressionable Sayers, for whom he felt no more than a passing fancy; his unsubtle flattery may well have been seen through, but the inexperienced and hungry Sayers would have been less than human had she not succumbed to hope:

> ... Himself has taken a violent fancy to the black jumper
> with the Tudor rose and the hair turned under ... You will
> be interested also that I have:
> pretty hands
> nice neck
> beautiful shoulders
> good legs
> good ankles!! (at this point I began to think him really
> besotted. The rest is true.)
> a good temper and
> a bit of the devil in me! ...
> I tell you all these absurdities because I know you trust me
> not to play the fool, or do the lad any harm, and because it
> is only little secrets that end badly, as I have had the
> opportunity of learning lately. Besides, what is a man to do
> in a place like this? Such a set of frumps you never did see.
> One had to let off steam somewhere. But you understand
> that Doreen Wallace wouldn't do for this job.[32]

Eric Whelpton's true nature—surface gloss without so much as an undercoat of discipline—emerges from another of her letters. She writes of his 'blethering' about his 'bad health' and 'blighted ambitions' and 'the girl who had failed him'

> and finally how he had no business to be telling me all this,
> but I was the only person who ever understood—with his
> head buried on my knees and making me smell of
> brilliantine in the most compromising manner![33]

She simply didn't see through him, writing that if she ever felt *she* was hurting *him* she would leave him 'like a shot': 'I didn't come over here to add to his burdens ...'[34] Whelpton didn't let his judgment of Sayers as the only person who ever understood him restrain his passions, however; one day while in London, he visited a theatre and fell in love with the girl in the next seat. Once her letters started arriving at the school, blazing rows between Sayers and Whelpton were the order of the day. The air cleared, but the end of the adventure was in sight:

> We are both rather estimable people and the whole thing would be most heroic and pathetic if one didn't see the comic side of it. Anyway we both nobly shouldered our own share of the blame—in fact Eric claimed it all, but to tell the truth I have been partly responsible—and at present mutual admiration stands at par.[35]

'If one didn't see the comic side of it'. In the unhappinesses and crises of later life, Sayers coped, not so much as she had in her youth—by an escapist refusal to face the facts—but by a determined acceptance of the comic nature of existence, of the absurdity which parallels every tragedy.

Later, Sayers was to be less generous to Whelpton: 'He is marked out for misfortune, but he doesn't distinguish between an honest woman and a dishonest one, so there is nothing to be done for him.'[36] The dream of love in ruins at her feet, Sayers now went down with mumps and, worse, had to endure a recurrence of alopecia. A specialist told her that it was the symptom of an internal upheaval of spirit which would ease only with contentment of mind. So where was she going to find that? Not in Oxford, which had failed her as do all revisited haunts of youth. Not in France, which had offered a brief and ultimately disappointing adventure. Sayers decided it was to be in London, a place she would characterize in *Unnatural Death*:

> To the person who has anything to conceal—to the person who wants to lose his identity as one leaf among the leaves of a forest—to the person who asks no more than to pass by and be forgotten, there is one name above others which promises a haven of safety and oblivion. London. Where no one knows his neighbour . . . Discreet, incurious and all-enfolding London.

5

Love's 'black and bitter deep'

Sayers left France at the end of summer 1920 at the age of twenty-seven. But not immediately for London. Instead she returned to Oxford as one of the 549 women only now permitted to receive Oxford degrees, in her case both Bachelor and Master of Arts. Such a happy day, when even 'the air scintillated with sunshine',[1] was the cruelly ironic prelude to the unhappiest five years of Sayers' life, a period she was to describe with a rare use of understatement as 'spiritually ragged'.[2]

To start with, far from being impressed with her educational status, employers seemed scared of taking one so erudite on to their books. Her friend Muriel, by contrast, was employed first by *Time and Tide*, then by *Vogue*, on each occasion failing to take advantage of the opportunity, and after rows with the management finding herself back on the streets. Without a salary, Sayers depended on sympathetic landladies to take pity on her, but accommodation was as elusive as employment. Her parents would have welcomed her home, of course, but Sayers saw that as a backward, perhaps irretrievable, move. Two poems written during this period not unnaturally are drenched in despair. 'Obsequies for Music' speaks only of dead hopes and dead loves:

> *'Dead past, go forth, bury thy carrion dead*
> *Because they do offend me grievously.'*
> *Full sternly thus I said,*
> *And my dead Past obediently*
> *Rose up to bury its dead.*[3]

'The Poem', here quoted in full, is the work of the passionate Sayers: her passion thwarted by circumstance and personal weakness, passion with nowhere to go, no one to embrace:

> *Kiss me! It cannot be that I*
> *Who wove such songs of pain and fire*
> *Last night—that fierce, desiring cry—*
> *It cannot be that I should tire?*
>
> *Prove to me, prove you're not grown weak,*
> *Break down this citadel of sense,*
> *Show me myself too faint to speak,*
> *Not armoured in my eloquence.*
>
> *I swear my singing was begun*
> *Out of love's black and bitter deep—*
> *But oh: The work was so well done*
> *I smiled, well-pleased, and fell on sleep.*
>
> *Now all day long I must rehearse*
> *Each passionate and perfect line,*
> *Mine the immaculate great verse—*
> *I do not know the thoughts for mine.*[4]

Sayers marked time by taking a succession of minor and unsatisfying teaching posts, thereby funding rooms at 44, Mecklenburgh Square, in Bloomsbury. It was hard going: she could afford to eat, but only if she dispensed with curtains. A letter sent to her parents in July 1921 is light in tone—no doubt for their sake—but a sense of panic lurks behind every line:

> I can't get the work I want, nor the money I want, nor consequently, the clothes I want, nor the holiday I want, nor the man I want!! And then people tell me of girls who are oppressed and embarrassed by the possession of an income of £300 a year, and feel that they ought not to have it and ought to be doing slum work and being useful to society. I call that pure egotism and spiritual pride. How thankfully would you or I support life under a load of similar embarrassments.[5]

In desperation, Sayers recalled those coffee parties and one particular narrative, and put pen to paper, unaware as she created one Lord Peter Death Bredon Wimsey that she was bidding farewell to financial, though not personal, insecurity. Manuscript completed, her father footed the typing bill, and off it went to publishers' readers. 'I've written a silly book, but I don't suppose any publisher will take it,'[6] she wrote in a fit of post-creation blues. It looked as though she was right, as the MS regularly thumped through her letter-box. But in November 1921, one reader expressed interest in the book—then titled *The Singular Adventure of the Man with the Golden Pince-Nez*, wisely changed for publication to *Whose Body?*—and Sayers found three 'small but very pretty'[7] rooms in Great James Street (her address for the next twenty years).

Was London going to prove that place of contentment, after all? It seemed so when early the next year she was taken on as a copywriter at Britain's largest and most progressive advertising agency, Benson's, at a salary of four pounds a week; she was inspired to start a second Wimsey novel, and heard that Liveright would publish *Whose Body?* in America, Fisher Unwin in Britain, and—the icing on the cake—*People's Magazine* wanted to serialize it.

Many are the figures pointed to as models for Wimsey—Whelpton among them—but Sayers was clear on the matter:

> I do not, as a matter of fact, remember inventing Lord Peter at all. My impression is that I was thinking of writing a detective story, and that he walked in, complete with spats, and applied in an airy don't-care-if-I-get-it way for the job of hero ... At this first interview, Wimsey informed me that he had a rather attractive mother, to whom he was much attached, and an immaculate 'gentleman's gentleman'—Bunter by name ... Lord Peter's large income ... was a different matter. I deliberately gave him that. After all, it cost me nothing, and at that time I was particularly hard up, and it gave me great pleasure to spend his fortune for him. When I was dissatisfied with my single unfurnished room, I took a

luxurious flat for him in Piccadilly. When my cheap rug got a hole in it, I ordered an Aubusson carpet. When I had no money for my 'busfare, I presented him with a Daimler double-six, upholstered in a style of sober magnificence, and when I felt dull I let him drive it . . .[8]

Contentment, then? Sadly, no. Her professional pride regained, her financial security assured, Sayers' private life resembled a jigsaw in which no two pieces fitted together: two affairs, pregnancy by one of them, and a lasting taste of bitterness from the consequences, lay ahead. Much of the blame can be placed at her own door but, if one considers Sayers' life to this point, one hesitates to point the accusatory finger or to make an unbending judgment. Sayers was to become a champion of absolute standards, but she was no less a champion of those who fall short of the ideal. Twenty years after these events she wrote:

> The point made . . . is that the story of the Crucified God appears irrelevant because people nowadays have no sense of sin. That, of course, is literally the *crux* . . . I'm a very poor person to appreciate modern man's feelings on all this, because I can't think of any personal misfortunes that have befallen me which were not, in one way or another, my own fault . . . I mean that I know jolly well that if anything unpleasant happened in my life I had usually 'asked for it'. Consequently, when I talk about carrying the sins of the world, I'm going outside my experience—anything I have to put up with looks to me like the direct punishment of my *own* sins, and not to leave much margin over for redeeming other people's! But I do see that most people to-day look upon themselves as the victims of undeserved misfortune, which they . . . have done nothing to provoke. Contemporary literature and thought seems to me to be steeped in self-pity . . .[9]

Which—and it is worth giving her some credit for this—was never one of Sayers' weaknesses. Men were—and the first of two was the Russian-born American writer John Cournos, who treated her shabbily and to whom she wrote in 1924 on hearing of his marriage to another: 'If I saw you, I should probably only cry—& I've been crying for about three years now and am heartily weary of the exercise.'[10] Cournos' stepfather, as a member of a sect called the Hasidim which 'placed spirit above dogma and exaltation above cold formalities of knowledge',[11] believed that divine energy prompted all creativity. As far as we know, the stepfather held to this dubious belief without causing any harm. Not so the stepson, who, puffed up with self-importance, came to England in 1912 to write novels, and pursued rather than knew the literary giants of the day. He was a man who spelt Art 'with a capital A'.[12] He was also sophisticated, idealistic, and—what probably first attracted Sayers to him— soaked in self-pity; indeed, in this regard, he made Whelpton look a novice. Cournos, as Brabazon notes, 'was the epitome of the Bloomsbury bedsitters, trying their luck with pseudo-profundities about free love, and often enough getting away with it'.[13]

The relationship lasted almost a year. She told her parents about it, but never actually introduced Cournos to them, perhaps doubting their ability to get on together. (On one occasion she told them: 'He and I have had a difference on a point of practical Christianity.'[14]) Sayers clearly believed Cournos was *the* man for her. She loved him, she wanted children by him, but what drove a wedge between them was his absolute commitment to freedom from the ties of wife and child so as to be 'free to live and love naturally'.[15] Just *how* absolute the commitment can be judged from his marriage in 1924 to Helen Kestner Satterthwaite (the writer Sybil Norton) and his becoming stepfather to her two children.

His *Autobiography*, written in 1935, mentions the marriage and his love for another Dorothy in America, but of Dorothy L. Sayers there is not so much as a line of print. Sayers sent him eleven letters during 1924 and 1925, which Cournos—just before his death—deposited in the library of Harvard University. These are invaluable, not only because their contents make apparent what happened between them, but, crucially, they allow us to see a Sayers with her defences down—and a very human and frail figure she is. I shall be quoting fully from these letters, but just one line will suffice here: 'Both of us did what we swore we'd never do, you see . . .'[16] For Cournos, that meant marriage. For Sayers, that meant 'free love' and loss of virginity outside marriage—the 'difference on a point of practical Christianity'.

One year before the earliest of her embittered letters—in April 1923—Sayers fell pregnant by somebody she 'didn't care twopence for'.[17] Cournos had finally rejected her, in October 1922, and left England, and on the rebound she formed a relationship in which the only tie was physical. 'Dearest mother, don't faint,' she wrote, 'I am coming home for Xmas on Saturday with a man and a motor cycle.'[18] She explained:

> It's a poor devil whom I chummed up with one week-end, finding him left lonely . . . He simply has not a red cent or a roof, and his job has gone bankrupt for a moment—the job being motors . . . the intellect isn't exactly his strong point . . . in fact he's the last person you'd ever expect me to bring back home.[19]

He was, however, the opposite of pretentious, and Sayers, in one brief burst of abandonment, enjoyed the rough and ready relationship, the intellect for once consumed by the physical. Her pregnancy confirmed, she rejected abortion on religious grounds, she rejected informing her parents whom she believed would not survive the shock, she rejected telling anyone at all in case it got back to them—and the man with the motor cycle rejected her.

Borne up only by wishful thinking that the 'father' might yet change his mind and share responsibility for the child—in which case her strong sense of sin and duty would have persuaded her to take the public consequences of private actions—Sayers took leave from Benson's and rented a small cottage close to London. A note shot through with panic reached her parents: 'Look here—I'm awfully rushed and rather bothered. Don't come up till the Spring. I want to get things straightened out, and I can't do that till I get my accounts from America and England

and have got my new book on to the Press both sides of the Atlantic...'[20]

Unsurprisingly, in the circumstances, the new book—*Clouds of Witness*, whose plot is riddled with sexual intrigue—moved at a snail's pace, and didn't reach the press for two years, but at least royalties were beginning to come in from the well-received *Whose Body?* It may seem astonishing that nobody noticed the pregnancy as the date of the birth drew closer, but Sayers' fondness for good food paid dividends: her ample figure invited simple acknowledgment that she had put on weight.

Just days before the birth, Sayers—reconciled now to the loss of the 'father'—wrote to her cousin Ivy Shrimpton, who, since her father's death two years earlier, had taken orphaned children under her wing in an Oxford apartment. Once she had written to Ivy: 'I think, old girl, that you are just a bit inclined to form a harsh judgement... of other people... Dear old girl, get out of the way of thinking that. It is terribly allied to Pharisaism, which, you know, is the one thing our Lord was always so down upon... I shouldn't like to feel, Ivy, that suppose sometime I sinned a great sin, I should be afraid to come to you for help...'[21] Sixteen years later, words written in idle superiority caught up with her. The day of the 'great sin' had arrived, although for the moment Sayers wasn't ready for the full confession:

> I have been wanting for some time to write to you on a matter of business. There's an infant I'm very anxious you should have the charge of, and I hope very much indeed you'll be able to take it. It isn't actually there yet, but will be before many days are over. It won't have any legal father, poor little soul, but I know you would be all the more willing to help give it the best possible start in life on that account. The parents want to do the very best for it and will be ready and willing to pay whatever your usual terms are, and probably something over. They especially want it to have affection rather than pomp: I know that nobody could do better for it that way than you. I am very personally interested in the matter, and will tell you more

about it later on . . . The point is, what would be the earliest
possible moment at which you could take it? At present
everything depends on the girl's not losing her job.
Everything has been most discreetly managed—her
retirement from public life is accounted for by 'illness'—
but naturally she can't turn up back at work plus a baby—
at least, not without letting stacks and stacks of people into
the secret, which might then leak out. So you see, the
sooner she could dump the infant on you and clear back to
work, the more chance there is of being money to support
it, as both parents are working and one of them alone
couldn't do much to support it. From the mother's history
it *should* be an extremely healthy child, having given not
the slightest trouble or bad time so far, and I understand
the doctor thinks everything should go easily. It will be a
little gent (or lady as the case may be) on both sides, and
would probably be in your charge for some years—till
circumstances enable the mother to take it herself . . .[22]

John Anthony was born in Tuckton Lodge, a private nursing
home in Southbourne, Hampshire, on 3 January 1924. Sayers
was thirty, and it wasn't an easy birth. Within two weeks of the
birth, Sayers sent her second letter to Ivy.

Excuse hasty note. Have been waiting to give you definite
news. Your baby arrived on January 3rd—a sturdy little
boy—and will be brought to you with all paraphernalia
and particulars on or about January 30th. Terms quite
satisfactory. Ever so glad you can take him. Will let you
know further.[23]

Sayers came clean in a letter written on 27 January, but even
now there is a marked absence of any tone of regret or remorse; no
confession at all, in fact. She says she is bringing the boy to Ivy
herself. As she may only be able to stay a minute or two she is
enclosing 'confidential particulars' about the child. 'I know you
are the most discreet woman in the world . . . I trust your discre-
tion absolutely'.[24] The 'confidential particulars' tell Ivy all

Sayers feels she needs to know:

> My dear, everything I told you about the boy is absolutely
> true—only I didn't tell you he was my own! I won't go into
> the whole story—think the best you can of me—I know it
> won't make you love the boy any less. He is really a fine
> little chap—I can't feel too bad about him myself now,
> because it will be so jolly to have him later on. I am thirty
> now, and it didn't seem at all likely I should marry—I shall
> have something for my later age anyway ... They know
> nothing about him at home, and they must know nothing.
> It would grieve them quite unnecessarily. You know, it's
> not the kind of ill-doing that Mother has any sympathy
> for ... So please, not a word of any kind to Christchurch.
> By the time I want the boy, they will be too old, if they are
> still alive, to worry much about anything, and they must
> have these last years in peace ... If you need anything more
> expensive, or doctors or advice, or anything in the world
> for him, let me know. I can manage it.—He is rather noisy
> & excitable—You'll find it doesn't do to nurse him or pet
> him much, or he'll keep you at it all day & night ... I'll tell
> you anything else there's time for when I see you—Good-
> bye till then, my dear—& be good to my son![25]

We have no record of the reclusive Ivy's response to this, but
there is nothing in Sayers' letters to suggest that she pried or
probed, lectured or judged; certainly no sign of any reference
to that pompous teenage letter. Ivy Shrimpton, loyal to her
friend now and in the years to come, possessed that rare and
precious virtue—acceptance.

Sayers, working full-time at Benson's, paid irregular weekend visits to her son, always followed by letters to Ivy. These
would remark on how well her child was doing, or remind Ivy
that it was time for some vaccination or other. Sometimes the
emotional cracks tore open. 'I must find out if his father wants
anything to do with him'[26] ... 'Don't take any notice of my
moods, I had just told J's father to go to hell—he's always be-
haved fairly badly & finally became intolerable, so I thought he'd

better push off . . .'[27]

Sayers undoubtedly believed a day would come when John Anthony would be a part of her own home. It was never to be, for when she did finally marry it was to a man who flatly refused to share his house with his wife's child by another man. It is doubtful if Sayers, even as hope drifted away, planned her lifelong silence, doubtful too that her parents would have been as unforgiving as she thought, but as time passed and demands of work papered over the emotional cracks, silence probably seemed the least painful solution.

Whatever the reasons, only Sayers' secretaries (who had to send on cheques) and John Anthony's schoolmasters were ever let in on the secret; her closest friends in middle age (and she had some very close friends) knew nothing of her son's existence until after her death in 1957. None of them have a convincing explanation for Sayers' behaviour, but perhaps it is simpler than sometimes thought—that wrung out mentally, spiritually and physically by the emotional torments of Whelpton, Cournos, an illegitimate son, a difficult birth, and rejections that seemed eternal in consequence, she never again possessed the strength to tell the story, nor perhaps the openness to admit to such human weakness. And as she became famous, with her name on the pages of newspapers and on the lips of thousands of Wimsey fans, she would have been yet more fearful of the truth emerging, knowing only too well that newspapers could take a basic truth and bludgeon it out of recognition.

Little in her letters to Ivy gives away the emotional cost of these years, the despairing misery, the sheer loneliness of her position, and all the time the need to keep up a cheerful facade at work or with friends. Her notebooks contain the occasional heartfelt entry: 'I have made a muck of all my emotional relationships and I hate being beaten, so I pretend not to care.' And the telling sequel: 'It isn't that I've failed and pretend not to care. I don't care; and that is why I've failed.' What *does* give away the emotional cost are the letters to John Cournos, written in 1924 and 1925—and it is these I quote now. I do so at some length, for here is the *emotional heart* of Sayers, never again to be so exposed, but always there to judge subsequent events against.

I've heard you're married—I hope you are very happy,
with some one you can really love. I went over the rocks.
As you know, I was going there rapidly, but I preferred it
shouldn't be with you, but with somebody I didn't really
care twopence for. I couldn't have stood a catastrophe with
you. It was a worse catastrophe than I intended because I
went and had a young son . . . & the man's affection
couldn't stand that strain & he chucked me . . . Both of us
did what we swore we'd never do, you see—I do hope your
experiment turns out better than mine . . .[28]

Have I really succeeded in astonishing you! . . . Since I
suppose it is something to come out of such a hell with
one's reason, one's health and one's job intact, I will accept
your congratulation . . . If I could have found a man to my
measure, I could have put a torch to the world. Would you
like to find me one, even now? . . . Now why in the world
should you want to meet me? If I saw you, I should
probably only cry—& I've been crying for about 3 years
now & am heartily weary of the exercise . . . It is very
irritating to have no one to whom I can boast about him,
but I'm afraid you did sound as though you would be a
very unsympathetic listener. It's a 'ard world—peopled by
savage women & tame men, isn't it, my civilised friend?—
Don't grudge me that jibe . . .[29]

. . . It's such headachey work going to the office after
howling all night . . . Final problem: Tea or no tea? It's
going to hurt like hell to see you, because Judah with all thy
faults I love thee still, & as you've no use for me I must be
in a very stupid & false & painful position. And I *won't* be
made to cry in teashops. But if you like to come here, I will
see you. And ask any questions you like—I can't imagine
the question I would not readily answer. But for Christ's
sake, no generalities. Good God:—do you think I am
unsexed? . . . And you condescend to find my wit

improved? It was always there—only you drilled &
sermonised the poor thing out of existence. I was really
fond of you & afraid of you. You were a rotten companion
for a poor girl. You wouldn't go to the theatre & you
wouldn't talk nonsense—can you imagine me sitting on
your knee turning out impromptu limericks, each
obscener than the last?—I'm reckless now, having nothing
to lose, & you seem to like rudeness. I'm sorry you found
our last conversation dull. It was rather desperately
exciting for me—the last whack that chucked me over the
cliff. Well, if we meet, I'll be witty—& don't you offer me
any more maxims. Women hate 'em. Be a brute if you like,
but *be personal* & you'll be irresistible. Come off Sinai—
I'm damned if I'll be patronised any longer.[30]

I dare say I wanted too much—I could not be content with
less than your love and your children and happy
acknowledgement of each other to the world. You now say
you would have given me all those, but at the time you
went out of your way to insist you would give me none of
them.[31]

I hope Anthony and I don't come to the workhouse! but
it's so hard to work. It frightens me to be so unhappy—I
thought it would get better, but I think every day is worse
than the last, and I'm always afraid they'll chuck me out of
the office because I'm working so badly. And I haven't
even the last resort of doing away with myself, because
what would poor Anthony do then, poor thing? . . . I still
want help, you don't know how badly . . .[32]

A lover must be a companion, because he cuts one off from
the world; a husband need only be a lover, because one
then remains in touch with the world, and can get
companionship from one's friends . . . You were right in
supposing that it is a husband that I really want, because I
become impatient of the beastly restrictions which 'free
love' imposes. I have a careless rage for life, and secrecy

tends to make me bad-tempered . . . Give me a man that's human and careless and loves life, and one that can enjoy the rough and tumble of passion . . .[33]

Do think—I was utterly inexperienced—passionately wanting to be loved & to be faithful, & deliberately you told me over & over again that you did not love me, did not want fidelity—that you had nothing for me but animal passion and 'kindly feeling'—Now, I know, it's different—I'm so battered about that even decent kindness would be a boon beyond price. But *then* I still had some hope & some faith, & the desire for better things. But I swear that if you had offered me love—or even asked for love—you should have had everything. Not easily, because I did not want to commit so bitter a sin—but you never asked me to love you—never said a word of anything but bodily desire . . . Absolute & utter faithfulness to the claims of lover or husband is a kind of fanaticism with me . . . It is the more dangerous that you—for it was *you*— should so have undermined the ideal of fidelity in me, that I *have* a Hyde personality as well as a Jekyll. It would be very easy for me to be completely 'episodic'—hence my early and persistent desire to find myself. I could very readily have become the complete courtesan—though I think I should always be faithful to the affair while it lasted, even so. I don't want to let Hyde kill Jekyll though . . . I am so terrified of emotion now . . . Well, well—the prizes all go to the women who 'play their cards well'—but if they can only be won in that way, I would rather lose the game.[34]

Shattering stuff. The hidden Sayers is a very appealing Sayers, especially as she grows older and expects less of life. Worth remembering as we go on with Sayers' story, and as 'terrified of emotion'[35] she builds up walls around her to keep the world out and the feelings in, is that the *hidden* self is the *true* self. It was reading these letters to Cournos that persuaded me that I genuinely liked this woman with 'a careless rage for life'.[36]

Two decades after these events, in a lecture on 'The Other Six Deadly Sins', Sayers—probably having come to terms with her weaknesses of the flesh and more at peace with herself—points up the cruel absurdity of the word 'immorality' having come to mean 'one thing and one thing only':[37]

> A man may be greedy and selfish; spiteful, cruel, jealous and unjust; violent and brutal; grasping, unscrupulous, and a liar; stubborn and arrogant; stupid, morose, and dead to every noble instinct— and still we are ready to say of him that he is not an immoral man. I am reminded of a young man who once said to me with perfect simplicity: 'I did not know there were seven deadly sins; please tell me the names of the other six.'[38]

She proposes two reasons for the sin of lust: sheer exuberance of animal spirits, or

> men and women may turn to lust in sheer boredom and discontent, trying to find in it some stimulus that is not provided by the drab discomfort of their mental and physical surroundings. When that is the case, stern rebukes and restrictions are worse than useless. It is as though one were to endeavour to cure anaemia by bleeding; it only reduces further an already impoverished vitality.[39]

Christ rebuked disreputable sins 'only in mild and general terms, but uttered the most violent vituperations against the respectable ones'. Caesar and the Pharisees 'strongly dislike anything warm-hearted or disreputable, and set great store by the cold-hearted and respectable sins, which they are in a conspiracy to call virtues'. The result, Sayers argues, is the 'identification of Christian morality with everything that Christ most fervently abhorred'.[40]

Elsewhere, during this same period, she acknowledges that forgiveness 'does not wipe away the consequences of the sin'.[41] In every case 'the consequences are borne by somebody'.[42] Often, of course, by the innocent, which makes the conscience of the guilty—forgiven by God and man, or not—

forever sensitive. Neither is it, she says, primarily a remission of punishment:

> Forgiveness is the re-establishment of a right relationship, in which the parties can genuinely feel and behave as freely with one another as though the unhappy incident had never taken place.[43]

Forgiveness, she accedes—as she has to, after such an optimistic definition—is a difficult business: 'No man living is wholly innocent or wholly guilty.'[44]

As for a man who was 'human and careless and loves life',[45] he came along—or she thought he did—in the shape of Oswald Atherton Fleming. She was to marry him and know some contentment from the marriage, but—as they were not really suited as a couple—it was a contentment born almost wholly of Sayers' weariness of searching any longer for the ideal, although lines from later essays are worth noting: 'The only way to deal with the past is to accept the *whole* past, and by accepting it, to change its meaning'[46] ... '[The disciples] did not allow any morbid and egotistical remorse to inhibit their joyful activities in the future'.[47]

This will do, she seemed to say. I am exhausted; I am alone; I need rest; I have financial security; I'll marry and get down to my work. And work, as it is for many whose private lives collapse around them, was her salvation. She was never in danger of losing her job at Benson's; her work barely suffered, because while she was doing it the rest was blotted out. Some take to alcohol, some to drugs. Others, like Sayers, take to work. As she knew when she penned the opening of *Have His Carcase*:

> The best remedy for a bruised heart is not, as so many people seem to think, repose upon a manly bosom. Much more efficacious are honest work, physical activity, and the sudden acquisition of wealth. After being acquitted of murdering her lover and, indeed, in consequence of that acquittal, Harriet Vane found all three specifics abundantly at her disposal; and although Lord Peter

Wimsey, with a touching faith in tradition, persisted day in and day out in presenting the bosom for her approval, she showed no inclination to recline upon it.

Work was to become much more than an escape, or an alternative to the fantasy world of her childhood; it was to be integral to her Christian faith. Work, she said in 1942, is to be seen

> not as a necessary drudgery to be undergone for the
> purpose of making money, but as a way of life in which the
> nature of man should find its proper exercise and delight
> and so fulfil itself to the glory of God. That it should, in
> fact, be thought of as a creative activity undertaken for the
> love of work itself; and that man, made in God's image,
> should make things, as God makes them, for the sake of
> doing well a thing that is well worth doing.[48]

Sayers kept the existence of a son from her parents in the belief they could never have withstood the shock. She could hardly keep her marriage from them, but knowing that marriage to a divorced man with two daughters would be a shock comparable in effect, she tossed off the news in a bright, breezy and wholly out-of-place style. In a letter dated 8 April 1926, having *first* gone over inconsequentials, she writes:

> ... In the meantime, I am getting married on Tuesday
> (weather permitting!) to a man named Fleming, who is at
> the moment motoring correspondent to the *News of the
> World* and otherwise engaged in journalism. No money,
> but a good job, forty-two and otherwise eminently suitable
> and all that.

In fact, Fleming was forty-four, twelve years older than Sayers. Mr and Mrs Sayers took the blow on their devout chins, but six days later another tactless missive arrived:

> Dear Mother, meant to send you a card last night, but
> nobody had any stamps and we had all overeaten and over-
> drunk ourselves. I understand that, the news having
> seeped out, the whole of Fleet Street, incapably drunk,

decorated the bar of the Falstaff last night, and for all I know they are still there.[49]

Sayers probably met Oswald Atherton Fleming at one of the many pubs frequented by journalists and advertising people. Scottish-born, with two sisters and six brothers, he had left home as a teenager to fight in the Boer War. After that he travelled widely, to the Far East, to the Hawaiian Islands, to the Continent. He never grew out of *his* fantasy world, promoting himself as the 14th Earl of Wigton, a wholly unsubstantiated claim; calling himself Oswald Atherton, when in fact he had been christened Oswald Arthur, and after World War One insisting on the title of Major when Captain had been his highest rank.

On 8 September 1911, he married Winifred Ellen Meyrick, a daughter of a vicar, and the couple lived in Coventry until 1914 when the wife (and one child by now) moved to the Meyrick home in Hartfield, Sussex, and Fleming entered the war. Commissioned in the Royal Army Service Corps as a second lieutenant in 1915 he saw out the war with the Twenty-Sixth Siege Brigade, Royal Artillery, and sent back from the front dispatches to the *Daily Chronicle* and *Sunday Chronicle*. He had no easy war. Gassed, shell-shocked, and hurt deeply by the death of two brothers, he wrote of his experiences in a book called *How To See The Battlefields*:

> October was one long nightmare to anybody unfortunate enough to be in the Somme area. Many and many a time did we pray that our particular lot would be sent up to comparative comfort of the 'Salient' at Ypres. I wonder if any of my readers remember the road to Hebuterne? That road broke the heart of more than one man on the ammunition supply. How the batteries ever got ammunition at all beats me hollow. And yet there are people who still think that the A.S.C. (M.T.) had a soft job! Some of them had, no doubt, at the bases, but what about the poor devils who—many times—worked forty-eight hours on end, at least half the time under shell-fire, plunging and wallowing in and out of shell-holes, lorries

heavily laden with shells and cartridges, well over the axles in mud, no lights, and very often no food, and not the slightest protection in the way of trench or dug-out when the road was under fire?

Like so many men changed, even crazed, by the war, Fleming couldn't fit snugly again into family life. He didn't return home, settling instead in lodgings in London. Their second daughter, Ann, said that on his occasional visits home 'mother found him very changed, and believed that the war had affected him psychologically'. His first marriage was dissolved on 15 May 1925, and although financial support was promised to Winifred it seldom materialized.

As with Sayers, Fleming's personal life floundered as his professional life prospered, and by the time they met he was a correspondent of the *News of the World*, specializing not only in motor-racing, as Sayers informed her parents, but also crime. Which probably convinced Sayers that they had enough in common to make a lasting marriage. Sayers would also have found attractive that he was a writer, a traveller, hale, hearty and uncomplicated. He also had 'plans'—although few of these ever came to anything. He loved good food and drink. He was charmed with the fateful ability to make a woman feel exclusively important. He had a certain panache, as when he drove his car home on whisky when the petrol ran out. He was also, it can be assumed, adequate in bed; Sayers, at this point in her life, was not interested in anyone who failed here. In a remarkable letter to Charles Williams in 1944, having got it into her head that Dante had been a passionate lover, she wrote of 'the distinguishing marks of True Bedworthiness in the Male', finding these 'to consist in the presence of Three Grand Assumptions':

1. That the primary aim and object of Bed is that a good time should be had by *all*.

2. That (other things being equal) it is the business of the male to make it so.

3. That he knows his business.

93

The first Assumption rules out at once all Satyromaniacs, sadists, connoisseurs in rape, egotists, and superstitious believers in female reluctance, as well as Catholic (replenish-the-earth) utilitarians and stockbreeders.

The second Assumption rules out the hasty, the clumsy, the lazy, the inconsiderate, the peremptory, the untimely and (in most cases) the routinier ...

The third Assumption rules out the tentative as well as the incompetent and inadequate.[50]

A cheerfully compelling vulgarity distinguished Sayers all her life, and in 1936 she actually delivered a lecture on 'The Importance of Being Vulgar':

It is, of course, all too easy to be vulgar without being great; it is not nearly so easy to be great without being vulgar—indeed it is almost impossible in any activity which brings one into contact with one's fellow creatures ... The two great queens who have adorned our history were each the very embodiment of the common people of their time and that was the secret of their greatness as rulers ... I am quite sure that my own notion of a lord as something to love and laugh at is not due ... to astuteness, but to my sheer unmitigated commonness. I like the common people and I heartily share their love of a lord because I am myself as common as mud in my likes and dislikes.[51]

Dorothy L. Sayers and Oswald Atherton Fleming were married on 13 April 1925, at the Registry Office close to her lodgings at 24 Great James Street. Sayers was two months short of thirty-three. The anguish of her parents can only be imagined: she had been christened in Christ Church Cathedral, Oxford, confirmed in Salisbury Cathedral, and they would have longed for a church setting at the very least. Henry Sayers could not even conduct the marriage; at the time Anglican clergy were forbidden from marrying in church even the innocent party in a divorce—and Fleming certainly wasn't that. Sayers must have felt it deeply, too, given her love of ceremonial, and her acute sense of sin.

The burden, a rooted dead weight in the soul, never left her—and in years to come, when she spoke out so vehemently on moral and doctrinal issues, driving—though she would have denied it—people into the Kingdom of God almost by physical force, it was as someone who had fallen and suffered and was desperate to warn others of the self-inflicted punishment lying in wait for the unwary.

6

'The deadlines of principles'

Throughout the emotional upheavals of the years from 1922, Sayers' one constant therapy was her working life at Benson's, where she equipped herself with material for arguably the best of her novels of pure detection, *Murder Must Advertise*.

> Of course, there is some truth in advertising. There's yeast in bread. Truth in advertising is like leaven, which a woman hid in three measures of meal. It provides a suitable quantity of gas with which to blow out a mass of crude misrepresentation into a form that the public can swallow.[1]

Benson's provided Sayers with a steady if unspectacular income until she was so well known as an author that she didn't need it, made her astute on such matters as contracts and book promotion, taught her about the use and abuse of language which she would put to good use in post-Wimsey writings, and reawakened in her a joyful sense of camaraderie unknown since Oxford days. Nonetheless, as *Murder Must Advertise* demonstrates, she never fell for the blandishments of the advertising world. She saw it as a worshipper at the feet of the false god of materialism. Essentially, advertising feeds one's bias towards covetousness:

> It was left for the present age to endow Covetousness with glamour on a big scale, and to give it a title which it would carry like a flag. It occurred to somebody to call it Enterprise. From the moment of that happy inspiration, Covetousness has gone forward and never looked back. It

has become a swaggering, swashbuckling, piratical sin, going about with its hat cocked over its eyes ... Its war cries are 'Business Efficiency,' 'Free Competition,' 'Get Out or Get Under!' and 'There's always room at the Top!' It no longer screws and saves—it launches out into new enterprises; it gambles and speculates; it thinks in a big way; it takes risks ... It looks so jolly and jovial, and has such a twinkle in its cunning eye, that nobody can believe that its heart is as cold and calculating as ever. Besides, where is its heart? Covetousness is not incarnated in individual people, but in business corporations, joint-stock companies ... which have neither bodies to be kicked, nor souls to be damned—nor hearts to be appealed to, either.[2]

It is possible to be too serious about all this, however, for Benson's, above all else for Sayers during those nine years, was tremendous fun. And the fact that colleagues long remembered her as exuberant, bouncy, vulgarly extrovert, says a lot for her ability to separate her working and private lives. She worked there, remember, during those long nights of weeping. Picture her: one hand stuck in the pocket of her masculine jacket, the other brandishing her long cigarette holder, hauling herself up and down Kingsway Hall's famous spiral staircase—the setting in *Murder Must Advertise* of Pym's Publicity and Victor Dean's murder.

She and the artist John Gilroy worked together on several imaginative and hugely successful advertising campaigns. For example, Gilroy painted the famous picture of the Toucan poised over glasses of Guinness, and Sayers added the jingle:

If he can say as you can
Guinness is good for you
How grand to be a Toucan
Just think what Toucan do!

Outstanding among their work, however, was the creation of the Mustard Club, and this was something Sayers worked on at home with her husband—possibly the only occasion in her adult life of an overlap of relationship and enthusiasm. J & J Colman's of Norwich had despaired of making mustard *sell*; it just wasn't a sexy enough object. True enough—but Sayers changed all that, and the country was suddenly aware of the Mustard Club, posters inviting one and all to join it, stories in newspapers of club members' sensationalist activities: 'Mustard Club in Court', or 'Mustard Club Member Blackballed'—all accompanied by Gilroy's superbly witty illustrations. Letters and cartoons appeared in the press. Jokes did the rounds: 'What is a canary? A sparrow who has joined the Mustard Club.' The Club had its own officers: among them Lord Bacon of Cookham, and secretary Miss Di Gester. There were rules and regulations: 'Every member shall see that the mustard is freshly made, and no member shall tip a waiter who forgets to put mustard on the table.' There was a prospectus which announced that the original Mustard Club was 'founded by Aesculapius, the god of medicine, in the days of Ham and Shem'. And this, 'in response to numerous enquiries', found its way into many newspapers:

> The Mustard Club (1926) has been founded under the Presidency of the Baron de Beef, of Porterhouse College, Cambridge. It is a Sporting Club, because its members are always there for the meat. It is a Political Club, because members find that liberal use of Mustard saves labour in digestion and is conservative of health. It is a Card Club, but members are only allowed to play for small steaks.
>
> The motto of the Mustard Club is 'Mustard Makyth Methusalahs,' because Mustard keeps the digestion young. The Password of the Mustard Club is 'Pass the Mustard please!'
>
> There are more than ten million branches of the Mustard Club —in fact, wherever a few people are mustered together at dinner, there you have a meeting of the Mustard Club. Every home where people respect their digestion is a branch of the Mustard Club . . .

And the objectives of this unique club?

To enrol all Grumblers, Curmudgeons, and other such persons who by omitting the use of Mustard have suffered in their digestions, and to bring such persons to a joyous frame of mind and a healthy habit of body by the liberal use of Mustard. To encourage the use of Mustard, not only with Beef and Bacon, but to show how it improves the flavour of Mutton, Fish, Cheese and Macaroni.

To teach the younger generation that the true foundation of health and good digestion is the Mustard Pot.

Occasionally, and only to be expected from Sayers, the text sank beneath the groaning weight of pun. This was published under the heading 'Mustard and Matrimony':

At Baconwell Police Court a case was brought by Mrs E. N. Pecker, of Nag's Head Lane, Barking, who complained of cruelty on the part of her husband. He was liverish, she said, and used words to her and was round at his club every evening. The Magistrate: Was it the Mustard Club? (laughter). Complainant: No, he always came back in such a bad temper that she thought it must be a political club.

The joke ran for about two years, and a country bowed down by strikes and the aftermath of a crippling war welcomed anything that lightened the gloom. Colman's, too, didn't do badly out of it. Sayers knew that, to succeed, the advertiser had to lead his storm-troopers in by way of 'the weak places', or the four gates:

By Fear-gate go in his formidable Death's Head Hussars: Are you Suffering from Halitosis, Body-Odour, Athlete's Foot, Pains in the Back, Incomplete Elimination? Are you Insured against Sickness, Old Age, Unemployment, Battle, Murder and Sudden Death? Is your Lavatory Clean? Does Dry Rot Lurk in your Roof? Do you Feel Too Old at Forty? . . . Take Vitamins under pain of Losing your Job: Wave your Hair, under Pain of Losing your Husband's Love: Use Blank's pure Dusting-Powder, under Pain of Poisoning your Baby: Beware of Substitutes: Beware of Germs: Beware of Everything!

By Sloth-gate go in the armies of Leisure: the Ready-Cooked Food, the Chromium that Needs no Cleaning, the Clothes that Wash Themselves, all the Gadgets and Machines that Take the Irk out of Work. And behind them come the devices for taking all effort out of the employment even of Leisure—the Cinema-posters, the Radio sets with easy tuning, the Gramophones that change their own records, the Gearless Cars, the Book-Societies that spare you the trouble of choosing your own reading . . .

Greed-gate is the entrance for all the schemes that promise Something for Nothing. The magistrates of the city work very hard to close Greed-gate; Lotteries can now scarcely find entrance in this country; Free-Gift Coupons have received a shrewd knock and Guessing-Competitions and Pools have sustained severe reverses. But surprise parties still bring off successful raids from time to time and carry off a good deal of loot before the authorities intervene . . .

The troops that attack Snob-gate are the best turned-out regiments in the army. They are made up of Discriminating Men and Smart Women, of Typists who Marry the Boss, of Men who can Judge Whisky blindfold and Hostesses who know how to give their parties that Air of Distinction. They offer Luxury Goods under the brand of the Life Beautiful; and perhaps the worst that can be said of them is that their notion of Beauty is trivial.

Sayers may not have fallen for the blandishments of the advertising world, but experience soon taught her not to lay *all* the blame at the door of the advertisers: 'Those who prefer their English sloppy have only themselves to thank if the advertisement writer uses his mastery of the vocabulary and syntax to mislead their weak minds.'[3] One must, she said, 'read advertisements carefully, observing both what is said and what is omitted'.[4] She was writing, or course, when there was *time* to take note of such subtleties. *Murder Must Advertise* includes this nice little exchange:

'That reminds me. You know that idiotic thing Darling's put out the other day—the air-cushion for travellers with a doll that fits into the middle and sits up holding an "ENGAGED" label?'

'What for?' asked Bredon.

'Well, the idea is, that you plank the cushion down in the railway carriage and the doll proclaims that the place is taken.'

'But the cushion would do that without the doll.'

'Of course it would, but you know how silly people are. They like superfluities...'

Fiction and fact merged marvellously in Sayers' honour in 1950, when she was asked to unveil a plaque in the reception area of Benson's. It reads:

DOWN THIS STAIRCASE
was precipitated to his death with malice
aforethought and for the gratification of all
who appreciate the fine art of murder
VICTOR DEAN OF PYM'S PUBLICITY
25 May MCMXXXIII
THIS TABLET WAS UNVEILED A.D. 1950
By Dorothy L. Sayers, M.A.

Whose Body? continued to sell well, the bibliophile, musician, connoisseur, multi-linguist, doggerel-loving Lord Peter having captured the public imagination. Now, after a long, midnight-oil, tear-stained struggle came *Clouds of Witness*; ever after the books came much more easily at the rate of about one a year. *Clouds of Witness*, published in 1926, is the story of Lord Peter's majestic defence of his older brother who has been falsely charged with murder. Impressively, albeit mechanically, he brings the true culprit to the shadow of the gallows. Wimsey is as affected as ever, but flashes of serious post-war reflection break through: 'I was ill, you know, and after I got the chuck from Barbara I didn't feel much like botherin' about other people's heart-to-hearts.'

Unnatural Death appeared just twelve months later. In this Wimsey allows centre-stage to one of Sayers' finest creations, a female sleuth called Miss Climpson, grey-haired, middle-aged, and—if a boardinghouse proprietress is to be believed—religious too: 'Miss Climpson is a nice lady, and that I must say, even if she is a Roaming Catholic or next to one.' Wimsey's description of her suggests dormant political passion, which his creator refused to develop.

> Miss Climpson . . . is a manifestation of the wasteful way in which this country is run . . . Thousands of old maids, simply bursting with useful energy, forced by our own stupid social systems into hydros and hotels and communities and hostels and posts as companions, where their magnificent gossip-powers and units of inquisitiveness are allowed to dissipate themselves or even become harmful to the community, while the ratepayers' money is spent on getting work for which those women are providentially fitted, inefficiently carried out by ill-equipped policemen . . .

Sayers for the first time touches upon moral causes and effects. Lord Peter inquires of a clergyman called Tredgold whether or not he should pursue investigations which could lead to another murder. He is told:

> Do what you think is right, according to the laws which we have been brought up to respect. Leave the consequences to God. And try to think charitably even of wicked people. You know what I mean. Bring the offender to justice, but remember that if we all got justice, you and I wouldn't escape, either.

This was Sayers' first novel written after her marriage, and

in the optimistic afterglow of lifelong commitment she has her
hero say:

> ... Read the divorce court lists. Wouldn't they give you
> the idea that marriage is a failure? Isn't the sillier sort of
> journalism packed with articles to the same effect? And
> yet, looking round among the marriages you know of
> personally, aren't the majority of them a success, in a hum-
> drum, undemonstrative sort of way? Only you don't hear
> of them. People don't bother to come into court and
> explain that they dodder along very comfortably on the
> whole, thank you ...

Hum-drum ... undemonstrative ... dodder ... Not the
words the Sayers we know would happily have associated with
an ideal marriage—she who had longed for a partner who was
human, careless and in love with life. But hers was no ideal
marriage, and this was what soon she would settle for. There
were two unexpected developments; unexpected, that is, to
Sayers who had married too much in haste to dwell long on the
nature or credentials of her husband, but sadly predictable to the
reasonably interested observer. First, Fleming shied away from
having his routine comforts disturbed by welcoming Sayers' son
into their home, and second, either because of post-war sickness
or laziness or, most likely, a combination of the two, he slumped
into unemployment blues and alcoholic haze. He didn't *have* to
work, of course; Sayers was earning enough to keep both of them.
But Fleming compounded the problem with sullen resentment
of her growing fame.

Sayers had been paying the eccentric, reclusive, but good-
hearted Ivy Shrimpton three pounds a month to look after John
Anthony, and visiting the boy most weekends. After a while, the
visits grew less and less, because Sayers—however burdened
with guilt about the past—was always someone resolutely to
look to the future and move on; and because she had little or
no encouragement from her husband. Letters to Ivy excusing
her attendance became commonplace.

The arrangement was under threat only once—in 1925 when

Ivy's mother died. Sayers stayed with her to help her through the bereavement. Ivy was now advised by well-meaning relatives to give up her caring for children in need, but a not disinterested Sayers argued that after so many years of independence Ivy would find not being her own mistress disagreeable. Sayers' view prevailed.

The public face of Sayers, even where her child was concerned, continued to be pugnaciously forthright. No mincing of words for her. On hearing that her son had broken a collar bone, she wrote: 'I am glad the kid has pluck anyhow—maternal affection is by no means my strong point, I must say, but if there must be children, it is preferable they should have some guts.'[5]

Such letters do her reputation no good at all, but two points should be heeded. The *tone* of such a missive, and the *relationship* between sender and receiver are crucial to interpretation. This was a long-standing friendship, in which on Sayers' side at least there had been honesty to the point of foolhardiness, and she may well have felt it was part of her image to exaggerate to the point of caricature her no-nonsense reputation. The other point is that friends of her latter years deny what many have seen as a dismissive dislike of children: her close friend Dr Barbara Reynolds will have none of it and has stories to prove her point:

> She hated to be asked by anybody if she was going to write another Wimsey story; and (my son) Adrian was about 14 and so excited to meet her... 'Miss Sayers, when are you going to write another Lord Peter?' You can imagine how my heart sank. But she was so sweet to him. She said, 'Well, you know, he is getting on a bit... and I don't really know that we can go on for ever with him'... And she used to send him stamps for his collection and mention the children in her letters. When my second baby was born she wrote to me and said 'This seems a good moment for remembering Adrian'. Not many people think of that. They send a present for the baby but they don't think that the older child may feel his importance diminished in the world. So she sent him rather special stamps.[6]

Sayers and Fleming started out well. The Bloomsbury flat was cramped for space, so Sayers accepted that they would have to move before John Anthony could join them. That seemed imminent, as her books, gaining in popularity with reviewers and readers alike, brought her respectable riches. Fleming, unlike his wife, had some interest in the political events of the day, and would spend historic occasions—the General Strike, for example—listening to the news on the wireless. He continued to write his motoring column, and on occasion organized race meetings. Only his weak stomach, a legacy from the war, betrayed anxiety—and then not enough to restrict his legendary skills in the kitchen:

> I have a first-class male chef, capable of turning out a
> perfect dinner for any number of people, who not only
> demands no salary, but also contributes to the support of
> the household. I came across this paragon some years ago,
> and having sampled his cooking and ascertained that he
> held sound opinions on veal (which I detest) and garlic
> (which I appreciate), married him. So far, the
> arrangement seems to work very well, and, since giving me
> notice would be a troublesome and expensive matter, I am
> hoping he will stay.[7]

But during her most productive year professionally—1928—Fleming's health deteriorated sharply. Commissions largely dried up—although he wrote cookery articles for the *Evening News* and a cookery book for Cross & Blackwell's. Then on 20 September, Sayers' father, at the age of 74, died—'suddenly, peacefully, mercifully'.[8] Sayers was at his bedside when he died. She had always loved her father, and it was a love communicated in her affectionate portrayal of clergy in the pages of her novels. Accommodation for Mrs Sayers and her sister, Mabel, now became a matter of some urgency. Fleming found just the place—24, Newland Street, Witham—an old-fashioned town on the main road between Chelmsford and Colchester. Sayers bought the house, with financial assistance from her mother, and the four of them moved in. Elderly people do not like disruption, and Helen Sayers was not immediately grateful.

> When mother went down with Mac the week before last to choose the papers etc she couldn't seem to see anything but gloom and difficulties, and that depressed poor old Mac (who is suffering badly from nerves) till he almost had a breakdown.[9]

Life improved, however, and Sayers' mother enjoyed a few contented months before, in August 1929, she too died at the age of 73. Her heart was unable to stand up to the stress of an operation on a strangulated hernia. She and her husband were buried side by side in Christchurch cemetery. Their daughter allowed no mournful hymns at the funerals, nor markers at the graves. But the parishioners erected a memorial tablet on the west wall of the church expressing thanks to God for the memory of the Rev. and Mrs Henry Sayers. Helen's sister continued to live with Sayers and Fleming until her death.

Sayers' fourth novel duly appeared that year—*The Unpleasantness at the Bellona Club*—in which Lord Peter establishes his blossoming reputation as both gourmet and master detective, and Sayers fails to hide feelings of exasperation for her real-life husband. War veteran George Fentiman—in much the same plight as Fleming had found himself after the war—complains:

> A man goes and fights for his country, gets his inside gassed out, and loses his job, and all they give him is the privilege of marching past the Cenotaph once a year and paying four shillings in the pound income tax ... It's pretty damnable for a man to have to live on his wife's earnings, isn't it?

And Lord Peter's diatribe on the marital state is in marked contrast to the cosiness of views expressed in *Unnatural Death*:

> 'It always gives me the pip,' said Wimsey, 'to see how rude people are when they're married. I suppose it's inevitable. Women are funny. They don't seem to care half so much about a man's being honest and faithful ... as for their

opening doors and saying 'thank you'... I've asked people, you know—my usual inquisitiveness—and they generally just grunt and say that *their* wives are sensible and take their affection for granted. But I don't believe women ever get sensible, not even through prolonged association with their husbands.

So established was she as a writer that her recently-acquired agent David Higham secured for her a contract with an American publisher which ended her days as slave to haphazard royalty cheques. She left Benson's, kept on Great James Street, used the Witham house as a weekend getaway, and commenced a new career as a freelance. No country lover—she had no interest in gardening, walking or animals (except pigs and cats)—she was to miss the camaraderie she had relished at Benson's until she discovered the seductive worlds of theatre and radio.

As the Witham property comprised two cottages knocked into one, and came complete with back garden, a cobbled yard and a greenhouse, it was no longer possible to pretend that lack of space alone prevented John Anthony joining his mother. The boy still lived with Ivy, though they too had moved—to a thatched cottage in the village of Westcott Barton, fifteen miles outside Oxford. Ivy called this cottage—without a single modern amenity and choked by undergrowth—The Sidelings. Sayers now blamed the potentially embarrassing presence of Aunt Mabel for the persistent separation.

John Anthony, in those early years of his life, knew her as Cousin Dorothy who could be expected to visit irregularly and bring presents at Christmas and birthdays. Sayers, who had no high opinion of the educational standards of the country, was content to leave tuition to Ivy—which didn't harm John academically, but did exact a price socially. He was never to move easily among his peers. Holding Sayers and Fleming together were his sporadic painting—which she over-praised—a parrot called Joey, a love of music on the gramophone, pub songs and pub conversation (she wore the lapel badge of the Froth Blowers), crosswords and the intricate marvels of the wireless.

Nothing that could be called permanent.

Professionally, 1929 was a prolific year for publications bearing the imprint of Sayers. Besides *Unpleasantness* there was a collection of short stories called *Lord Peter Views the Body* (all but one very substandard; Sayers knew she was no short story writer, but that didn't stop her persisting); a translation of Thomas the Anglo-Norman's *Tristan in Brittany*, a collection of twelfth-century romantic fragments, and the first of three series of *Great Short Stories of Detection*, whose sixty classic tales she selected. Her Introduction has been called 'authoritative... concise... containing in its relatively brief compass virtually all that was to be said about the detective story up to the date of its composition':[10]

> The art of self-tormenting is an ancient one, with a long and honourable literary tradition. Man, not satisfied with the mental confusion and unhappiness to be derived from contemplating the cruelties of life and the riddle of the universe, delights to occupy his mind in leisure moments with puzzles and bugaboos... It may be that in them he finds a sort of catharsis or purging of his fears and self-questionings. These mysteries made only to be solved, these horrors which he knows to be mere figments of the creative brain, comfort him by subtly persuading that life is a mystery which death will solve, and whose horrors will pass away as a tale that is told... The fact remains that if you reach the second-hand bookstall for his cast-off literature, you will find fewer mystery stories than any other kind of book. Theology and poetry, philosophy and numismatics, love-stories and biography, he discards as easily as old razor-blades, but Sherlock Holmes and Wilkie Collins are cherished and read and re-read, till their covers fall off and their pages crumble to fragments.[11]

Wilkie Collins was a favourite of hers. In fact, in June 1928 she wrote to the *Times Literary Supplement* requesting from readers access to letters, manuscripts and papers to assist her in a 'critical and biographical study of William Wilkie Collins'. The projected biography was never finished, but in 1977 the incomplete version was published by the Friends of the University of Toledo Libraries.

Also in that year she responded enthusiastically to an approach from another crime novelist, Anthony Berkeley, to be part of the Detection Club. The idea was for twenty or more writers of detective fiction to meet at regular intervals for dinner and discussion. Premises in Gerrard Street were paid for out of the proceeds of joint detective radio serials, to which notables of the day like Agatha Christie, Freeman Wills Croft, E.C. Bentley, John Dickson Carr, and Sayers herself each contributed an episode.[12]

The Detection Club was no exception to the rule that a club's genuineness can be judged by the bizarreness of its ceremonies, and from handwritten copies still existing of 'The Uncommon Order of Initiation of New Members of the Detective Club' and 'The Order of Solemn Installation for a President of the Detective Club', it is quite clear that Sayers took a precocious lead. Some members thought she took the whole business far too solemnly; apparently she threatened with expulsion those who divulged ceremonial secrets, and showered with invective those who put other commitments before the Club's monthly meetings. This is part of the initiation ceremony:

> The Company being Assembled, and the Lights
> Extinguished, the President (or the Ruler of the Feast
> appointed in his Room), shall proceed to the Place
> Designated for the Ceremony, with his Attendants & the
> Candidates in manner following.

THE ORDER OF THE PROCESSION

1. Two Torchbearers

2. Eric the Skull borne on a Black Cushion

3. The Secretary

4. The Candidates

5. The Sponsors bearing Torches

6. The President . . .

The Candidates are cross-examined by the President:

'Do you promise that your Detectives shall well and truly detect the Crimes presented to them, using those wits which it may please you to bestow upon them and not placing reliance upon nor making use of Divine Revelation, Feminine Intuition, Mumbo Jumbo, Jiggery-Pokery, Coincidence or the Act of God?'

Answer: 'I do.'

The President: 'Do you solemnly swear never to conceal a Vital Clue from the Reader?'

Answer: 'I do.'

The President: 'Do you promise to observe a seemly moderation in the use of Gangs, Conspiracies, Death-Rays, Ghosts, Hypnotism, Trap-Doors, Chinamen, Super-Criminals and Lunatics, and utterly and forever to forswear Mysterious Poisons unknown to Science?'

Answer: 'I do.'

Once elected, the new members face one more ordeal should they renege on their promises:

. . . may other Writers anticipate your Plots, may your Publishers do you down in your Contracts, may Total Strangers sue you for Libel, may your Pages swarm with Misprints and your Sales continually Diminish. Amen.

Approaching forty, Sayers—settling for a quiet personal life—made several binding decisions: to stay with Fleming, despite the uneasy tension between the two (as she was to tell her friends: 'He gets so impatient with me and I irritate him appallingly when I am at home; but he can't bear me to be away'[13]); to accept that her husband, who was growing more irascible by the day, would never now accept John Anthony into the home, and—linked to that—to arrange an informal 'adoption' of her son so that, as he embarked on school life, she would have some official place in his life. Only the latter decision called for action, and in 1933 Anthony was told to call Sayers 'Mother' and Fleming 'Father'; adoption in any legal sense was impossible for it would have been necessary to produce his birth certificate complete with Sayers' name as sole parent.

1930 saw the publication of her fifth novel, *The Documents in the Case*, startlingly different from anything attempted before or after. Minus Wimsey, it is a collection of letters and documents which reconstruct events leading to the death of one George Harrison and to the execution of his murderer. As we read the letters, layer after layer of deceit is exposed, and people's understanding of each other is shown to be dependent on falsehood and circumstance, rather than on any objective truth. Scientific blunders in the murder method exist, despite technical collaboration from Robert Eustace, alias Dr Eustace Barton—but these take nothing away from what is at its heart Sayers' first attempt to relate Christian doctrine to the modern world; even the solution emerges from a religious and philosophical discussion. *Strong Poison*, published the same year, introduces her *alter ego*, Harriet Vane:

> Let me confess that when I undertook *Strong Poison* it was with the infanticidal intention of doing away with Peter; that is, of marrying him off and getting rid of him—for a lingering instinct of self-preservation, and the deterrent object-lesson of Mr Holmes's rather scrambling return from the Reichenbach Falls, prevented me from actually killing and burying the nuisance.[14]

Harriet Vane, a writer of detective stories, is charged with murder. Peter Wimsey intuitively knows that she couldn't have done it, and proceeds to unravel the truth in his debonair fashion. Except that he isn't quite so debonair as in the past. There is a hint of the human about him as Sayers 'rather timidly introduced

111

the love-element into the Wimsey story'.[15] Vane is not ready, however, for Wimsey's romantic advances; she is too bruised to respond to affection. Over several books she will keep Wimsey at a distance, reducing him to a forlorn and lonely figure:

> I could not marry Peter off to the young woman he had . . . rescued from death and infamy, because I could find no form of words in which she could accept him without loss of self-respect. I had landed my two chief puppets in a situation where, according to all the conventional rules of detective fiction, they should have had nothing to do but fall into one another's arms; *but they would not do it*, and that for a very good reason. When I looked at the situation I saw that it was in every respect false and degrading; and the puppets had somehow got just so much flesh and blood in them that I could not force them to accept it without shocking myself.[16]

The lacklustre *Five Red Herrings* followed a year later: a complex puzzle, cardboard characterization, devoid of humour as well as Harriet Vane. The couple's holidays in Galloway inspired both plot and setting, and one can imagine Fleming dabbling with his paints (he was fully retired from journalism now and flitting from one hobby to another) while Sayers researched the Scottish idiom and interrogated stationmasters about rail schedules.

The next novel, *Have His Carcase,* is quite different again. The re-emerging Harriet Vane takes the first forty-seven pages just to discover a corpse on a rock—and as she unravels the mystery with Wimsey the pace is slow, gentle and beguiling. By the end, however, there is still no sign of entanglement:

> 'Let's clear out of this,' he said. 'Get your things packed and leave your address with the police and come up to Town. I'm fed to the back teeth.'
> 'Yes, let's go . . . It's all frightening and disgusting.

We'll go home.'

'Right-ho! We'll go home.'

Such was the explosion of creative energy after this that Sayers was ordered by her doctor to rest for three weeks. She wrote *The Nine Tailors* and *Murder Must Advertise* almost simultaneously, and between the publication of the two came another collection of short stories, *Hangman's Holiday*.

The Nine Tailors set out as a labour of love: Wimsey solves the crime of a body in a church's bell-chamber, but the truly unforgettable hero is the Rev. Theodore Venables, clearly an affectionate portrait of the Rev. Henry Sayers; the church, Fenchurch St Paul, is an amalgam of several churches in the Fens; and the first sixty-three pages provide no mystery, rather a gentle portrait of a community to which Sayers wanted to pay tribute. In fact, the book—by nature of the research required into campanology—took two years to write, and 'to keep the wolf from the door'[17] Sayers put it aside to toss off *Murder Must Advertise*.

Campanology is essential to the plot of a book subtitled 'Changes Rung on an Old Theme in Two Short Touches and Two Full Peals', and Sayers well knew the bell-ringing fraternity as sticklers for accuracy. 'Incalculable hours' were spent 'writing out sheets and sheets of change ringing'. She had to visualize 'from the pages of instructions to ringers, both what it looked like and what it felt like to handle a bell and to acquire "rope-sight"'. She studied 'a good deal of technical stuff about bell cages, bell inscriptions, upkeep of bells and so on'.[18] It paid off; in the novel she wears her learning lightly, experienced bell-ringers could find only three tiny technical errors, and she was made Vice-President of the Campanological Society of Great Britain. She felt, she said, sinfully proud.

The Nine Tailors has always been her best-selling novel. On initial publication it ran quickly into three impressions, 100,000 copies being sold in two months in the United Kingdom alone. By now many of her novels had been translated into half-a-dozen languages. Interviewed by the *Daily Express* she said she was 'a scholar gone wrong'. Sayers may have been wary of the press, but as long as there was a door open behind her she enjoyed basking in the sunlight. Her proudest moment came on 13 June 1934, her birthday, when she was invited to the Somerville College Gaudy Dinner to 'propose the toast of the University'; in her speech she thanked a university education for 'that habit of intellectual integrity which is at once the foundation and the result of scholarship'.

Murder Must Advertise came relatively painlessly, for she fondly caricatured the people she had worked with, and drew with zest and skill the helter-skelter hypocrisy of an advertising agency. Death comes to Pym's Publicity in more ways than one: Victor Dean is pushed down the spiral staircase, and Wimsey in the guise of Death Bredon joins the workforce to solve the mystery. Sayers didn't rate the book highly, critical of its melodramatic sub-plot of drug-peddling among the 'Bright Young People' of the day. But she accepted that it had its moments:

> In this place, where from morning till night a staff of over a
> hundred people hymned the praises of thrift, virtue,
> harmony, eupepsia and domestic contentment, the
> spiritual atmosphere was clamorous with financial storm,
> intrigue, dissension, indigestion and marital infidelity.
> And with worse things—with murder wholesale and
> retail, of soul and body, murder by weapon and murder by
> poison. These things did not advertise, or, if they did, they
> called themselves by other names.

Fleming's book, *Gourmet's Book of Food and Drink*, also slapped onto the bookstalls in 1933. Dedicated to his wife, 'who can make an Omelette', in sales and publicity it didn't begin to compare with her work—which only served to widen the gulf between them and send him scurrying for his paints and whisky bottle.

Gaudy Night is the novel in which Sayers finally achieved her ambitious goal of fusing social comment with detection. Personal relationships can never be trusted, she writes out of desperate personal experience. Only in work and craftsmanship can be found satisfaction of the mind and salvation of the soul. Intriguingly, *Cat o' Mary* and *My Edwardian Childhood*, both written in the early thirties, end as she begins *Gaudy Night*, and the reason is not hard to find: Harriet Vane takes the place of Katherine Lammas, and says all the things that Sayers is bursting to say. So it is that in this book Harriet takes centre stage: she doesn't require Wimsey until page 265—to be fair, there isn't a murder in *Gaudy Night*—and, when he does appear, gone is the silly ass who, we are told, was merely the affectation of a man who had to make himself believable to the criminal classes; all along he was really a serious scholar with a stunning mind, a sensitive soul.

Intellectual integrity—Sayers' conviction that just as intellectual honesty is essential to scholarship, so it is to the conduct of life—is not only the theme of the book; it is also that which finally brings Peter and Harriet together. Sayers' basis for a true and lasting relationship has been seen to triumph—in a work of fiction, at least.

> On the intellectual platform, alone of all the others,
> Harriet could stand free and equal with Peter, since in
> that sphere she had never been false to her own standards.
> By choosing a plot that should exhibit intellectual
> integrity as the one great permanent value in an
> emotionally unstable world I should be saying the thing
> that, in a confused way, I had been wanting to say all my
> life. Finally, I should have found a universal theme which
> could be made integral both to the detective plot and to the
> 'love-interest' which I had, somehow or other, to unite
> with it.[19]

It is a dubious basis for a lasting relationship, and Sayers in her heart of hearts must have known it, but she could well have argued from painful experience that it had probably as much chance as any other:

> She stood still; and he stopped perforce and turned
> towards her. She laid both hands upon the fronts of his

gown, looking into his face while she searched for the word
that would carry her over the last difficult breach. It was
he who found it for her. With a gesture of submission he
bared his head and stood bravely, the square cap dangling
in his hand.

'*Placetne, magistra?*'

'*Placet.*'

There is so much of Sayers' personal life in this novel that
examples can be taken at random: the setting draws exclusively
on Somerville days—Harriet thinks of the 'bitter years' when she
had gone to London 'to write mystery fiction, to live with a man
who was not married to her'—she had 'broken all her old ties and
half the commandments'—in a trunk she finds a 'faded tie that
had once belonged to a dead lover'—Harriet muses 'To be true
to one's calling, whatever follies one might commit in one's
emotional life, that was the way to spiritual peace'—Peter urges
Harriet to write out her bitterness: 'What's the use of making
mistakes if you don't use them?'

> The young were theoretical; only the middle-aged could
> realize the deadlines of principles. To subdue one's self to
> one's own end might be dangerous, but to subdue one's
> self to other people's ends was dust and ashes . . . Could
> there ever be any alliance between the intellect and the
> flesh? . . . Experience, perhaps, had a formula to get over
> this difficulty; one kept the bitter, tormenting brain on one
> side of the wall and the languorous sweet body on the other
> and never let them meet.

Sayers worried about the public reception of *Gaudy Night*;
predicting that 'if it didn't strike lucky it would be a sensational
flop'. But, published in November 1935, the first edition of
17,000 copies was sold out at once, and five impressions were
hurried through by the end of the year. Not everybody was
happy: for example, Mrs Q. D. Leavis, a respected critic and
wife of the academic F. R. Leavis, was very scathing, but her
arguments were blunted by snobbery and ill-humour. Sayers,

however, was hurt disproportionately by the attack—probably because she had put so much of her *hidden* self into the work.

> Sayers displays knowingness about literature without any sensitiveness to it or any feeling for quality—i.e. she has an academic literary taste over and above having no general taste at all . . . evidently Miss Sayers' spiritual nature, like Harriet Vane's, depends for its repose, refreshment and sustenance on the academic world, the ideal conception that is of our older universities—or let us say a rationalised nostalgia for her student days.[20]

Even when Sayers was going through the darkest hours, or enduring social and sexual deprivation in an unsatisfactory marriage, or penning the profoundest thoughts from out of the depths of her psyche, she herself was never less than boisterously extrovert, able to wither lesser mortals on the spot, and—as all her friends insist—immense fun to be with. So it was E. C. Bentley, the author of the classic detective story *Trent's Last Case* (highly praised by Sayers, who wrote a foreword for later editions), who in a spoof called *Greedy Night* much more successfully caught the mood of *Gaudy Night*:

> *Lord Peter Wimsey*
> *May look a little flimsy,*
> *But he's simply sublime*
> *When nosing out a crime.*

Bentley's crime has been committed at Janus College, where late one evening the great detective listens nostalgically to the Aquinas Club in song:

> He heard the tremendous burden of 'On Ilkley Moor Baat'At,' the stirring swing of 'Auprès de ma Blonde', the complex cadences of 'Green Grow the Rushes Oh', the noble organ-music of 'Slattery's Mounted Foot', the crashing staccato of 'Still His Whiskers Grew', the solemn keening of 'The Typist's Farewell'. Once there were indications that a Rhodes Scholar was trying, with as little

success as usually waits on his countrymen's efforts in that direction, to remember the words of his own national anthem. Then there fell a hush . . . Wimsey sighed. The luxurious, self-conscious melancholy of those no longer ridiculously young, but having—with any luck—half a lifetime still before them, possessed him. Elbows on sill, chin in hands, he gazed into the now untenanted gloom, recalling lost binges of old years.

Gaudy Night was intended to be the end of Lord Peter, and would have been but for Muriel St Clare Byrne's insistence that she and Sayers should put him on the stage. Sayers agreed, as long as Muriel would deal with all the technicalities. The result was *Busman's Honeymoon*, which opened to mixed reviews at London's Comedy Theatre on 16 December 1936, with Dennis Arundell as Wimsey and Veronica Turleigh as Harriet. The BBC broadcast its own version two months later, and in June 1937 the novel version appeared. Subtitled 'A Love Story with Detective Interruptions' it places Wimsey firmly back in his pastoral English roots and he and Harriet turn their honeymoon cottage into a lost Eden. Love and death, that explosive mixture, are given Sayers' intoxicating verbal treatment.

It was *Busman's Honeymoon* that gave Sayers the stage bug, never to leave her. At the time she must have feared the outcome, as her one excursion into another medium had ended in disaster. She wrote the script for a film called *The Silent Passenger*, in which Wimsey looked like a member of the Mafia. Sayers never touched the film world again, turning down an offer of $10,000 from MGM for *Murder Must Advertise*, and refusing even to see the film version of *Busman's Honeymoon* with Robert Montgomery:

> I do not like the films and I do not want them. I do not need their publicity, which is likely to do me more harm than good. I do not need their money, for I can live very well without it. They have nothing to offer me which I would not very much rather be without. They will find it difficult to believe this, but it is a fact.[21]

So, more or less, ended the career of Lord Peter Wimsey. The public career, anyway. For when Sayers said there would be no more Wimseys, she hid away in her attic 170 pages of a sequel to *Busman's Honeymoon*, called *Thrones, Dominations*. The title is a quote from Milton's *Paradise Lost*. The fallen angel Lucifer addresses his fellow devils: 'Thrones and Imperial Powers, off-spring of heaven,/ Ethereal Vertues . . ./ These titles now/ Must we renounce, or changing still be called/ Princes of Hell?'

Sayers told her friend Helen Simpson that the quotation gave 'the whole theme of the book in a nutshell'. The MS was purchased by the Marion E. Wade Center at Wheaton College, Illinois, in 1976, where it can be read but not copied. The right to publish rests with the Sayers Estate and remains under nego-tiation. It is believed that Sayers' son was on the verge of granting permission just before his death in 1984. Sayers' biographer Alzina Stone Dale is convinced that this is vintage Sayers, and that she didn't complete the book either because it is explicit about sex in a way no crime novel of the thirties could be, or because she found her fiction, in its emphasis on the significance of marriage as an institution, imitating too closely a public event (the accession and later the abdication of King Edward VIII so that he might be free to marry 'the woman I love') not to prove embarrassingly controversial.[22] A simpler reason would seem to be that Sayers had tired of Wimsey, who in the MS is a pallid image of his former self, and committed her energies to the theatre. She might also have felt some shame that after 170 pages there is not so much as a hint of a crime.

A final collection of short stories, *In the Teeth of the Evidence*, appeared in 1940, and three Wimsey short stories including *Tallboys*—picturing Wimsey as a nappy-changing father—were written during the war but not published until 1973. In some of her short stories, Sayers toyed unsuccessfully with a travelling salesman detective called Montague Egg. One post-Wimsey pleasure was to work at literary spoofs of the great man's ex-ploits and family connections: a letter in *The Times* on the Wim-sey chin; a series of mock Elizabethan poems allegedly by one of Wimsey's ancestors, Roger Wimsey; an 'Account of Lord

Mortimer Wimsey, Hermit of the Wash', a memoir prepared as a Christmas present for friends. She did much the same for Sherlock Holmes, treating Holmes as a real character, and subjecting him to analytical treatment in essays like 'Holmes' College Career', 'The Dates in the Red-Headed League', and 'Dr Watson's Christian Name':

> It has always been a matter of astonishment to Dr Watson's friends ... to observe that his wife apparently did not know her own husband's name. There can be no possible doubt that Watson's first name was John. The name 'John H. Watson' appears conspicuously and in capital letters, on the title page of *A Study in Scarlet* ... Yet in 1891 we find Watson publishing the story of *The Man With the Twisted Lip*, in the course of which Mrs Watson addresses him as 'James'.[23]

Sayers twice contributed analyses on the true life murder case of Julia Wallace—in *Great Unsolved Crimes* and *The Anatomy of Murder*. She also, from June 1933 to August 1935, reviewed over 350 crime titles for the *Sunday Times*, kind to the likes of Carter Dickson, who wrote well, and Agatha Christie, who wrote ingeniously, but scathing of Maurice Dix's 'preposterously melodramatic style' and Ellery Queen's 'determination to be literary or die':

> [Carter Dickson] can write ... He has staggered me by producing a perfectly correct gerund: 'Something about the servants' hearing things in the house' ... I would forgive him more sins than one for that blessed apostrophe!

> The Week's Worst English—Shaking him like a dog shakes a rat. We all say it, but not in print, Mr Burton—not in print!

> 'A puff of the cosmic effluvium'—'horses the warp and woof of the outdoors'—'his alabaster bosom' (it is only a white shirtfront)—'he slid, almost slithered over the rug.

He was like a cat on his feet' (do cats slide over rugs?)

In her last column of 1934 she made this New Year's Resolution:

> I will not cease from mental fight nor shall my sword sleep in my hand till I have detected and avenged all mayhems and murders done upon the English language against the peace of our Sovereign Lord the King, his Crown, and dignity.

Sayers was often invited to speak on 'whether or not it is possible to treat the detective story with any marked literary dignity'. Sayers had only one answer for that, of course, but she delivered it in style. She did nothing better than 'Aristotle on Detective Fiction', in which she claimed that Aristotle was 'not so much a student of his own literature as a prophet of the future . . . what, in his heart of hearts, he desired was a good detective story'. And she goes on to prove it:

> . . . Aristotle, by one of those blinding flashes of insight . . . puts the whole craft of the detective writer into one master-word: *Paralogismos*. That word should be written up in letters of gold on the walls of every mystery-monger's study . . . paralogism—the art of the false syllogism . . . 'Homer,' says he—if he had lived in our own day he might have chosen . . . Father Knox or Agatha Christie . . . —'Homer more than any other has taught the rest of us the art of *framing lies in the right way* . . . Whenever, if A is or happens, a consequent, B is or happens, men's notion is that, if the B is, the A also is—but that is a false conclusion . . . Just because we know the truth of the consequent, we are in our own minds led on to the erroneous inference of the truth of the antecedent.' There you are, then; there is your recipe for detective fiction: the art of framing lies.[24]

Her auditor, Mary Ellen Chase, remembered another of these occasions, at Cambridge. She had never come across 'one

so magnetic to listen to'; students listened 'spellbound, transformed, entranced'.[25] This was all the more remarkable, she
said, because of Sayers' personal appearance (at the age of
forty-two):

> There can be few plainer women on earth than Dorothy
> Sayers; and the adjective is an extremely kind one. She
> seemingly had no neck at all ... She had a florid
> complexion, very blue, near-sighted eyes, and wore
> glasses which quivered. Her thinning hair rarely showed
> evidence of care ... She was large, rawboned, and
> awkward.[26]

Sayers' physical decline was marked: a sedentary life contributed, but the sustaining interest in personal love having
deserted her she probably felt no compelling need to take care
of herself. Any physical decline was not matched by a mental
one—indeed, as she left behind her the comforts of Wimsey,
she took enormous leaps in mental and spiritual energy which
took her into the theatre, theology and the Church of England.
And, as we shall see, Sayers could make theology every bit as
exciting as a detective story:

> The golden age for all who live by their brains is the period
> from forty to sixty. They have learnt their technique and
> are ready to create freely in their chosen medium, and with
> wider knowledge they have gained wider interests ...
> They have become more entertaining and easier to get on
> with, because they no longer take themselves with such
> agitated seriousness. The delight of middle-age is a
> paradox: that as one becomes more important to others
> one becomes less important to oneself ... Only in middle-
> age is it gloriously revealed to one that what one says and
> does makes little difference in the long run to anybody,
> and that therefore one may as well say and do what one
> likes.[27]

Sayers once used the phrase 'all very good fun while it lasted'.
That was the point. Whether committed to novels, advertising,

drama, theology or social commentary, she found it huge fun while it lasted, and her gift was to communicate this sense of enjoyment to others. But nothing lasted very long, one obsession always led to another, and it is necessary now to consider the next in line—the stage.

7

The Greatest Drama

The Zeal of Thy House, by Dorothy L. Sayers, opened in Canterbury Cathedral on 12 June 1937, and subsequently made appearances at London's Westminster, Garrick and Duke of York Theatres. Ostensibly the story of the French architect, William of Sens, its theme was a passionately held belief in the importance of creation.

Prior to the play's London opening in 1938, an intrepid reporter from the *Church Times* cornered Sayers during rehearsals. Refusing to be cowed by her opening salvo: 'Please don't begin by saying how odd it is to find a detective novelist writing a play about Christian dogma. I am so tired of that remark'[1]—he plunged in with prepared questions on fiction, dogma, romance, work, and dullness and zeal in religious drama. She responded vigorously. She had written detective stories, she said, because she was 'hard up'.[2] Detective novels had an unashamedly romantic appeal.

> Life is often a hopeless muddle, to the meaning of which [people] can find no clue; and it is a great relief to get away from it for a time into a world where they can exercise their wits over a neat problem, in the assurance that there is only one answer, and that answer a satisfying one.[3]

Sayers saw a similarity of theme in *Gaudy Night* and *The Zeal of Thy House*: 'Integrity of work overriding and redeeming personal weakness.'[4] Zeal was not always enough: a dramatist 'must understand what he is writing about, and he must try to put the Christian point of view fairly',[5] but laudable motives on the part of sincere Christian folk may end in 'hopeless failure from the dramatic point of view because in playwriting piety and good intentions are not enough'.[6] Dullness she thought unforgivable.

> I am afraid that the pious themselves are partly to blame.
> Artists who paint pictures of our Lord in the likeness of a
> dismal-looking, die-away person, with his hair parted in
> the middle, ought to be excommunicated for blasphemy.
> And so many good Christians behave as if a sense of
> humour were incompatible with religion; they are too
> easily shocked about the wrong things. When my play was
> acted at Canterbury, one old gentleman was terribly
> indignant at the notion that the builders of that beautiful
> Cathedral could have been otherwise than men of
> blameless lives.[7]

One hopes that the *Church Times'* reporter discovered a bonus in that week's pay packet.

The commission for a play to mark the Canterbury Festival of 1937 had come from the Friends of Canterbury Cathedral, who were looking for a worthy successor to the plays of previous years—*Murder in the Cathedral* and *Thomas Cranmer of Canterbury*. (The latter was written by Charles Williams, who in later years was to whet Sayers' appetite for all things Dante.) Sayers, reluctant initially, capitulated when the wise—and perhaps advised—Miss Margaret Babington, Festival Manager, suggested she dramatize Gervase of Canterbury's account of the gutting by fire of the Norman Choir in the twelfth century, and magnificent rebuilding of the new Choir by William of Sens, who, during the masterminding of proceedings, had injured himself in a fall from scaffolding.

Here was Sayers' chance to further explore the relationship between a workman and his work, and in medieval language and style so dear to her. The title was taken from Psalm 69:9—'For zeal for thy house has consumed me, and the insults of those who insult thee have fallen on me'—and the play dealt with issues applicable equally to artist and Christian: that God who grants artists their talents will not tolerate spiritual pride, that what happens to a man caught between the justice of God and the jealousy of man is one of life's great imponderables, and that to achieve a great and godly work one should always employ a good architect who lives an immoral life rather than a poor architect who lives a blameless life.

Once started, the play proved labour intensive, not least because Sayers persisted in writing everything out longhand. She did have the sense, however, to employ a secretary to look after mundane administrative matters. At this point in her life, her obsession with these experience-soaked beliefs of hers about work and private life was total—so much so that they even dominated letters to her son. People, she said, always believed that if they shook a writer 'something exciting and illuminating' would drop out of him, whereas . . . 'What's due to come out has come out, in the only form in which it can ever come out . . .'[8] The letter ends with an extract from the play.

> *Death gnaw upon me, purge my bones with fire,*
> *But let my work, all that was good in me,*
> *All that was God, stand up and live and grow.*
> *The work is sound, Lord God, no rottenness there—*
> *Only in me. Wipe out my name from men*
> *But not my work; to other men the glory*
> *Send to Thy Name alone. But if to the damned*
> *Be any mercy at all, O send thy spirit*
> *To blow apart the sundering flames, that I*
> *After a thousand years of hell, may catch*
> *One glimpse, one only of the Church of Christ,*
> *The perfect work, finished, though not by me.*[9]

Within hours of the play's first performance the Cathedral opened its doors further to a Service of Arts and Crafts, intended as

> . . . a Thanksgiving to God for His gifts to mankind through artists and craftsmen: also a service of dedication, in which the artist recognised that the exercise of his art was a religious act, and asked the blessing of God on his vocation.[10]

Sayers herself was part of the procession comprising 'eminent persons associated with architecture, painting and sculpture, literature and music'.[11] It must have been a gratifying occasion. Less so perhaps was the response of press and public to the play. The reviewers were kind, and the audiences capacity, but typical of the reviews was 'everybody who feels that theatre still has a contribution to make to our religious life should take an early opportunity of visiting it',[12] and audiences, unable to make the connection with *Gaudy Night* which Sayers deemed so obvious, saw the play as a total change of direction for the author of crime novels. What everybody agreed upon, however, was the wondrous accessibility of her language:

> Her monks are human beings, mixtures in varying proportions of the sublime and ridiculous, and her pilgrims, just because they express themselves in the language of the twentieth-century trippers, are sufficiently quick with life to be of Chaucer's company...[13]

Sayers was content, a condition not disturbed by an invitation to become President of the Modern Language Association. As someone who wondered aloud whether she was 'a scholar gone wrong' it would have been comforting to read in the Association's magazine: 'We are fortunate in having in our... President a lady who is not only a distinguished novelist but also a fine scholar.'[14]

Scholar or no, Sayers had lost none of her talent for encouraging support of her own ventures: for her poems it had been a fictitious clash of opinion in the religious press, for her play it was a series of publicity hand-outs which included this from her own pen (to be read with the imminent *The Man Born to be King* in mind):

> Miss Sayers finds it much more entertaining to be a playwright than a novelist. 'Because when a novel is written, it is finished, but with a play you have all the fun of putting it together on the stage... I am bound to admit',

added Miss Sayers, with a twinkle 'that I am probably the most "interfering" playwright in London. I shove my oar in at every rehearsal, and how my long-suffering producers put up with me I don't know'—In actual fact Miss Sayers is extremely popular with her cast...

Ever after, the public expected religion from Sayers, an irritant at first undoubtedly. But Brabazon's judgment that she 'did her best to depersonalise the whole thing by scrupulously sticking to a restatement of Church doctrine, and refusing to be drawn at any time into "what Christ means to me" or any other form of personal avowal'[15] is not the whole story: that's how it began, but as letters written in the last years of her life substantiate, and friends of her latter years insist, being compelled to dig deep into the well of theology reawakened her own very real but slumbering faith. But first:

> One day I was asked to write a play for Canterbury about William of Sens... I liked the story, which could be so handled as to deal with the 'proper truth' of the artist—a thing on which I was then particularly keen... I never, so help me God, wanted to get entangled in religious apologetic, or to bear witness for Christ, or to proclaim my faith to the world... When the show came to London, I couldn't escape the normal press interviews... And as a result of one of them, I wrote the article 'The Greatest Drama Ever Staged' which eventually appeared in the *Sunday Times*... That did it. Apparently the spectacle of a middle-aged female detective-novelist admitting publicly that the judicial murder of God might compete in interest with the corpse in the coal-hole was the sensation for which the Christian world was waiting.[16]

Sayers of course could not write dully to save her life, and only she could have imbued with such swingeing wit and bile the simple thesis that it wasn't dogma that made Christianity dull, but the Church's shameful neglect of it. I quote generously from that 2,000-word article in the *Sunday Times*:

The young Sayers: an appealing photograph now lodged with the Bodleian Library, Oxford.

The Rev. Henry Sayers moved his family to Bluntisham Rectory, Huntingdonshire, in the Fens, when Sayers was four years old. It remained her home for the next twenty years.

At Oxford Sayers joined the Bach Choir, directed by the eccentric Dr Hugh Percy Allen, for whom she developed an unconcealed passion.

Sayers impersonates Dr Allen, stylishly conducting the Bach Choir.

1930: a sketch of Dorothy Leigh Sayers by artist John Gilroy, with whom she worked at Benson's.

My Goodness My GUINNESS

In 1922 Sayers was taken on as a copywriter at Benson's, Britain's largest and most progressive advertising agency. She wrote the copy lines for these two Guinness advertisements, to John Gilroy's illustrations.

If he can say as you can
Guinness is good for you
How grand to be a Toucan
Just think what Toucan do

1939: Sayers with 'Eric', the all-electric skull mascot of the Detection Club, Gerrard Street, London.

6 February 1942: Dorothy L. Sayers signs the Visitors' Book at St Martin-in-the-Fields, after giving an address at the lunch-time service.

The famous writer of detective stories relaxes in the lounge of the Detection Club.

The title page of *The Zeal of Thy House*, signed by Dorothy L. Sayers. The play opened in Canterbury Cathedral in 1937.

In the 1949 performance of *The Zeal of Thy House*, Michael Goodwin appears with Jill Balcon *(right)* and Hugh Miller *(below)*.

THE ZEAL
OF THY HOUSE

by

DOROTHY L. SAYERS

Acting Edition
for the Festival of the Friends of Canterbury Cathedral
1937

Canterbury:
H. J. GOULDEN, LIMITED
(by kind permission of the Author and Victor Gollancz, Ltd.)

Dorothy Leigh
Sayers: the writer.

A recent revival of
Busman's Honeymoon
by Sayers and Muriel
St Clare Byrne, at the
Lyric Theatre,
Hammersmith,
London—with Emily
Richard as Lady Peter
Wimsey, Edward
Petherbridge as the
famous detective.

... The Christian faith is the most exciting drama that ever staggered the imagination of man—and the dogma is the drama. That drama is summarized quite clearly in the creeds of the Church, and if we think it dull it is because we either have never really read those amazing documents or have recited them so often and so mechanically as to have lost all sense of their meaning. The plot pivots upon a single character, and the whole action is the answer to a single central problem: *What think ye of Christ?* ...

The Church's answer is categorical and uncompromising, and it is this: That Jesus Bar-Joseph, the carpenter of Nazareth, was in fact and in truth, and in the most exact and literal sense of the words, the God 'by whom all things were made'. His body and brain were those of a common man; his personality was the personality of God, so far as that personality could be expressed in human terms. He was not a kind of demon pretending to be human; he was in every respect a genuine living man. He was not merely a man so good as to be 'like God'—he was God ... This is the dogma we find so dull— this terrifying drama of which God is the victim and hero.

If this is dull, then what, in Heaven's name, is worthy to be called exciting? The people who hanged Christ never, to do them justice, accused him of being a bore—on the contrary, they thought him too dynamic to be safe. It has been left for later generations to muffle up that shattering personality and surround him with an atmosphere of tedium. We have very efficiently pared the claws of the Lion of Judah, certified him 'meek and mild', and recommended him as a fitting household pet for pale curates and pious old ladies. To those who knew him, however, he in no way suggests a milk-and-water person; they objected to him as a dangerous firebrand. True, he was tender to the unfortunate, patient with honest inquirers, and humble before heaven; but he insulted respectable clergymen by calling them hypocrites. He referred to King Herod as 'that fox'; he went to parties in disreputable company and was looked upon as a 'gluttonous man and a winebibber, a friend of publicans and sinners'; he assaulted indignant tradesmen and threw them and their belongings out of the temple; he drove a coach-and-horses through a number of sacrosanct and hoary regulations; he cured diseases by any means that came handy, with a shocking casualness in the matter of other people's pigs and property; he showed no proper deference for wealth or social position; when confronted with neat dialectical traps, he displayed a paradoxical humour that affronted serious-minded people, and he retorted by asking disagreeably searching questions that could not be answered by rule of thumb. He was emphatically not a dull man in his human lifetime, and if he was God, there can be nothing dull about God either ...

  '*And the third day he rose again*'. What are we to make of this? One thing is certain: if he were God and nothing else, his immortality means nothing to us; if he was man and no more, his death is no more important than yours or mine. But if he really was both God and man, then when the man Jesus died, God died too; and when the God Jesus rose from the dead, man rose too, because they were one and the same person ... There is the essential doctrine, of which the whole elaborate structure of Christian faith and morals is only the logical consequence. Now we may call that doctrine exhilarating, or we may call it devastating; we may call it revelation, or we may call it rubbish; but if we call it dull, then words have no meaning at all.[17]

It was an article to excite meek and mild clergy, if nobody else; they had never realized what a revolutionary leader had called them, or what a thrilling task had been entrusted to them. One elderly reader said it was the most practicable exposition 'of our religion in plain English' which he had seen or heard in eighty years' church membership. At about the same time a similar article appeared in the *St Martin's Review*, although this included a prime example of Sayers' satirical skills: an imaginary examination paper, complete with answers, on the Christian faith.

Q: What does the Church think of God the Father?

A: He is omnipotent and holy. He created the world and imposed on man conditions impossible of fulfilment; He is very angry if these are not carried out. He sometimes interferes by means of arbitrary judgments and miracles, distributed with a good deal of favouritism . . .

Q: What does the Church think of God the Son?

A: He is in some way to be identified with Jesus of Nazareth. It was not His fault that the world was made like this, and, unlike His Father, He is friendly to man . . .

Q: What does the Church think of God the Holy Ghost?

A: I don't know exactly. He was never seen or heard of till Whit-Sunday . . .

Q: What is the doctrine of the Trinity?

A: 'The Father incomprehensible, the Son incomprehensible, and the whole thing incomprehensible' . . .

Q: What was Jesus Christ like in real life?

A: He was a good man—so good as to be called the Son of God . . . He was meek and mild and preached a simple religion of love and pacifism. He had no sense of humour . . .

Q: What is meant by the Atonement?

A: God wanted to damn everybody, but His vindictive sadism was sated by the crucifixion of His own Son, who was quite innocent, and, therefore, a particularly attractive victim . . .

Q: What does the Church think of sex?

A: God made it necessary to the machinery of the world, and tolerates it, provided the parties (a) are married, and (b) get no pleasure out of it.

Q: What does the Church call Sin?

A: Sex . . .; getting drunk; saying 'damn'; murder, and cruelty to dumb animals; not going to church; most kinds of amusement. 'Original sin' means that anything we enjoy doing is wrong.

Q:What is faith?

A: Resolutely shutting your eyes to scientific fact.

Q: What is the human intellect?

A: A barrier to faith.

Q: What are the seven Christian virtues?

A: Respectability; childishness; mental timidity; dullness; sentimentality; censoriousness; and depression of spirits.

Q: Wilt thou be baptized in this faith?

A: No fear![18]

The Zeal of Thy House lost Sayers money, principally due to a disastrously ill-timed tour: it opened in Norwich, for example, just as Hitler invaded Czechoslovakia, which took people's minds off a play's theological blandishments. It fared no better in Southport, where ferocious gales and floods kept not only the audiences away, but most of the cast as well. Sayers was too much in love with the theatre, however, to be put off by such minor setbacks: just being with actors was one of the happiest things to happen to her, and as she had written to Ivy Shrimpton on the play's London opening: 'I am preoccupied with "Zeal" to the exclusion of all memory and commonsense.'[19]

Her enthusiasm succeeded in finding another backer, but still she needed to supplement her annual income of £3,500. Her solution raised the eyebrows of her friends and the temperature of *The Times*' leader column: she loaned her name for an advertising campaign run by Horlicks. One of the company's famous 'before-and-after' stories was headed: 'TIGHT-ROPE. A true-life story by Dorothy L. Sayers, author of *The Five Red Herrings, The Nine Tailors*, and part author of the recent West End success *Busman's Honeymoon*.' It told of how an ambitious young man's prospects were being foiled by Night Starvation, rectified quickly and painlessly by bedtime Horlicks. *The Times*, surprised that the Chairman of the Modern Language Association should so soil herself, regretted the absence of Lord Peter Wimsey: 'Noblemen, so far as is known, are not immune from night-starvation . . .' Sayers' reply struck just the right tone:

> You are curiously out of date in your information if you
> suppose that this is the first time that either Peter Wimsey
> or myself has been connected with the advertising
> profession. Peter was himself an advertising copy-writer
> for a short time . . . while I for nine years held a similar
> position . . . I heartily agree that the style of advertisement
> in question is not up to Peter's standard or mine—but
> then the advertisers refused to make use of the elegant
> copy I prepared for them and re-wrote it according to their
> own notion of what was fitting . . . It may be of interest if I
> add that I undertook this advertising job when a small
> amount of capital was needed to finance the provincial
> tour of my play *The Zeal of Thy House* . . . Since no
> assistance was forthcoming from the Church for a play
> written and performed to her honour, I unblushingly
> soaked Mammon for what I could get in that quarter . . .[20]

The appealingly honest Sayers again. And, nothing daunted by her experiences, she accepted a further invitation to write a play for Canterbury—as long as they would improve their offer of thirty guineas! Ambition ran riot second time round, with Sayers attempting a new version of the Faust legend:

... I do not feel that the present generation of English people needs to be warned against the passionate pursuit of knowledge for its own sake: that is not our besetting sin. Looking with the eye of to-day upon that legendary figure of a man who bartered away his soul, I see in him the type of the impulsive reformer, over-sensitive to suffering, impatient of the facts, eager to set the world right by a sudden overthrow, in his own strength and regardless of the ineluctable nature of things.[21]

Sayers' promise of a Faust doing evil that good might come, of an intelligent man betrayed by an unrealistic vision, of an honourable man unleashing anarchy and destruction precisely because of a naive belief in imposed Utopia, boded well for another Canterbury Festival success and perhaps a strong London run. (Sayers' Pope recommends 'the slow and stony road / To Calvary', to which Faust replies: 'Follow Christ? That way is too long and uncertain.'[22]) *The Devil To Pay* reached London, certainly, but met with pertinent criticism from the likes of James Agate: 'I suggest that this is a play for mystics who confound, and are comforted in confounding, plain-song with plain thinking.'[23] Sayers, by overloading a play with theological argument and supernatural wisdom, had made a mistake she was not to repeat: that the market-place should somehow be expected to understand the language of Zion.

One more play followed almost at once, a trifle called *Love All*, which opened in the diminutive Torch Theatre (affectionately known as the Torture Theatre) in Knightsbridge, on 9 April 1940. A light comedy, which boasts as its best line 'Every great man has a woman behind him ... And every great woman has some man or other in front of her, tripping her up', it closed before the end of the month. It warranted no other fate.

Love All is such sub-standard Sayers that one suspects her heart was elsewhere during its writing: in the imminence of war, most likely, which Sayers, while not ghoulish enough to relish, would have greeted with the soul and shout of a hitherto slumbering Musketeer. In a series of articles for the *Spectator* she resurrected Lord Peter and Harriet, the Rev. Theodore Venables, Miss Climpson, and other favourites, to make patriotic propaganda and personal hobby-horses digestible. The 'Wimsey Papers' were tolerably amusing, and occasionally—like this example from Wimsey to Harriet Vane—an unashamed and unmistakable attempt to let the nation know *Sayers'* way of winning any war:

> You are a writer—there is something you must tell the people, but it is difficult to express. You must find the words. Tell them, this is a battle of a new kind, and it is they who have to fight it, and they must do it themselves and alone. They must not continually ask for leadership— they must lead themselves. This is a war against submission to leadership, and we might easily win it in the field and yet lose it in our own country . . .
>
> It's not enough to rouse up the Government to do this and that. You must rouse the people. You must make them understand that their salvation is in themselves and in each separate man and woman among them. If it's only a local committee or amateur theatricals or the avoiding being run over in the black-out, the important thing is each man's *personal responsibility*. They must not look to the State for guidance—they must learn to guide the State. Somehow you must contrive to tell them this. It is the only thing that matters.[24]

Such imperiousness. Such repetition, too, with Sayers saying much the same thing three times over, a failing even in her novels, but usually forgivable for the zest with which it is written. What is different is a tone of tetchiness creeping into her work, marring sometimes the wisdom and the wit. It culminates in her correspondence with the BBC at the time of *The Man Born to be King*, after which she settles in calmer waters and is perhaps still more effective. There is no lack of explanation for the tetchiness. Her husband, suffering increasingly from rheumatism and the sense of a failed life, now relied heavily on the whisky bottle to dull both body and mind:

Mac [as he was affectionately known] is getting so queer and unreliable that it is not safe to trust him to do anything at all, and if he is told that he has forgotten anything, he goes into such a frightful rage that one gets really alarmed. The doctors say that he *is* getting definitely queer—but there doesn't seem to be much that one can do about it.[25]

Sayers' son had won a scholarship to Malvern College, and as she met him at the start and finish of terms, or joined him in shopping for school clothes, or wrote friendly but not motherly letters to him, she must have suffered regrets that no matter what she did now she could never reclaim the time and enjoy a mother's true relationship with her son. She was so very busy, committed to a hugely ambitious range of work, while tied to a bloody-minded husband and tiresome household chores:

Well, dash it, if it comes to that, how about a Day in the Life of an Inoffensive Citizen, anxious only to toil for the nation's good.

8.30—Breakfast—2 letters from persons applying about the situation.

9.30—Invent new kind of batten while waiting for husband to vacate bath.

9.40—Bath and dress.

10.10—Secretary arrives, dizzy with anti-cholera inoculation.

10.15—Cook says another young person has called about the situation.

10.17—Interview young person.

10.25—Send Secretary to buy screws to mend cigarette-box broken by outgoing housemaid. Order meals.

10.30—Ring M.S.B. [Muriel St Clare Byrne] about W.E.A. [the Workers' Educational Association, for whom Sayers lectured on 'The Great Economic Obsession'].

10.45—Start on letter to Sec. of W.E.A.

10.50—Stop to mend cigarette-box—unsuccessful.

11.00—Continue letter to W.E.A. Sec.

11.10—Listen to Secretary's symptoms and say she had better go home after lunch.

11.20—Continue letter to W.E.A. Sec.

11.30—Irritated by failure of cigarette-box to function. Mend it again . . . Successful.

11.50—Draft letter to W.E.A. Sec., and further letter to Sec. of C.S.U. at Newnham, offering to lecture on Nov. 9.

12.30—Feel it is too late to start on Christmas Message to Nation. Saw batten preparatory to experiment with new idea . . .

1.00—Lunch. Remind Cook prospective housemaid arriving 2.15 and will she meet her at station.

1.30—Present housemaid says, can I tell Cook name of prospective housemaid. Tell her Dora Wybrook.

1.35—Suddenly recollect, not Wybrook but Wymark. Convey correction to Cook.

1.40—Feel disintegrated. Cut out and hem grey border.

2.00—Front-door bell rings. Nobody to answer it. Cook at station, housemaid changing.

2.5—Call housemaid down to answer door.

2.6—Caller turns out to be Dora Wymark, train having arrived 15 mins earlier than Passenger Enquiries said it would, so that Cook missed her at station.

2.8—Explanations. Take D.W. to kitchen and leave her there.

2.10—Uneasy feeling of expectation. Sew border.

2.30—Hearing Cook return, apologize for error in information. Sew border. Cook and D.W. exploring avenues, & the house.

3.00—D.W. returns. Interview. Says she would like to come.

3.5—Interview Cook separately. She is willing.

3.10—Engage D.W.

3.12—Hunt house for change to pay D.W.'s fare.

3.20—Return to library. Secretary says she is feeling better.

3.25—Telephone. Mysterious caller for husband. Fetch husband.

3.30—Husband says message is from local baker, asking why we have changed to rival baker. Did not know we had. Refer husband to Cook.

3.35—Return to library. Sign letters, and try to understand where everything is.

3.40—Ring Bun, and tell her must urge Ed. Spectator to make up his mind about Wimsey letters and must soothe Gollancz about blurb. Bun says Hodder & Stoughton interested in booklets provided they are a) religious or educational & b) edited under my supervision; hopes of really embracing scheme for getting stuff out. Say, Excellent—perfectly ready to edit anything provided others do most of the work.

3.45—Return to library. Dismiss Secretary with good wishes and wedding-present.

3.55—Try to think about Christmas Message to Nation.

4.10—Local joiner arrives to ask what it was I wanted done about battens & fly-gallery. Explain model theatre to him and work the curtains. Place order. Ask about spot lights and cleats. Local joiner says he has friend with diploma for making models of things, but he is in R.A.F. Reserve & may go any minute—also he is 'busy courting'.

4.40—Try to think about Christmas Message to Nation. Disintegrated.

4.45—Disintegrated.

4.50—Abandon Message to Nation. Try to put batten together.

4.57—Joiner's friend arrives unexpectedly.

5.00—Tea-bell rings. Tell husband I am engaged with joiner's friend. Explain too hurriedly and have to explain again.

5.05—Joiner's friend very intelligent and voluble. Says he will explore avenues.

5.20—Tea (cold).

5.50—Come up to library and write letter to M.S.B. So there you are. At any rate, I have engaged the housemaid.[26]

Sayers' testiness is observed again when, having offered her services to the Ministry of Propaganda, she was invited to be on the Authors' Planning Committee of the Ministry of Information. Told that its purpose was to advise how best to use authors in time of war, she wrote back curtly informing the Ministry that it wasn't part of their brief to tell writers what to write. Such early disaffection did not prevent her joining a committee which boasted such names as L. A. G. Strong, R. H. S. Crossman and A. P. Herbert. But within a month she was writing to a fellow author:

At the moment I feel there is nothing to be done with the Ministry of Information. I have tried myself to get them to exercise a little sense, and to make proper use of trained writers. But they are in a hopeless muddle, and will never get anything done until they have carried out a ruthless purge of parasites.[27]

In fact the solitary sufferer from any such purge was Sayers herself. One week a cross appeared against her name, with the accompanying words 'Very difficult and loquacious'; the next, her name had disappeared altogether. She didn't allow the natural disappointment to weigh too heavily on her; there was much else to do. Articles flowed from her pen. One, written a week before Neville Chamberlain declared Britain was at war with Germany, asked 'What Do We Believe?':

> When a strong man armed keepeth his palace, his goods
> are in peace. But when a stronger than he shall come . . . he
> taketh from him all his armour wherein he trusted. So to us
> in war-time, cut off from mental distractions by
> restrictions and black-outs, and cowering in a cellar with a
> gas-mask under threat of imminent death, comes the
> stronger fear and sits down beside us. 'What,' he demands
> rather disagreeably, 'do you make of all this? Is there
> anything you value more than life, or are you making a
> virtue of necessity? What do you believe? Is your faith a
> comfort to you under the present circumstances?'[28]

Another asked a very different kind of question: 'Devil, Who Made Thee?' The sub-heading said it all. 'Have Hitlers a place in the Divine Scheme of Things? Dorothy L. Sayers says that rods are not specially manufactured in Heaven; men put them in pickle for their own backs':

> The Divine 'scheme of things', as Christianity
> understands it, is at once extremely elastic and extremely
> rigid. It is elastic, in that it includes a large measure of
> liberty for the creature; it is rigid in that it includes the
> proviso that, however created beings choose to behave,
> they must accept responsibility for their own actions and
> endure the consequences.[29]

Occasionally she took time off from the war to fire broadsides against the press, who angered her for what she listed as sensational headlines, false emphasis, suppression of context, garbling, inaccurate reporting of facts, plain reversal of facts, random and gratuitous invention, and flat suppression:

> What they do clearly show is an all-pervading carelessness about veracity, penetrating every column, creeping into the most trifling item of news, smudging and blurring the boundary lines between fact and fancy, creating a general atmosphere of cynicism and mistrust. He that is unfaithful in little is unfaithful also in much; if a common court case cannot be correctly reported, how are we to believe the reports of world-events?[30]

Sayers' crucial work as war broke out, however, was *Begin Here*, a book of some 160 pages written in response to Victor Gollancz's request for a Christmas message to the nation. Typical of Sayers, she wastes no space bemoaning the calamity fallen upon the earth, the fear and loss and grief; instead she hammers home the insistent Christian truth, that the work of Christ is to bring good out of evil:

> War is an ugly disaster; it is not a final catastrophe. Whatever men may have said in their haste and terror, let us get that fact firmly into our heads. There are no final catastrophes. Like every other historical event, war is not an end, but a beginning.[31]

She calls people to spirituality and individuality; she pleads with them to revise their attitude to work. And as a sequel to arguments in *Gaudy Night* and *The Zeal of Thy House*, she contends that the whole point of work is satisfaction, not financial reward. Theological man is the ideal, with man viewed as a whole being, body and spirit, both good. Humanist man, rational man, biological man, sociological man, psychological man, economic man, all represent a decline in the wholeness and dignity of man. A fresh conception is called for, and Sayers' suggestion is *creative* man:

He it is whom we have of late most sadly forgotten and neglected; he it is who sums up in himself all human faculties and inspires them with the driving energy of will and emotion; yet, in the nature of things, he can never pretend to be absolute altogether. His creation is self-justified and valid in itself, but it can never be more than relative; for though man can make new things out of old, he cannot create anything out of nothing. He is a part of time and space, like every other material being; and he knows (none better) that he is only the mirror of that absolute Creation that created time and space . . .

We must think creatively as individuals, always remembering that we are not only individuals, but responsible to the church and state, nation and empire, continent and world of which we are living parts and which have no meaning without us. And we dare not wait too long. Change there will have to be, and if our civilisation will not change itself from within, it will be altered by force from without. If we really want a United States of Europe, we must combine now by good-will or be compelled into a united state of tyranny. If we want our own state to make reforms, we must learn to control the state, lest the state end by controlling us. If we want some hard thinking done, we must think for ourselves, or others will do the thinking. There are only two ways to move the world: the way of the Gospel and the way of the Law, and if we will not have the one we must submit to the other. Somehow we have got to find the integrating principle for our lives, the creative power that sustains our balance in motion, and we have got to do it quickly.[32]

One excited reader was Sir Richard Acland, who saw Sayers' creative man as 'forming part of something bigger which I believe is beginning to happen'.[33] So excited, in fact, that he formed 'The Nine Point Group', comprising likeminded people who 'realise that this War is a part of a world-wide revolution, and who recognise with pleasure that a part of this revolution is the attack on all privileges, including the privileges in our own country, and the repudiation of imperialism'.[34] Not only that, but they 'hold all these views on the basis of Christianity, and not on a basis of agnosticism and humanism'.[35] Sir Richard, therefore, had not the slightest doubt that Sayers would join.

Sayers swiftly disabused him. She could not possibly give her allegiance to such a group. To begin with, she distrusted the phrase 'Christian principles'. Also, she had no objection to the acquisition of property or privilege. And, finally, she would always warn people *against* 'serving the community', because this came perilously close to reversing the order of the first two Commandments.[36]

True blue politically Sayers may have been, but this did not blind her to the faults of capitalism; when she pointed them out, however, she was lapped up as a socialist. Sayers was clear that to be interested only in economic equality—whether as capitalist or socialist—is to be tragically shortsighted because it puts one's ultimate values in money.

What she *was* willing to join—possibly because it sounded a lot less pompous—was the Church's Committee for Work among Men Serving with HM Forces. Briefed to 'go about and instruct the serving soldier in the Christian Faith', Sayers wrote feelingly to a friend in the Forces, 'that to be harangued about religion by a middle-aged female must add very greatly to the horrors of war for these helpless and unhappy young men'. She took it on, nonetheless.

A schoolboy is reputed to have written of Sayers, that she had 'turned from a life of crime to join the Church of England'. Nothing could have more convinced a Wimsey-besotted public that this was so than an address she gave to the Archbishop of York's Conference on 'The Life of the Church and the Order of Society'. Less for what she said overall than for what the press made of parts of it—what she would have called 'suppression of context' and 'false emphasis', no doubt. At Malvern at the invitation of Archbishop William Temple—an increasingly outspoken fan of Sayers—she spoke on the church's place in society, and once again proved herself able to hold all things in balance,

battling for an honourable place between dishonourable ex-
tremes, without succumbing to compromise of spirit or principle. The church cannot isolate itself from a corrupt society: at its
head is a God who became man and thereby sanctified material
life. But neither can the church demand that it runs society: all
human institutions and dogmas are fallible and short-lived, and
no place for the keeper of eternal truth. Instead, the church must
make its voice heard in every area of human concern, but never
identify wholly with any one organization or policy:

> ... The Church can only order the affairs of the world
> when, and so long as, she is not involved in or identified
> with them. That this conclusion presents a number of
> difficulties in practice I am very well aware. The Church is
> in the world, and her members are men. Both as men and
> as Churchmen, Christians have to cope with social,
> economic, political and moral questions. The Church has,
> however, this unique assistance: that she believes that God
> was also a man. And this particular Man it has never been
> possible to identify with any social, political or economic
> system, or with any moral code. He seems literally all
> things to all men; to the rebel, a revolutionary; to the lover
> of political order, the sanction for the tribute paid to
> Caesar; to the virtuous, the King of Virgins; to the sinner,
> the friend of harlots and publicans; to the pacifist, Prince
> of peace, to the warrior, a sword in the earth; to the gentle,
> meek and lowly; to the impatient, armed with vituperation
> and the scourge of small cords; to the light-hearted, the
> guest at Cana, to the melancholy, the Man of Sorrows; to
> the once-born, simple as a little child, to the twice-born,
> rent in sunder in Gethsemane; to the humanist, perfect
> man, to the theologian, perfect God; filling all the
> categories and contained by none; and with all this, a
> single, recognizable, and complete Personality. That the
> Church should resemble her Founder is no doubt
> impossible. She is in the world and subject to the Law of
> Nature: it is idle to demand figs under natural conditions

which make the production of figs impossible. Very well, then: 'Let no fruit grow on thee for ever.' We must, it seems, do the impossible, or perish.[37]

That was how Sayers concluded her address. As a summary of her case it cannot be improved upon. Earlier, however, she had included phrases like 'nosing out fornication', 'denounced adultery', and 'if every man living were to sleep in his neighbour's bed'—and it was perhaps a little ingenuous of her to believe that the press would publish the sombre summarizer rather than the racy raconteur:

> Suppose, during the last century, the Churches had devoted to sweetening intellectual corruption one quarter of the energy they spent on nosing out fornication—or denounced legalized cheating with one quarter the vehemence with which they denounced adultery. But the one was easy and the other was not. The Law cares little for sacraments; but it is reluctant to alter marriage laws because the alterations upset the orderly devolution of property. And of fornication it takes little cognizance, unless it leads to riot and disturbance. But to upset legalized cheating, the Church must tackle government in its very stronghold; while to cope with intellectual corruption, she will have to affront all those who exploit it—the politicians, the press, and the more influential part of her own congregations. Therefore she will acquiesce in a definition of morality so one-sided that it has deformed the very meaning of the word by restricting it to sexual offences. And yet if every man living were to sleep in his neighbour's bed, it could not bring the world so near shipwreck as that pride, that avarice, and that intellectual sloth which the Church has forgotten in the tale of the capital sins.[38]

A popularizer of Christianity: Sayers may have despised the term, but that was the role increasingly being allocated to her by a church rubbing its hands in holy glee and a public rubbing its eyes in whimsical disbelief. Her next project would serve only to intensify the image: a serialized dramatic life of Christ in the BBC Children's Hour slot, to be called *The Man Born to be King*. As we have seen, stormy encounters between two great—some might say self-important—institutions lay ahead, but these didn't take place in a vacuum; Sayers and the BBC had seldom seen eye to eye.

8

'Life is no candidate for the Detection Club'

Sayers' initial contact with the BBC, in the early thirties, had nothing to do with religion at all. She was, as we have seen, one of half-a-dozen writers who collaborated on radio serials such as *Behind the Screen* and *The Scoop*, each one responsible for picking up and running with a plot set up by another:

> ... The Plot of *The Scoop* was planned in rough outline by all the authors in committee before the broadcasting of Chapter 1. After this, each writer worked to a sketch-outline of what his instalment was to contain ... As regards the actual writing, each author was left free to develop his own style & method. Generally speaking, the writer who first introduces a new character is responsible for laying down that character's general appearance, method of speech, & other writers dealing subsequently with that character are, of course, expected to carry it along on the same lines.[1]

This was very much to the public's taste, although a number of listeners criticized Sayers' characters for using 'God' as an expletive. She could see nothing objectionable about 'God', and if the BBC didn't like the bad language it was up to the BBC to cut it out.

By now faint tremors could be felt in the relationship. Sayers was upset that the BBC couldn't get her name right, omitting her middle initial in most of its announcements, so she wrote several typically curt letters along the lines of: 'Will you please take steps to see that my name is removed from any further programme announcements.' In fact, Sayers had right on her side in this instance, as the BBC had on its payroll a music-hall artist called Dorothy Sayers and, not unnaturally, she wanted audiences to distinguish between the two.

Sayers also believed she knew her own worth, and one of her running battles with the BBC was over the size of her fees: such was the fear she could instil that an 'Any Questions' producer, querying 'rather excessive' luncheon expenses of six shillings and sixpence, was told by a higher authority to drop it and pay it. Sayers dismissed scornfully the blandishments of programmes like 'The Brains Trust':

> ... quick wits and superficiality ring the bell every time,
> whereas the sounder people, who never advance any
> statement without verifying their references are put at a
> great disadvantage. This seems to me a pity, because
> people are already sufficiently inclined to despise facts and
> authority, and to prefer snap judgments and personal
> opinions.[2]

And she was no great fan of religious broadcasting either:

> I always thought it unfair to put 'Lift Up Your Hearts'
> [equivalent to today's 'Thought for the Day'] just before
> the 8 o'clock News so that one can't escape it—like the
> vicar waylaying the congregation at the church door. But
> now Derek McCulloch has started it on the 6 o'clock I am
> foaming at the mouth, and the blasphemy in my household
> would shock Satan himself. I *won't* be prayed at and over
> and round like this! It's slimy, that's what it is, simply
> slimy. I think I shall apostasize and become a Zoroastrian
> or a Buddhist, or something that doesn't take a mean
> advantage of a person.[3]

She was no less hard on what seems to have been a primitive version of 'Desert Island Discs'. A poor innocent called Stephen Williams wrote to her requesting participation in a programme of her favourite operatic records. Sayers declined on the basis of knowing little about opera, but also felt it necessary to point out that she was allergic to 'this kind of bosh'.

Sayers, to her credit, was one of the few to lambast the BBC about its treatment of P. G. Wodehouse, who, having been taken prisoner by the Nazis and shunted from interment camp to interment camp, found himself at the age of sixty placed under house arrest and invited by the German Foreign Office to do a series of broadcasts to America. The title of the talks—'How to be an Internee in Your Spare Time without Previous Experience'—was typical of the creator of Jeeves and Wooster, as was the unabashed humour of their content. Unfortunately, British sensibilities were not up to it; Wodehouse seemed simply to be another Lord Haw-Haw broadcasting Nazi propaganda.

Attacks on him reached an unhealthy pitch when, in a BBC broadcast on 15 July 1941, William Connor—'Cassandra' of the *Daily Mirror*—accused him of treason. Sayers rose to Wodehouse's defence: did anybody actually know what he had said? what of the principle that a man should be assumed innocent until proved guilty? and shouldn't the political naivety of a man like Wodehouse be taken into consideration? She very much hoped that the Religious Broadcasting Department would have something to say about it . . .

The Department knew Sayers well. For Christmas Day, 1938, she had written a radio nativity play for Children's Hour, called *He That Should Come*. Produced by Val Gielgud and a clear forerunner to *The Man Born to be King*, this consisted of one scene—the Bethlehem inn 'crowded with as many and various types as possible'. No controversy here; just fulsome praise from an appreciative audience:

> For the first time for years I listened to a broadcast play, and thoroughly enjoyed *He That Should Come*. So, you may be interested to know, did my 'pub audience', roughly speaking the older generation of the village. As one of them put it, 'it's nice to think that people in the Bible were folks like us'.

Which prepared the way for the altogether more ambitious

project, *The Man Born to be King*, but stocked still with 'folks like us'. There followed, as we have seen, the notorious battle of the scripts, the triumphant broadcasts, and Sayers' skirmish—a sort of coda—with those who hailed the plays as 'one of the greatest evangelistic appeals'. Once the sound and the fury had died away, the impact was revealed in the hundreds of letters Sayers received—and answered, usually at length—from listeners intrigued but unsure about her version of Judas, or trying to make sense of God become man, or so overwhelmed by the complexities and sorrows of life that any portrayal of a good yet powerful God seemed almost blasphemous. Sayers could bitch with the bitchiest of her correspondents, but when it was a case of the heart or the head crying out to her she seldom refused a serious reply. She wrote movingly about Judas, whom she had cast as an impatient man, an egotist, eager for revolution overnight and on his terms, and I quote the letter at length:

> Avarice and swindling are mean sins; any sin, carried far enough, can make a man false in grain. Well-meaning stupidity does usually lead to catastrophes far greater than one might expect. But there are worse sins than any of these. I don't know; but given the Gospels give so little clue to the real inner motive of the betrayal we are left free to guess, and I think the softest thing is to choose the motive which might be most likely to lead one's self into such a treason, and say, 'God help me, it might well have been like *that*.' Almost certainly it was a sin which looked to the sinner like a virtue, for those are the sins which lead to the worst betrayals. And I expect that every age, and every person, has his own way of acting Judas. Of course, no sin is beyond forgiveness—but Judas would not wait to be forgiven. In my play I suggested that he did not *want* to be forgiven and therefore could not repent or receive forgiveness, and so lost himself. Because God damns nobody. People damn themselves. They have what they choose. 'It is a fearful thing to fall into the hands of the living God, for they give to every man that which he has

desired.' The fact that God can bring good out of evil does not abolish the guilt of the sinner. That's the point, isn't it? of the sayings about 'it must needs be that offences come . . .' and 'the Son of Man goeth as it is written . . .' And I imagine that the guilt is just the same, whether the consequences are obviously disastrous or not. I mean, I have not Hitler's opportunity for massacring people on a big scale, but if I am as cruel and beastly as I can be to a few people I have the opportunity to hurt, then I am surely as bad as he is, or worse . . . I made [Judas] a clever man without charity, who lost faith as a result, and finally hope. If one is one's self a clever person without much charity, it's easy to imagine one's self inside the skin of that particular Judas. But that, of course, is just a writer's trick—one writes about one's own sins just because one understands them from the inside and can make them convincing. I don't happen to care a great deal about money, and therefore I shouldn't make a very good job of an avaricious Judas, because of the difficulty of imagining how that kind of mind would work. I say this, because it doesn't do to trust writers too far. However much they may set out to relate facts or interpret an actual event, there will be moments when they find themselves trying to tell the world something they know from personal experience. That is why, when there is room for guessing, they make such different guesses.[4]

Long letters like this, some gentle, others bilious—increasingly the former as she grew older—were written by the thousands during the thirties, forties and fifties. Criticism, deserved or undeserved, brought out the best in her; she could take it, but she could never let it lie. So when an academic criticised Sayers among others for judging literature on the basis of whether or not it promoted the cause of Christianity, she shot off a few rounds of venom: this just isn't true, she begins . . .

. . . it would be inconsistent, since I have repeatedly warned people against judging works of art in this simple, not to say naive, manner . . . To be sure, it is of no disadvantage to a book that its underlying assumptions should be in accordance with the facts; but neither correctness of data nor piety of intention will suffice to make a good work of art out of a bad one. Every such work must be judged primarily by the standard of its proper technique; if it is not true to that standard it is true to nothing, and good for nothing . . . [If] it is a question of criticizing, not the work of art itself, but the philosophy which . . . it expresses, then it is surely not improper for the critic to say whether, in his opinion, that philosophy is true or false . . .[5]

Simultaneously with *The Man Born to be King*, Sayers wrote *The Mind of the Maker*, which, though less popular with the broad public, stands as her greatest, most lasting, most original work. She described it as 'a brief study of the creative mind', which is a modest summary of what others have called 'one of the most illuminating inquiries into the creative process ever written'.

In the opening pages she quotes Nikolai Berdyaev—'In the case of man, that which he creates is more expressive of him than that which he begets. The image of the artist and the poet is imprinted more clearly on his works than on his children'— and issues her well-worn disclaimers:

This book is not an apology for Christianity, nor is it an expression of personal religious belief. It is a commentary, in the light of specialised knowledge, on a particular set of statements made in the Christian creeds and their claim to be statements of fact. It is necessary to issue this caution, for the popular mind has grown so confused that it is no longer able to receive any statement of fact except as an expression of personal feeling.[6]

What she then does with remarkable clarity and conviction is to take one of the more baffling theological conundrums—the Trinity—and prove beyond all reasonable doubt that it is something seen at work whenever a human being puts hand or mind to creation. Sayers uses as her starting-point the concluding speech of St Michael in *The Zeal of Thy House*:

> Praise Him that He hath made man in His own image, a maker and craftsman like Himself, a little mirror of His triune majesty.
>
> For every worth of creation is threefold, an earthly trinity to match the heavenly.
>
> First: there is the Creative Idea; passionless, timeless, beholding the whole work complete at once, the end in the beginning; and this is the image of the Father.
>
> Second: there is the Creative Energy, begotten of that Idea, working in time from the beginning to the end, with sweat and passion, being incarnate in the bonds of matter; and this is the image of the Word.
>
> Third: there is the Creative Power, the meaning of the work and its response in the lively soul; and this is the image of the indwelling Spirit.
>
> And these three are one, each equally in itself the whole work, whereof none can exist without the other; and this is the image of the Trinity.[7]

The Father is the moment of vision for the artist. The Son is the long, often arduous incarnation of that vision, which in its culmination awakens those feelings of power and joy that drove the Father to begin the process. The Holy Spirit is that power and joy being communicated. These three—Father, Son and Holy Spirit; inspiration, incarnation, joyful power—are inseparable: three persons, one God, three aspects of one creative act.

> It has become abundantly clear of late ... that something has gone seriously wrong with the conception of humanity and of humanity's proper attitude to the universe. We have begun to suspect that the purely analytical approach to phenomena is leading us only further ... into the abyss of disintegration and randomness, and that it is becoming urgently necessary to construct a synthesis of life. It is

dimly apprehended that the creative artist does, somehow or other, specialize in construction, and also that the Christian religion does, in some way that is not altogether clear to us, claim to bring us into a right relation with a God whose attribute is creativeness.[8]

Sayers' achievement in *The Mind of the Maker* is to bring God and man closer to each other, yet a book hailed as 'an essay of great penetration and acumen, which will be much valued in theological circles',[9] is no dense academic tract. Sayers compellingly discusses what happens—in religion or art—when one of the three persons is stronger or weaker than the others, what happens when an artist falls in love with his characters, and why the consequences of a creator *compelling* a creation to follow him are always catastrophic. Sayers' later detective fiction, as we have seen, illustrates her arguments, and she scatters clues as to why she moved away from the genre:

> The desire of being persuaded that all human experience may be presented in terms of a problem having a predictable, final, complete and sole possible solution accounts, to a great extent, for the later extraordinary popularity of detective fiction ... It is significant that readers should so often welcome the detective-story as a way of escape from the problems of existence. It 'takes their minds off their troubles'. Of course it does; for it softly persuades them that love and hatred, poverty and unemployment, finance and international politics, are problems, capable of being dealt with and solved in the same manner as the Death in the Library ... Life is no candidate for the Detection Club...[10]

Sayers, it needs to be remembered, was writing in the early years of world war, when life itself and everything that made it dear seemed to be coming apart at the seams. To deal with a crisis of such immense proportions, she argued, all branches of learning—the humanities, science, theology—had to be reassessed to see what they could provide as remedies:

Any witness—however small—to the rationality of a creed assists us to an intelligent apprehension of what it is intended to mean, and enables us to decide whether it is, or is not, as it sets out to be, a witness of universal truth.[11]

One means of reassessment was to be a series of books under the title of *Bridgeheads*, edited by herself and Muriel St Clare Byrne. Four were planned, only two—including *The Mind of the Maker*—were published, probably because Sayers in particular just didn't have the time or energy to match her initial enthusiasm. She did, however, prepare a 'Statement of Aims' for the series, and I quote this almost in full because it sums up the sheer breadth of her concerns, and the audaciousness (on occasion the arrogance) that led her to pontificate on education, capitalism, work, government intervention, war, as well as the underpinning or undermining of moral and spiritual laws. It remains a remarkable document, not least because every so often she seems to say something pertinent *for today*:

(1) We believe that the chief trouble among the nations today is fear—the fear of death and especially the fear of life. Human life is 'fear-conditioned': this is what depresses men's spirits and paralyses constructive effort. We believe that this fear can only be driven out by a strong awareness of the real value of life. Our aim is to give the people of this country a constructive purpose worth living for and worth dying for.

(2) A real value for life must be such as to satisfy man's nature as a whole. No value for life is real that involves the denial of any part of human personality.

(3) We believe that absolute value cannot and must not be ascribed to any objective or authority within the framework of history. Any such ascription can only lead to an increasingly violent conflict of dialectical opposites. When this happens man sees himself as the helpless puppet of uncontrollable demonic forces, and loses the will to live.

155

(4)   While, therefore, we do not deny, but strongly assert, the principle of 'relativity' in the sphere of physics, biology and psychology, we contend that this principle also, if erected into an absolute, displays man as a puppet of demonic forces, and either destroys his hold on life or causes him to revolt into some form of authoritarianism. The question 'relative to what?' must be asked, and it can only be answered by reference to an absolute reality outside the 'drift of becoming' and knowable at any moment in history. This absolute reality is the sole sanction for the sanctity and value of the individual personality.

(5)   We believe that peace and stability are not attainable if considered as static in their nature or pursued as ends in themselves. They are the by-products of a right balance between the individual and the community. This balance is attainable only by a ceaseless creative activity directed to a real standard of value.

(6)   We believe that liberty and equality are not attainable by considering the individual man as a unit in a limited scheme of society (e.g. 'economic man', 'political man', 'the worker', etc.), but only by considering him as a complete personality, capable of self-discipline in a self-disciplined community; the aim of such discipline being the fulfilment of man's whole nature in relation to absolute reality.

(7)   We recognize that the past is irrevocable, and ought not to be otherwise. We shall not therefore advocate the return to outworn or discredited structures of society (e.g. feudalism, Marxist communism, etc.) or any programme that aims at 'putting the clock back' (e.g. national isolation or the abolition of machinery). We realize that 'the future can only be built upon the foundation of the real past.' We shall not represent the present war, or any other human calamity, as an evil necessarily destructive of all civilized

effort, but as an opportunity which, by breaking up false standards, opens the way to fresh creative effort. We believe that the only way to overcome evil is to transform it into a greater good.

(8) We shall not primarily concern ourselves with methods—such as economic systems, or theories of government—though these will no doubt emerge. We shall try to quicken the creative spirit which enables man to build such systems in the light of his spiritual, intellectual and social needs. We aim at the Resurrection of Faith, the Revival of Learning and the Re-integration of Society . . .

Thus we shall endeavour, among other things:

To urge on creative activity, keep people interested in life, and combat lethargy, defeatism and depression of spirits.

To keep firmly before the minds of the people the true nature of man and the importance of the individual in the community and in the universe.

To remind people incessantly, while the War continues, of the spiritual aims for which it is waged and thus to prepare for a real energy of reconstruction in peace.

To explain to people, as well as we can, what is happening, why it is happening and how it concerns themselves, and to encourage them to form instructed opinions and act upon them. To emphasize the value of active, individual thinking and feeling, and to do away with the prevalent reliance upon 'spoon-feeding' and mental 'dope'.

To stimulate enjoyment in spiritual and mental exercise, and to correct the over-emphasis upon bodily comfort and 'conspicuous waste' in the better-off sections of the population. To lay stress, at the same time, on the necessity of a proper standard of physical well-being in all sections.

To open people's minds to the idea (a) that those whose work is interesting and stimulating should be given freedom to pursue it without crippling distractions, and (b) that those whose work is of necessity mechanical and uncreative should be given leisure for recreation.

To point the way to the proper employment of leisure (i.e. one which gives full play to creative energy . . .)

To recognize, encourage, and bring into action all the valuable qualities in which our nation is rich, and set them consciously working for the kind of society that shall be fully expressive of man's nature.

To examine into grievances, misunderstandings, etc., in the public mind (especially at the moment with regard to war aims and war restrictions) and to get these removed by the spread of correct information and the encouragement of a right spirit (whether in the public or in the governing bodies).

To observe and examine instances of social obstructiveness (e.g. contempt of the churches, resentment against intellectualism, readiness to cheat the government, etc.); to analyse the underlying causes (often unconscious) beneath their sometimes misleading expression; to discover and show how far such obstructiveness is justified by defects in the bodies concerned and how far an objection rightly made to those defects has been wrongly carried over to (e.g.) religion, learning and government as such; and to dispel, by explanation and argument, obstructiveness that arises from mere ignorance and misunderstanding of the facts.

To awaken the nation to a livelier understanding of the importance of the creative arts in the life of the community, and to secure for these a national and political recognition commensurate with their great actual and still greater potential influence.

To make the nation aware to how great an extent modern thought has been governed by scientific method, and, while strongly encouraging the application of scientific method to everything within its own sphere, to make it plain that this sphere is not unlimited.

To emphasize, in particular, that economics, though considered today as constituting the fundamental structure of society, was not always so considered, and has, in fact, been already found unworkable.

To explore suggestions for international settlement, bearing in mind the following considerations:

(a)   While it is certainly at present impossible, and probably at any time undesirable, to abolish nationality or national feeling, nationalism must not be 'deified' (i.e. regarded as an absolute).

(b)   Treaties determining territorial boundaries must not be regarded as Divine Acts insusceptible to revision. An extreme rigidity in the administration of treaties or any other legal instrument ends inevitably in the opposite extreme of the denunciation of treaties, rebellion against law and an appeal to force.

(c)   The establishment of international control (whether in such a form as the League of Nations or that of the suggested Federation of Europe) is bound to fail if the forms of justice and legality are or become, in fact, only a disguise for the forensic protection of vested interests.

(d)   The existence of enormous world-resources of food and other materials (made available by science) side by side with extreme want among large numbers of the population has become a world scandal that is wholly intolerable. Means must be formed of distributing supplies to meet world needs even if this means a complete reconstruction of economic structure.

(e)   A non-economic structure of the kind established in

159

Russia and Germany, which depends upon a low standard of living for whole populations, is wholly undesirable, and must be unnecessary in view of the world surplus in production.

To awaken the nation to the need for an entire overhaul of the aims and methods of education in this country. This is at present directed chiefly or wholly to the end of securing gainful employment, and is neither satisfactory in itself (i.e. in producing wise and happy citizens) nor even successful in its avowed purpose (i.e. it is powerless to check unemployment and does not fit people for the useful employment of leisure). The nation must be encouraged to take a very much wider view of the function of education, in better accordance with the needs of human nature and good citizenship, and to demand of its government that the necessary money for this better education shall be forthcoming. That is to say, that education which fits the citizen for peace must be taken at least as seriously as the armaments which fit him for war, and the necessary expenditure of thought and money cheerfully incurred.[12]

Ironically, the planning of such heady goals was followed by a lull in the writer's life, as though all the constituencies under fire and at risk of change came together and found ways of drawing the teeth of the would-be revolutionary. Sayers seemed now to be marking time, taking a breather between *The Man Born to be King* and *The Mind of the Maker* and her next all-consuming project, which would last to the end of her days, the translation of Dante's *The Divine Comedy*. But then came the strange affair of the Lambeth Degree.

Dr James Welch of the BBC wrote privately to William Temple, the Archbishop of Canterbury, unashamedly advocating her for the rare honour of a Lambeth Degree as reward for *The Man Born to be King*. His heart was in the right place, though Sayers would not have approved of what he called his 'serious judgment':

These plays seem to me to be her *magnum opus* . . . I have

been astonished at the religious effect of these plays on regular churchgoers; but very much more striking than that is the way in which the Gospel has been made to mean something to people totally divorced from the churches to whom the Christian Gospel has little relevance or meaning. My serious judgment is that these plays have done more for the preaching of the Gospel to the unconverted than any other single effort of the Churches . . . and so I wonder . . . whether it would be possible and right to offer Dorothy Sayers a Lambeth D.D. for this piece of evangelism . . . I have not asked her, but I think I know her well enough to say that nothing would give her such deep pleasure as the conferring of that degree.[13]

Dr Welch should have been proved right. Sayers hungered after honours and awards, revelled in pomp and ceremony, and some years later was to accept a lesser honorary degree from Durham University without hesitation. The Archbishop, himself convinced that the plays had been 'one of the most powerful instruments in evangelism which the Church has had put into its hands for a long time past',[14] offered Sayers a Lambeth DD in September 1943, with what should have been the clinching argument in favour of acceptance: 'You would be the first woman actually to receive the Degree.'[15] But Sayers refused. Prevaricated at first, and then refused. And reading between the lines of her letters—legitimately, I feel, in the context of the Sayers we have come to know—it is possible to detect both a very real fear of press intrusion into her private life and, perhaps more so, a very real guilt about her past which she had never been able entirely to shake off.

In her first response to the Archbishop, she confessed that she would feel happy about accepting such an honour if she were a better kind of Christian. Was she really one at all? she mused. Or was she only in love with an intellectual pattern? And suppose one day she were to break free professionally from her religious shackles, and write something that might bring a blush to the Archbishop's cheeks?[16]

The Archbishop's reply gently pointed out that it would be 'a great mistake' to suppose that a Lambeth DD was somehow 'a certificate of sanctity or incompatible with the production of a thoroughly secular work in literature'.[17] Sayers sent a holding note, to which Temple expressed regret that he had put her 'all in a flutter'.[18] Then came the refusal: in this letter she rejected ecclesiastical labels or official ties to the church, on the grounds that if ordinary people were to take any notice of her she should remain on ther own, separate, a freelance. Also, she didn't want to be put under the scrutiny of the sensational press, which just might suggest she had planned to be honoured when she moved from crime to theology.[19]

Who was she kidding? Temple, perhaps, but never herself. She would have loved the rough and tumble of the scrum, as she had proved a mere two years earlier in the controversy over *The Man Born to be King*. Anyway, the Archbishop accepted her decision as final, and the matter was not raised again. Her first letter is the most revealing, with its expression of doubts that she is a Christian at all, and its agonizing over where her true love lies—in Christ, or in a pattern. Sentiments which betrayed Sayers' mild inner doubts of the time, but which also proved prophetic of an uncomfortable spiritual crisis in her later years. Meanwhile, in the run-up to Dante, there were correspondents to battle with, causes to decline—including, controversially, that of Zionism—and an irate husband to care for.

Solidarity in Guilt

At Witham, where Sayers now lived permanently, she was looking after Aunt Maud, as well as an increasingly querulous Fleming, who no longer helped even with the cooking. Secretaries came and went. Cats purred in and out. And a pig called Fatima, raised in the back yard, was immortalized in Sayers' Christmas poem to her friends.

> *This is our yard, and in it stands*
> *Our mistress (on hind-legs, with hands);*
> *The other one (the quadruped)*
> *Was Fatima—but now she's dead.*
> *When our establishment took charge*
> *of Fatima, she was not large;*
> *But lord, how she did feed and feed,*
> *A very prodigy of greed!*
> *She was, in short, a perfect Pig;*
> *And, when she got very big,*
> *A lorry came, and she was taken*
> *To where pigs vanish into bacon.*
> *Hear Pussius Catus moralize—*
> *To be a Pig is most unwise;*
> *Better by far to be a Cat,*
> *Who, if he likes, can put on fat*
> *And grow majestic and immense*
> *Regardless of the consequence,*
> *Since, though he bulge with fish and meat,*
> *He never will be fit to eat.*
> *So, because Pussies and Mankind*

Are so enlightened as to find
Each other quite uneatable,
Puss can afford to wish you well,
Hoping your Christmas may be good,
And beautiful with glorious food.

Not all her poetry was quite so frivolous, and Fräulein Fehmer, who had taught Sayers the piano at Godolphin, was the recipient of a war poem written in rhymeless style, called 'Target Area'. (Sayers hated looking back—'I thoroughly dislike all retrospect'[1]—but she never lost her affection for her piano teacher, and indeed had always sent her a copy of the latest Wimsey novel.)

. . . There is a particular nocturne
that I cannot hear to this day without thinking of her;
when it is rendered
by celebrated musicians over the aether
I see the red-brick walls, the games trophies,
the rush-bottomed chairs, the row of aspidistras,
that garnished the edge of the platform, and Fräulein Fehmer,
gowned in an unbecoming dark-blue silk,
lifting the song from the strings with a squaring of her strong
*   shoulders;*
the notes on the wireless are only an imperfect echo
of that performance . . .

When the great Lancasters,
roaring out of England, making the sky boil like a cauldron,
stooped at last upon Frankfurt from the blackness
*   between the stars*
did the old, heartbreaking melody cry to you,
Poland's agony through the crashing anger of England?
Did we strike you, perhaps, quickly
tossing the soul out through the rent ribs or merciful
splitting of the skull? Or did you
find yourself suddenly awake at midnight,

peering from the blankets, fumbling for your glasses, to see,
by flare-light and fire-light,
the unexpected precipice by the bedside,
the piano shattered aslant, with all its music
coiling out of it in a tangle of metallic entrails,
dust, books, ashes, splintered wood, old photographs,
the sordid indecency of bathroom furniture
laid open to the sky? Or are you, I wonder,
still waiting the personal assault, the particular outrage,
expiating the world's sin in a passion of nightly expectation
till the unbearable is reiterated
and the promise fulfilled? . . .

This I write
with the same hand that wrote the books I sent you,
knowing that we are responsible for what we do,
knowing that all men stand convicted of blood
in the High Court, the judge with the accused.
The solidarity of mankind is a solidarity in guilt,
and all our virtues stand in need of forgiveness,
being deadly . . .[2]

Such a poem exposes Sayers in a tender, compassionate vein. But she retained her ability to write the spectacularly withering letter. One Methodist minister, poor unsuspecting soul, harangued her to take up the cause of abstinence and to fight alongside him the demon drink. Sayers controlled herself—just—for the first reply:

> It must be a great grief to you that our Lord should have been so ill-informed, or so lacking in common moral and Christian sense, as to use wine both for His Sacraments and for his pleasure. What a pity he had not the advantage of being able to study Miss Baker's pamphlet on the subject . . .[3]

Not knowing when to leave well alone, the minister pursued the matter, and this time Sayers let herself go:

I will put to you two questions, and will trouble you to answer them in two words or not at all.

(1) 'The Son of Man came eating and drinking and ye say "Behold a gluttonous man and a wine-bibber".' Do you agree with this criticism, yes or no?

(2) If the answer to the above is yes, then please state in one word whether you consider that Our Lord, in drinking wine, showed himself to be: (a) wicked or (b) ignorant...

If you believe that Jesus was wholly God, then to condemn his conduct is presumptuous. If you believe that he was not wholly God, but only partly or in some respects divine, you are a heretic. If you think he was not God at all, you are an infidel.[4]

The minister didn't trouble Sayers again. She had no patience with clergy who piously denounced 'sin' which, privately, they defined as 'weaknesses of the flesh' or even 'weaknesses of the flesh we of course are not subject to'. She had no patience, either, with correspondents who let slip the odd loose phrase which betrayed their own prejudices, especially in the sexual area. One of these referred to Christ as 'apparently sexless'.

This is a very wild statement, supported by no documentary evidence whatever. Of his 33 years of life, we know about only 3. By that time we certainly find a person in whom the passion for the work that was to be done had swallowed up all other passions. But whether that state was arrived at without struggle we simply do not know at all. A single devotion will, in fact, destroy all lesser devotions; the single-hearted person has usually no attention to give to competing interests—but this has nothing to do with physical peculiarities but with dominant purpose. One thing at least is very remarkable: that Christ, alone of all religious teachers, made no difference between women & men, laid down no separate rules for female behaviour, was equally unselfconscious with both sexes, gave just the same serious attention to the questions & opinions of women as of men, never used female faults & failings to point any particular moral, and indeed, made sex no part whatever of his teaching, except to say, when challenged, that men were as much to blame as women for sexual sins, & that dirty thinking was just as bad as dirty living. He appears, in fact, to have been completely sane on the subject—a thing quite impossible to any abnormal person, & unusual in anybody.[5]

Another correspondent rhapsodized about women—and Sayers retorted with the example of Christ:

He alone . . . among great religious teachers, had no whimsies about women . . . He never held them up either as a menace, or a snare, or an inspiration; never delimited their sphere of action, or told them to stick to the kitchen . . . or to take their ideas from their husbands and stop talking about what they did not understand. He treated them quite ordinarily as individual persons—and seemed to look on them neither as 'Women, God help us!' nor 'The Ladies, God bless 'em!' but just as specimens of humanity, who happened to be female. I find this fact fortifying, and consider it as tending to clear the mind of cant.[6]

After letters like these, it might be supposed that Sayers would have been a woman ahead of her time and a staunch, not to say aggressive, proponent of the ordination of women. In some senses she was, but she perceived the complications: she told one corresondent that although she saw no strictly theological reason why women should not be ordained, the ministry of the sacrament undoubtedly raised a few difficulties. After all, the priest represented Christ, and Christ was a man. She paraphrased the apostle Paul as support: 'All things may be lawful, but all things are assuredly not expedient'—and inferred that for any church to break with apostolic tradition was to invite schism for schism's sake. She wanted women to preach and teach, however, and wondered if some special order might be created.[7] Sayers was uncharacteristically loose in her thinking on the issue: the fact that 'Christ was a man' is irrelevant; he was also a Jew, but who would demand that all priests be Jewish?

Sayers often addressed the exclusively male clergy—once, memorably, on one of her favourite themes, work. In her talk, called 'Why Work?', she advanced three propositions: work is not, primarily, a thing one does to live, but the thing one lives to do . . . it is the business of the Church to recognize that the secular vocation, as such, is sacred . . . and the worker's first duty is to serve the work:

> The popular 'catch' phrase of to-day is that it is everybody's duty to serve the community. It is a well-sounding phrase, but there is a catch in it. It is the old catch about the two great commandments. 'Love God—and your neighbour; on those two commandments hang all the Law and the Prophets.' The catch in it, which nowadays the world has largely forgotten, is that the second commandment depends upon the first, and that without the first, it is a delusion and a snare. Much of our present trouble and disillusionment have come from putting the second commandment before the first. If we put our neighbour first, we are putting man above God, and that is what we have been doing ever since we began to worship humanity and make man the measure of all things. Whenever man is made the centre of things, he becomes the storm-centre of trouble—and that is precisely the catch about serving the community.[8]

Worthy societies bombarded her with requests to ally herself to their cause, or at very least to address their membership. Sayers lost interest the moment they said she could take up any subject she chose—she alone was the principal attraction. To Sayers, this denoted 'stupidity', and stupidity, in her book, was the sin of Sloth: 'There are times when one is tempted to say that the great, sprawling, lethargic sin of Sloth is the oldest and greatest of the sins and the parent of all the rest.'[9] As she saw it, it was unforgivably stupid to be more interested in a person than in the truths he or she might utter.

It was in 1943 that first General Sir Wyndham Deedes, then Miss L. M. Livingstone, wrote to ask Sayers' support for the cause of Zionism. Anti-semitic feeling wasn't exactly rife in the country, but there were disturbing signs of it gaining a foothold, and they no doubt reasoned that the proven propaganda skills of someone like Sayers would help refute the dangerously emotive arguments. She declined, however, on the grounds that anyone who tried to be objective would end up by offending both Jews and Christians. Also, if her fellow-countrymen were taking to anti-semitism it was because, having had to put up with 'bombs, black-out, restrictions, rations, coal-targets, bread-targets, clothes-coupons, call-ups, income-tax, lack of domestic help and general bedevilment',[10] the arrival of an alien culture in their midst was one problem too many. Nothing, she believed, could change the 'otherness' of Jews, and as it was an 'otherness' they themselves encouraged they could not reasonably object to it being resented. That 'otherness' Sayers would have traced back to the time of Christ:

> I cannot, you see, bring myself to approach the question as though Christ had made no difference to history. *I* think, you see, that He was the turning-point of history, and the Jewish people, whose religion and nation are closely bound up with the course of history, missed that turning-point and got stranded: so that all the subsequent course of their history has to be looked upon in the light of that frustration . . . Naturally I cannot expect Jewish people to sympathize with this point of view, but I do find it rather difficult to discuss a problem if I have to leave out what appears to me to be the major factor.[11]

Asked to write an article for a symposium on 'The Future of the Jews', Sayers produced twenty-six pages on the coming of Christ as the 'turning-point of history', and the frustrations of the Jews as the predictable outcome of failing to recognize Jesus as Messiah. Some Jewish contributors to the symposium, having demanded to see what she had written, then played into her hands by refusing to have their articles published in the same volume. Sayers believed she had proved her point and wrote self-righteously to the publishers:

> In this country, where self-criticism and the toleration of criticism are practised almost to excess, nothing can so alienate sympathy from the Jewish cause as the policy at present pursued by a certain section of its apologists. And indeed neither goodwill nor co-operation is possible when the expression of opinion by one party is resented or stifled by the other. I beg these people, Christians and Jews alike, not to stir up anger in this country against the Jewish nation by continuing in this deplorable attitude of mind. They may succeed in silencing criticism, but it is when the English are silent that they begin to think.[12]

However one comes to this story, it does little credit to Sayers. It is true that she may well have taken a more sympathetic line had she known of the alarming extent of anti-semitism elsewhere in the world; and Brabazon is surely right when he points out that 'awareness of others' faults is not the same as hostility'.[13] Also, Sayers was a woman of her time, and should not be judged outside history and with the gift of hindsight. Nonetheless, it is hard to see how she could soften her basic conviction—that the Jewish people bring trouble upon themselves by rejecting the true Messiah. So appalling has been that 'trouble' that they could justifiably ask: where was he? and if he ignored their cries because they had ignored him, what sort of punishment fitting the crime was that? Take him away. We'll go on waiting ... As Sayers had penned to Fräulein Fehmer: 'The solidarity of mankind is a solidarity in guilt, / and all our virtues stand in need of forgiveness, / being deadly ...'

1 0

'You will never be able to pass the beasts until you understand yourself'

In 1943, in her fiftieth year, Sayers discovered the last and perhaps truest love of her life—the poetry, the spiritual world, of Dante Alighieri the Florentine. She owed the discovery to Charles Williams, an extraordinary if eccentric novelist, and one of a small group of lay-people whose work influenced the Church of England—T. S. Eliot, C. S. Lewis, Williams and Sayers. She reviewed one of his novels thus:

> To read only one work of Charles Williams is to find oneself in the presence of a riddle—a riddle fascinating by its romantic colour, its strangeness, its hints of a rich and intricate unknown world just outside the barriers of consciousness; but to read all is to become a free citizen of that world and to find in it a penetrating and illuminating interpretation of the world we know.[1]

Williams, all his adult life, clung to a belief in romantic love, comparing the very first uncomplicated view lovers have of each other with the relationship between God and his creation before the Fall. He believed in Affirmation—the acceptance, in love, of all things, not for their own sake, but as images, however imperfect, of the Divine. Like Sayers, his imagination thrived in legendary times, the days of Camelot and Arthur, and his spirit rejoiced in the clear-cut designs of the Catholic faith. Unlike Sayers, whose deepest religious conviction was the conviction of sin, he seemed continually to experience the valleys of damnation and the mountains of ecstasy. She was well aware of the difference.

> I can enter into Charles's type of mind to some extent, by imagination, and look through its windows, as it were, into places where I cannot myself walk. He was, up to a certain point, I think, a practising mystic; from that point of view I am a complete moron, being almost wholly without intuitions of any kind. I can only apprehend intellectually what the mystics grasp directly.[2]

In 1943 Sayers got hold of Williams' new book on Dante, *The Figure of Beatrice*, in which the author penned a portrait of a man not only of his own time but of all time, a man like other men: 'We have looked everywhere for enlightenment on Dante, except in our lives and our love-affairs,' he wrote.[3] Beatrice, Dante's lover, dies and is transformed into the rapturous creature who transports him into paradise—and, like Williams after him, Dante saw love as a foretaste of eternity, and a motivating force to aim at perfection on earth. The eternal is in the everyday, and what we do with the everyday determines where we spend eternity.

Williams' book convinced Sayers of Dante's greatness:

> But it was still some time before I made up my mind to tackle Dante in person; after all, fourteen thousand lines are fourteen thousand lines, especially if they are full of Guelphs and Ghibellines and Thomas Aquinas. A friendly critic can often give the impression that a poem is more colourful than it is by picking out the jolly bits and passing over the rest... Besides, the world always hinted that Dante, besides being great, grim, and intellectual, was also 'obscure'.[4]

She *did* tackle Dante in person—'finding him, for some reason which I cannot explain, upon that shelf of my library which is devoted to English poets of the 19th century'[5]—and immersed herself in Hell, Purgatory and Paradise. The impact ensured that whatever sorrows and troubles came her way in the last fourteen years of life, she would never lack for intellectual satisfaction as she laboured with love over her own translation—and that, after all, was what she always most craved.

> I can remember nothing like it since I first read *The Three Musketeers* at the age of thirteen. Neither the world, nor the theologians, nor even Charles Williams told me the one great, obvious, glaring fact about Dante Alighieri of Florence—that he was simply the most incomparable story-teller who ever set pen to paper. However foolish it may sound, the plain fact is that I bolted my meals, neglected my sleep, work, and correspondence, drove my friends crazy, and paid only a distracted attention to the doodle-bugs which happened to be infesting the neighbourhood at the time, until I had panted my way through the Three Realms of the Dead from top to bottom and from bottom to top; and that, having finished, I found the rest of the world's literature so lacking in pep and incident that I pushed it all peevishly aside and started out from the Dark Wood again.[6]

What Sayers was to write later about Hell in Dante's vision supports Williams' contention that the Florentine was a man of all time. It is, she says, 'a picture of human society in a state of sin and corruption',[7] and to her the signs in Dante's day were not different from the signs in her own:

> Futility; lack of a living faith; the drift into loose morality, greedy consumption, financial irresponsibility, and uncontrolled bad temper; a self-opinionated and obstinate individualism; violence, sterility, and lack of reverence for life and property including one's own; the exploitation of sex, the debasing of language by advertisement and propaganda, the commercialising of religion, the pandering to superstition and the conditioning of people's minds by mass-hysteria and 'spell-binding' of all kinds, venality and string-pulling in public affairs, hypocrisy,

dishonesty in material things, intellectual dishonesty, the fomenting of discord (class against class, nation against nation) for what one can get out of it, the falsification and destruction of all the means of communication; the exploitation of the lowest and stupidest mass-emotions; treachery even to the fundamentals of kinship, country, the chosen friend, and the sworn allegiance; these are the all-too-recognisable stages that lead to the cold death of society and the extinguishing of all civilised relations.[8]

Sayers speaks of her 'mania' for Dante, and in those early besotted days she taught herself 'to read the medieval Italian in a very few weeks' time, with the aid of Latin, an Italian grammar, and the initial assistance of a crib'.[9] She determined to translate *The Divine Comedy* herself, not put off at all by the existence of other translations of high repute: 'I think that the trouble with all of them is that they have far, far too much reverence for their author. They are afraid to be funny, afraid to be undignified; they insist on being noble and they end by being prim. But prim is the one thing Dante never is.'[10] One only has to read Sayers' summary of the life and work of Dante to accept the contention of her biographer Ralph E. Hone that 'all her previous life had been a preparation: her skill in languages, her successful apprenticeship as a writer in many genres, her bristling sensitivity to theology, her wide social awareness, her enormous reading in many fields'.[11]

Dante Alighieri was born in Florence, in 1265. He fell in love with Beatrice, who 'was to him much less a bodily passion than a spiritual revelation'.[12] Beatrice married another, but Dante continued to adore her from a distance; indeed it seems as though he never exchanged so much as a passing word with her. In 1290, however, she died, and quite emotionally shattered he turned for consolation to philosophy, although first he had to marry one Gemma Donati, to whom he had been engaged as a boy, and who was to bear him four children. Politically active—'he believed in a single world government, a kind of United States of Europe, under a single Emperor holding his authority direct from God, while a purified Church should act as a check on tyranny'[13]—in 1301 he found himself ruined and in exile from Florence after getting embroiled in troubles between two rival parties.

For twenty years he led the life of a wanderer, studying at the universities of Bologna and Paris, leaving unfinished a philosophical work called *The Banquet*, and dependent on the benificence of noblemen who made use of him as they pleased. Amid the wreckage of his life—he died in 1321—he penned *The Divine Comedy*.

> The 'Comedy' is an allegory of the way to God. Whether one reads it as an allegory of human society or of the individual soul, it is the story of Everyman's passage from the dark wood of error, through the knowledge of and the death to sin; after that, the toilsome climb up the mountain of repentance to the recovery of lost innocence, and thence upwards by the mystical way of illumination to the vision of God. Literally, it is shown as a journey through Hell, Purgatory and Paradise, but allegorically it figures the soul's pilgrimage in *this* world . . . His journey is the journey back to Beatrice . . . As love had once shown him the glory of eternity realised and communicated in the person of a living woman, so now the love from which all loves derive shows him the everlasting realities communicated through the whole visible world of creatures. He sees the affirming of all the symbols, the awful identity of the infinite with the finite; and in the culminating vision he sees that which is at once the means, the pledge, and the explanation of all such identities—the identity of God and man in Christ.[14]

Undismayed by her husband's caustic comment, 'What on earth do you want to read that stuff for?'[15] and undeterred by the intermittent threat of 'doodle-bugs' over Witham, Sayers bustled into her reading and translating with enviable gusto, sending Williams over the next nine months nineteen letters of rising excitement and gushing enthusiasm. He responded with eleven of his own. It is in these letters that one is aware of

Sayers mellowing: she is less dismissive, less overbearing: it is as though the warmth at the heart of the Affirmation steals into her soul, and begins its seductive work. For example, this to Williams during an aside on John Milton:

> I think that if, in a great writer, one finds something which causes a serious lack of sympathy, one may have the right to say so ... and that ... such a lack of sympathy may not prevent one from genuinely appreciating the purely poetic achievement. But I do think it is a serious disqualification for writing a book on that writer; and what I *cannot* understand or stomach is this present-day notion that it is a positive qualification, if not the chief and only qualification for the task. I am, for example, allergic to Charles Lamb—I can't help that—but why should I go out of my way to say so in a long, peevish and impenetrably stupid book? I find J. M. Barrie at once a brilliant stage craftsman & a nauseating sentimentalist ... but why should I analyse the nausea to the tune of 60,000 words ... One unfortunate clergyman, very busy, was badgered by reporters to write an opinion of *The Man Born to be King* at the time of the uproar, which he kindly did. It was not published, & he enquired why ... The Editor replied: 'Oh, but you approved of it—that isn't News' ... Love for anything is Not News—except in Heaven—& that is why the *Inferno* is so full of people angrily beating & biting one another in the slough; they *like* that sort of thing. They *want* to be cross & miserable. They *enjoy* chewing things to pieces—the little nasties! It must be part of the frustration of Hell that there is nothing good there to chew up—the good is beyond their reach; they can only chew one another.[16]

Abandoned as she was to Dante's way, Sayers thankfully separated the complexities of the *Comedy* from the naivety of the political vision, and some of his attraction for her—it is a relief to see—lay in the power of a mirror image:

The charm of his character (in the poem—God knows what he was like on the domestic hearth) is that he takes himself very seriously as a poet but not at all seriously as a man. Is it feminine of me to say so? Perhaps—but G.K.C. observes somewhere that everybody dislikes a man who stands on his dignity & a woman who doesn't, & I can agree with him about the first part, though with reservations about the second.[17]

I suppose there is nothing in Dante's Heaven against which the contemporary mind rebels so uneasily . . . To be content *for ever* with a lower place, without either possibility or desire of 'improvement' or 'progress', has become quite alien to our way of thought . . . To be sure, what we *say* we want to abolish is the artificial inequality of goods & social status; but I am not sure that this is being accompanied as it should by any recognition of a real hierarchy of merit. I seem to detect a general disposition to debunk the natural hierarchies of intellect, virtue & so forth, & substitute, as far as possible, an all-round mediocrity.[18]

. . . I cannot share that mystical excitement about sex, or even really sympathise with it . . . I do not care how many 'unrefined' sonnets he wrote about Nella, or what nameless orgies he indulged in . . . during his passage through the Dark Wood—down at the bottom of him there is something that knows where it lives & and is not really *bothered* about 'this woman business'.[19]

It is no small achievement to have made [Virgil] consistently good, kind and wise, through two long epic books, in which he is *never once* tedious or pompous or patronizing or superior.[20]

Was there ever a heaven so full of nods and becks and wreathed smiles? So gay and so dancing? . . . Surely nobody ever so passionately *wanted* a place where everybody was kind, and courteous, and carried happiness so lightly.[21]

Williams, on the staff of the Oxford University Press, had once written to Sayers in similar bubbling vein, about her novel *The Nine Tailors*—'It's a marvellous book; it is high imagination'[22]—but he was quite bowled over by her relentless ecstasy, and suggested that he might publish her Dante letters, or something similar—'I do very much want people to get all you say about the laughter and lightness and fun—even—of Dante... Oh do, do!'[23] It is indicative of Sayers' mood that she didn't immediately squash the idea:

> I write to you a series of innocent, carefree, personal letters about a great poet, & your immediate reaction is to contrive how they can be turned into a pamphlet to improve other people's minds. And I, instead of replying, 'Charles, don't be disgusting!' begin to dally with the project, & shall end by saying 'If you like—provided *you* do all the work & *I* get some of the money'![24]

Any plan to publish, if such it was, came to nothing with the untimely death of Williams in May 1945. Sayers received the news from his friend, Margaret Douglas, and wrote back at once:

> This is very grievous news. Charles Williams was unique in his work & his personality; there is nobody who can take his place. It comes as a great blow to me personally—I was very fond of him & proud of his friendship, & especially at this moment, the work I am trying to do owed so much to him & to his encouragement & inspiration that I feel as though the whole direction of it has been cut off.[25]

Sayers struggled on, however, lost still in her passion for Dante, and encouraged afresh by friendship with the Williams family who—impressed with her contribution to a memorial volume on Williams and thankful that an agreement ensured that all royalties came their way—first sent reprints of some of Williams' novels, and then arranged meetings with her. Later, she would fittingly dedicate her versions of *Hell* and *Purgatory* to

'The Dead Master of the Affirmations, Charles Williams'.

Her versions might never have appeared at all, however, but for a chance encounter with E. V. Rieu, who had supported the *Bridgeheads* series and was now the editor of Penguin Classics. More importantly, he was looking for a new translation of Dante. Sayers' early nervousness as to whether she was equipped to carry such a project through is illustrated by the fact that over lunch together at the end of 1944 she didn't so much as mention the work she was doing on the opening Cantos. It was left to Muriel St Clare Byrne to whisper into Rieu's receptive ear. He in fact had in mind a prose translation, but finding Sayers in convincing form he agreed to hear her read stanzas she had completed. The result was never in doubt:

> It is full of fire, swift movement, poetry and vigour, and
> above all, for my purposes, it is clear . . . I have great
> pleasure therefore in accepting your offer to translate the
> Divine Comedy for my series of Penguin Classics . . . May
> I tell them that you could deliver Inferno by January 1,
> 1946, Purgatorio by January 1, 1947, and Paradiso by
> January 1, 1948?[26]

In their dealings with authors, publishers have never lost their innate and invariably misplaced optimism about dead-lines, and Rieu's credulity was greater than most. Sayers actu-ally asked for four years instead of three to finish, but it was four years before the publication of *Hell*, a further six before *Purgatory* appeared, and her unfinished *Paradise* was com-pleted by her friend Barbara Reynolds.

Sayers lectured widely on Dante, mostly under the auspices of the Summer School of Italian Studies, and it was one of these lectures that made Reynolds—at the time a lecturer in Italian at Cambridge—blink, sit up and take notice. 'I got so excited,' she wrote later, 'that I had to be held down by [my husband] Le-wis.'[27] She was conquered by Sayers' portrayal of Dante as a *contemporary* writer stating critical *truth*, and of course by her very presence, in silver evening dress and extravagant earrings, speaking with vibrant passion, and caring little for technical expectation or intellectual pretension. She probably wouldn't have believed that Sayers herself found that lecture 'rather an ordeal':

> ... the audience was made up of (a) about 6 people who know *all* about Dante—sitting like sharks, just under the platform with their jaws wide open; (b) about 50 people who know more about Dante, and far more Italian, than I do; (c) about 400 people who (to judge by the looks of them) had never even *heard* of Dante! However, I did fairly well, because, the acoustics of Jesus Hall being bad, and most of the other lecturers academic gentlemen who mumbled serenely along with their noses in their papers, I turned out to be the only lecturer whom, so far, the audience had been able to hear properly. Thus I had an unfair advantage—merely because being no academic but a common popular soapbox lecturer, I didn't mind shouting at them in a loud and brassy voice, without regard for my own dignity or that of my subject.[28]

Letters were exchanged between Sayers and Reynolds; Sayers took tea with the Reynolds family; a professional relationship developed, out of which emerged a deep, lasting and fruitful bond. Reynolds was among the first to congratulate Sayers on publication of *Hell*: '*Greed* is the only word which describes my sessions with it; indeed it has thrown all my time-table out of joint.'[29] The translation had praise heaped upon it, although *The Times*' reviewer, while admitting she had caught the directness of the original, believed she had failed to catch the poetry. C. S. Lewis probably had its measure:

> You have got (what you most desired) the quality of an exciting story. On that side you may record almost complete success. Next; I think the metric audacities are nearly all effective in their places, i.e. as things in *your* poem. How far they are like anything in Dante ... is another matter. They have on me the effect of making Dante rather like Browning. That is certainly better than

making him like Milton. I shd. say that they are
everywhere doing more good than harm . . . Every live
rendering must sacrifice some things to achieve others . . .
It is a strong, exciting view from one particular angle, and
that is worth any number of timid, safe versions.[30]

Sayers was content. Content enough to reply at length to
genuine but often intricate letters of inquiry from puzzled correspondents. As I have hinted before, gone is the desire verbally
to maim the ignorant amateur; she seems now to care, and to want
to help:

The terror that seizes upon Dante in the Dark Wood is—
isn't it?—a kind of ignorant and unreasoning terror, such
as afflicts a good many people to-day: 'We are lost—we
don't know where we are going—something is wrong
somewhere—we want to pursue happiness (the ascent of
the mountain) but we are being prevented by daemonic
forces (the Beasts) which seem to be outside us and beyond
our control.' Whereon Reason illuminated by Grace
intervenes and says, in effect, 'You will never be able to
pass the Beasts until you understand yourself. The Beasts
are the exteriorisation of the corruption within. You must
face it there, and you must not be afraid of learning the
truth about it. There is your reluctance to commit
yourself—there is your lack of a living faith—there is what
you feel to be a rather excusable weakness in emotional and
sexual matters—you recognise these, do you? All right, let
us see where they lead to. Self-indulgence, a little gold-
digging, discontent and a nasty, quarrelsome spirit—that
worries you, does it? I am glad to hear it. But now, I fear,
we come to a blank wall, which is your self-opinionated
obstinacy. Every devil in you is determined that you shall
not know what lies behind that barrier of pride in your own
judgment. But there is no going back, and, God help you,
you must and shall go through with it. There, now you can
begin to know the worst of yourself. There is no sin,
however foul, whose seeds are not recognisable in

181

yourself; no depth, however hideous, to which you are not capable of descending. Once you have admitted this, you are safe; you can look up on the face of evil unscathed, with fear and trembling you shall work out your salvation, and you shall be saved by understanding.' So at the bottom of this descent there is no crisis, except one of relief. The worst is known, or, as Virgil says, 'We have seen all'. The soul has died to sin, down to the roots of sin, and in its most hidden and abominable aspects, which one does not like to confess even to one's self . . . In accepting the guilt it is released from the guilt and can go on to purge the stain.[31]

Sayers has begun her own journey home, tantalizingly on the fringes of the Dark Wood, an arduous path ahead, but with refreshing glimpses of the presence of God to persuade her along it. Dante the man, Dante the poet, were for all time, she believed, and in her majestic Introduction to *Hell* she unconsciously conjures autobiography out of a timeless vision:

To gaze upon the mirror of the sun and stars and in himself to mirror forth the truth. This was the task which Dante had set himself . . . in the wreck of all his earthly hopes. He had lost love and youth and earthly goods and household peace and citizenship and active political usefulness and the dream of a decent world and a reign of justice. He was stripped bare. He looked outwards upon the corruption of Church and Empire, and he looked inwards into the corruption of the human heart; and what he saw was the vision of Hell. And, having seen it, he set himself down to write the great comedy of Redemption and of the return of àll things by the Way of Self-Knowledge and Purification, to the beatitude of the Presence of God.[32]

For Sayers, who often said that the only business of the Christian, in the end, is to be crucified, Dante's vision—if she could only keep it before her—must have come as a gratifying relief. But the emotional highs of *The Divine Comedy* could not eclipse the emotional lows caused by an increasing awareness of her husband's ill-health and her own mortality. Even in the middle of her most joyful letters to Williams, reality could break through and the mood become darker:

> Yesterday I broke a teapot & a plate. The day before that, I broke a hot-water bottle. Nerve going, meaning going—& tonight I overcooked a piece of steak. These thoughts lead to melancholy.[33]

11

Saying the Unsayable

Dante did not take up all Sayers' waking thoughts and energies, as this chapter will abundantly prove. St Anne's House, Soho, in the heart of London's theatreland, enticed her to its calling in 1942, and refused to ease its hold on her until her death fifteen years later: the compensations offered—meaty argument among friends, a chance to get away from a quarrelsome and often drunken husband, and the revival of a life in London unknown since the twenties—probably ensured that her work there gave her as much physical relief as Dante did spiritual.

St Anne's itself had been destroyed during the war by a land-mine, leaving standing the parish house and the tower with its clock stopped at the moment of destruction. Two Anglo-Catholic priests, the Rev. Patrick McLaughlin, whom Sayers had met when he was a vicar near Witham, and the Rev. Gilbert Shaw, thought the parish house ideal for the realization of a shared vision—a centre where open-minded agnostics could find reasoned and reasonable debate about Christianity. Sayers, at McLaughlin's request, added her voice to their plea to the Archbishop of Canterbury, who then instructed the Bishop of London to open up the House for their ministry.

So far so good. The cracks started to open when it became clear that, shared vision or not, Shaw and McLaughlin had very different ideas as to how to make the vision reality. For Shaw it was ascetic practice, prayer and meditation, almost a withdrawal from the world; for McLaughlin it was an exploration of the social environment and determining its spiritual significance. Sayers, of course, sided with McLaughlin: even more so after her experience of Williams, Dante and the Way of Affirmation, which convinced her that life is to be enjoyed, not denied.

In November 1944 she joined the Advisory Council of the House, and was elevated to Chairman a few years later. She had little choice: it was her lecture on Drama, given at St Anne's House first course of lectures—'Christian Faith and Contemporary Culture'—that really launched the project with publicity and style. (Such was its impact on her official biographer, James Brabazon, that he knew from that moment he wanted only to enter the world of theatre; T. S. Eliot on literature, Lady Rhondda on journalism, and James Welch on broadcasting, paled beside Dorothy L. Sayers on drama.) She also had little suspicion of what she was getting into: St Anne's supporters divided into two groups, one for Shaw, the other for McLaughlin, a division compounded by both men's lack of organizational sense.

It was chaotic. But Sayers never shirked a challenge, and in she strode, fighting off the Diocesan Reorganization Committee's attempts to abandon the project and sell off the site, drafting memoranda, sitting through long, tedious meetings, writing letters to newspapers and officials, appealing for funds, and somehow holding on to the vision while around her perished Gilbert Shaw and dozens of assistants and advisers, none of whom could make much sense out of the personal and financial complications immediately encountered. But St Anne's House—a Centre of Christian Discourse, according to the Bishop of London; a Centre of Cultural Studies, according to those involved—survived. That it would never have done so without Sayers is not only true but also a tremendous compliment to her unquenchable enthusiasm for a cause she saw as just. How she achieved what she did has to be left to the imagination, although perhaps she only had to be herself: energetic, rumbustious, committed, and unhesitatingly decided in her opinions.

I see that the Conference ended by passing a resolution about private property. I observe thankfully that we succeeded in securing the insertion of a cantel against identifying the Church with a political programme—so apparently the meeting, unlike the Press, was able to recognise a few words in the papers addressed to them other than the word 'fornication'. Something has *got* to be done about the Press.[1]

Tension eased at St Anne's with the departure of Gilbert Shaw, if the following account by Patrick McLaughlin is to be believed:

> My colleague, 20 years my senior whom I respected enormously . . . wanted to concentrate more and more on all sorts of curious things, like mysticism, visions, levitation and exorcising people possessed by devils. Several times, when we were having Seminars on the upper floor of St Anne's House, blood curdling shrieks would come up from the basement where Gilbert was exorcising somebody; and snakes were supposed to be slithering up the stairs! I had to soothe my group by saying 'Please don't be alarmed. It's only my colleague dabbling in devilry.'[2]

It was while McLaughlin was off sick and Sayers off guard that a Mission to London was launched, 'specifically about religion, the one thing not to be talked about at St Anne's House'.[3] McLaughlin was furious, particularly as the press called it a campaign to 'clean up sin', sin being understood 'as sexual, never pride, or greed or dishonesty'.[4] Sayers fumed and fretted, replying to those who said they didn't like the way missioners talked about religion that neither did she; the only Mission authenticated by St Anne's was 'to give intelligent people an opportunity of hearing an orderly exposition of the Christian Faith and of asking as many questions as they like and having those questions intelligently discussed and answered'.[5]

She was put out by a *Daily Sketch* report that 'Dorothy Sayers, the playwright, will write "Thrillers" from the Bible, with modern dialogues and characterisation, which will be performed for Dean-street, Soho, audiences'.[6] 'May I make it quite plain,' she responded, 'that I am *not* writing "thrillers from the Bible", or anything of that kind?'[7] To a more congenial audience she went further: 'All these sensational reports were the fantasy of a sick brain . . . My own job at the moment is translating *The Divine Comedy*—fortunately I did not mention *that* to the reporter, or he might have said I was composing a religious farce!'[8]

As if all this was not enough—and Dante back home, remember—Sayers was commissioned in April 1945 to write a play for performance at the 750th anniversary celebrations of Lichfield Cathedral the following year. The result was *The Just Vengeance*, 'a miracle-play of Man's insufficiency and God's redemptive act, set against the background of contemporary crisis'.[9] An airman dies, his plane crashing on Lichfield, and the action of the play takes place at the moment of his death: it ends with his triumphant acceptance, first of the cry of the crowd—'Say that the guilt is Mine; give it to Me/ And I will take it away to be crucified'— then of the cry of the Persona Dei—'Instead of your Justice, you shall have charity;/ Instead of your happiness, you shall have Joy; Instead of your peace the emulous exchange/ Of love.'[10]

Sayers thought it her finest work. Others were not so sure. Certainly it isn't her most original, saturated—some would say suffocated—as it is by the influence of Charles Williams. And she didn't have his skill to so fuse the natural with the supernatural that there seems no yawning gap between them. Perhaps the give-away is found in a letter she wrote to Muriel St Clare Byrne:

> I think I shall have to write a warning preface, indicating that 'nobody can give an intelligent opinion of this play without having undergone the tremendous intellectual discipline of reading *The Divine Comedy*', so that they won't ever be sure whether they are falling foul of me or of an elder and better poet! Anyhow, nearly all the argument and most of the best lines are Dante's—I shall say so, and leave them to entangle themselves.[11]

This from someone who believed that a play ought to explain itself. However, the actual production—overcoming every visual and aural defect of the Cathedral—seems to have been a splendid spectacle. Articles on this, that and everything continued to appear. Predictably on Heaven and Hell:

> God *sends* nobody to Hell . . . But He has so made us that what in the end we choose, that in the end we shall have . . . Neither can he force any soul into beatitude against its will; for He has nothing but Himself to give it. And it is precisely the light of His presence which the self-centred soul can know only as burning and judgment. So the Lady Julian said that in her visions she 'saw no Hell but sin' . . .[12]

Less predictably on political matters, like a letter she wrote to a national newspaper following flooding in the Fens:

> I think the time has come to protest against the use, whether in appeals or in Press and Radio announcements, of phrases like '*the Government* have given £1,000,000', '*the Government* will give a £ for every £ subscribed'—as though 'the Government' had any money of their own with which to make liberal gestures. The plain fact is that all the money comes from the tax-payers (including, incidentally, the flood-victims themselves) . . .[13]

Sayers was true-blue Tory all through. Socialist principles, to her, were unrealistic and a denial of individual responsibility. During the war, with a Labour Government in power, she wrote an article warning that 'the Socialists are setting up in this country all the familiar apparatus of a tyranny':

> When the Socialist process is completed, nobody will be able to have a roof over his head or a shirt to his back, or a bit to put in his mouth, without Government permission. Since the Government will be the only employer, every worker will lie wholly at the tyrants' mercy, unable to change or to get employment except on the tyrants' terms . . . The Conservative Manifesto explicitly recognises that the man who works hard and makes money ought to benefit by his labour, instead of being penalised by crushing and vindictive taxation . . .[14]

One can agree or disagree with that, depending on one's own political prejudice. It is harder to sit on the fence over the kind of remarks she made in a letter to Dr James Welch, who had moved from the BBC to be part of the Groundnuts Scheme farce in Tanganyika. To be charitable, she was tossing off a paragraph in a chatty and private letter, and had not thought through the implications of her remarks; to take the letter at anything like face value is to go some way towards endorsing the view of some, that Sayers at heart was a somewhat unattractive reactionary:

> I do wish somehow we could have let all these foreign people *alone*. A little Christianity would doubtless have done them no harm, if only it didn't have to be mixed up with things like industrialism, European institutions, party politics and the savage waste and greed of our kind of agriculture. If we go on like this much longer, there won't be a scrap of surface left on the earth anywhere. It *sounds* all right to heal the sick and preserve the lives of babies and so on, but if one goes on multiplying the population and destroying fertility, where does one end? We are doing away with all nature's safeguards . . . and as soon as we've broken down the defences of another bit of soil, we develop it until we develop it right away. I sometimes feel it would be an excellent thing if the native population murdered all the Europeans and proceeded to 'let in the jungle'.[15]

Collections of Sayers' articles and addresses were published by Gollancz and Methuen: *Unpopular Opinions* in 1946, and *Creed or Chaos* a year later. Penguin published her translation of Dante's *Hell* in 1949, and the same year saw a revival of *The Zeal of Thy House* at Canterbury, and acceptance of a request by the Bishop of Colchester to write a play for their Festival.

1950 was to prove a mixed year. In the spring Sayers unveiled a plaque at her old employers', Benson's, to commemorate her novel *Murder Must Advertise*. And in May she went to Durham University to receive an Honorary Degree in Literature, squirming no doubt at the Public Orator's rather strained form of wit as he set up the presentation:

> An examination of the claims of Miss Sayers to appear
> before us today must raise a preliminary doubt whether
> this is quite the sort of platform upon which she should be
> standing. The Documents in the Case, unobscured by
> Clouds of Witness, cannot be dismissed as Five Red
> Herrings in establishing this point. Long before the
> evidence of Unnatural Death, which had itself come out
> before Lord Peter Viewed the Body, there could be no
> doubt Whose Body had been in question. In the Teeth of
> the Evidence, even after the Unpleasantness at the Bellona
> Club—and it will be remembered that this did not follow
> but preceded the notorious Gaudy Night—Miss Sayers
> publicly took the unfortunate view that a book called
> Murder Must Advertise had no personal application. As
> for her victim, before anyone could Have His Carcase,
> Strong Poison proved to be present: and it is my feeling
> that there would have been no need to cite the Nine Tailors
> or to take the case further had not Hangman's Holiday
> intervened.

Sayers cut her visit to the University short, wanting to be at
home with her husband who was now extremely ill. One month
later, in June 1950, she was by his side when he suffered a stroke
and died instantly. It was a not unexpected death. Three years
earlier Sayers had written to a friend:

> The doctor, when I saw him yesterday, took a rather poor
> view of his blood-pressure, and told me a number of things
> *I* could have told *him* years ago if I had had the
> opportunity. This was the first time he had ever happened
> actually to see Mac in that kind of giddy and unco-
> ordinated state . . . The trouble, of course, with blood-
> pressure people who have *uncontrolled tempers*, is that they
> may work themselves up into a stroke at any moment. But
> one can't do anything about it, because nobody else can
> control their tempers for them.[16]

By 1949 Fleming's health had deteriorated alarmingly, and a hospital examination revealed enlargement of the heart and 'marked calcification of the aorta'.[17] The only cure was the one he couldn't maintain: to reduce his dependence on cigarettes and alcohol, and take to his bed for ten hours every day. 'Mac was better yesterday and the day before, but relapsed into gloom today,' Sayers noted.[18] And a descent into gloom was usually the signal for a trip to local pubs, where he had a reputation for drinking to excess. More than once he had to be assisted home, or he would order someone to put him 'on the rail', which meant help him to the wrought-iron fencing by which he could support himself to his front door. He was a disappointed man, and felt he had little to live for: he had not been able to make a stable living, his hobbies of portrait painting and photography had long since blurred into the past, and his own gnawing sense of inadequacy and failure had been fed by his wife's very public success.

'It will seem very queer without Mac,' Sayers wrote three days after his death. 'I shall miss having him to look after, and there will be no one to curse me and keep me up to the mark!'[19] And again: 'It seems impossible there should be so many uninterrupted hours in the day.'[20] Sayers would miss the habit of her husband, little more, and creative life would go on. That there was an absence of mourning is hardly surprising: what love she had ever felt for him must have died when he refused to have her son in the house. Barbara Reynolds is quite clear on the point: 'People don't understand that her intention was to bring up Anthony herself. Then she married Mac and he would have none of it.'[21] Predominant feelings over the years seem to have been exasperation tinged with compassion. Patrick McLaughlin recalled Sayers telling him that in Fleming's last years:

> ... he got so bad that he would follow her from room to room, or come and stand in the door of the library and pour the most appalling abuse over her while she was writing. She would say: 'Go away, Mac; for God's sake, go away. If you must go and have some more whiskey, go and have some more whiskey, but don't bother me. I'm busy, I've

got some writing to do.' She told me many times how awfully difficult life was and how she could hardly write anything.[22]

A close friend at this time was the artist and scenic-designer Norah Lambourne. She had been responsible for the sets and costumes of *The Just Vengeance* and *The Zeal of Thy House*, and if that hadn't been enough to cement a friendship she also shared Sayers' love of cats. She stayed at the Witham house many week-ends while Fleming was alive, and her memories are important for a fair portrait to emerge:

> He could be extremely welcoming, extremely kind, and he could be quite the reverse and rather difficult. He was always perfectly charming and delightful to me. He was a very attractive man, but in a curious way he was extremely jealous of Dorothy's interest in the theatre, particularly because it took her away from home . . . He never wanted to know about it except, I think, to make disparaging remarks about any theatrical activity in which Dorothy was involved. Dorothy did tell me . . . I must realize he was a badly shell-shocked case from the Great War, and you never could predict what mood he would be in. This I found to be true when other people came into the house. He could become quite abusive.[23]

Sayers' tribute to her husband is the word she used on his death certificate to describe his occupation: Artist—a sensitive man broken and befuddled by war, struggling to make artistic sense of the world through paint and pictures. Here was one of Sayers' own great Affirmations.

Fleming was cremated at Ipswich, and his ashes scattered in the churchyard at Biggar in Scotland, home town of the Fleming family. Sayers wrote to his daughter Ann to assure her that the 'voluntary allowance' she had been paying over the years to his first wife would continue. She went through his papers, sent his clothes to be distributed among poor ex-Army officers, and—content that there was nothing more to be done—settled down to work. Typically, that meant a theological skirmish.

The popular scientist, Professor Fred Hoyle, in one of a series of broadcast lectures, calmly asserted that there was no evidence for God as Creator of the universe, and went on to debunk the Christian concept of immortality, calling it 'horrible' because he himself would hate to live more than three hundred years. Public indignation—predictably trite and ill-informed—flared briefly, with letters to newspapers accusing the BBC of atheistic and left-wing propaganda. Sayers, in more measured fashion, and at the invitation of the BBC, pointed out in a similar broadcast that eternity means the annihilation of time, not its prolongation.

> I am going to ask you to make a little effort of the imagination. Can you imagine that I am writing a book whose characters are divine creations—in the sense that they possess a measure of free will and are conscious both of themselves and of the action of the story going on about them. Have you done that? Good. Now you are going to see some very funny things happening to time. Two time-schemes are involved—my time (which we will call 'real time') and the 'created time' inside the story. The characters are aware only of the created time. I—and you as privileged onlookers—are aware of both. The two times do not interfere with one another. Thirty years of created time may pass under my pen in a moment without adding one grey hair to my head; or I may devote months of my time to describing one of their days. I may even lay the story aside, and after a long period of time take it up again where I left off. But no corresponding gaps or irregularities will be apparent to the characters, whose own time will present itself to them as an orderly succession of twenty-four-hour days proceeding at an even pace. Though I may choose to begin my story in the middle and narrate previous events in a series of 'flash-backs', the characters will not be aware that they are being used in this topsy-turvy fashion; for them, the past will be

the past and the future the future whatever the order of
their appearance in my 'real time'. Moreover, for you and
me the story has a beginning and ending—it starts, let us
say, when the hero is already forty, and ends after the
marriage of his grandson; but to the hero it will seem that
he was born in the usual manner and has lived through all
the unwritten days. For I have endowed him and all his
fellow-characters with created memories, which can call
up history at will to an infinite period in the past, and
arouse expectation of an equally extensible future. The
characters will, in fact, experience all that nightmare of
infinitely prolonged time which so horrifies Mr Hoyle.
But you and I know that in their case this 'bad infinity' is
an illusion: their times are in their author's hand ... The
analogy is, of course, only an analogy. I am *not* saying that
God is just a Great Big Novelist. But I do say that many
apparently 'obscure' theological doctrines ... have quite
familiar parallels in everyday life—if only we will take the
trouble to find out what the doctrines mean.[24]

That bit of bother out of the way, Sayers turned her atten-
tions exclusively to the play—or historical pageant—she had
planned for the Colchester Festival. Even Dante had to be set
aside as the July 1951 deadline was swiftly approaching, and she
had aimed ambitiously high: one of the kings of Colchester was
grandfather to Constantine, who presided over the Council of
Nicaea where the Christian Creed was hammered into shape, and
so—as she confided to Norah:

... the play ... would be about Constantine and the
Council of Nicaea—period 4th century—beginning at the
court of King Coel (old King Cole to you), and proceeding
to the court of Constantine at Rome, and afterwards to the
Council (lots and lots of bishops and people in fantastic
mitres and Constantine in full Imperial togs) ... the
bishop has readily agreed to my having a completely free
hand with the production side ... [25]

Considering that *The Emperor Constantine* had a cast of nine-ty-six, a running time of nearly four hours and twenty-five scene changes, it was a commendable feat just staging it at all. It opened on 3 July at the Playhouse Theatre, where it proceeded to earn respect rather than applause. Even Norah Lambourne calls it 'a bit of a marathon' and admits that Sayers 'tried to cover too large a canvas'. But the *Church Times* liked it. Its reviewer commended Sayers for having made drama out of dogma, in this case a turn-ing-point in the history of Christendom when at the Council of Nicaea the church decided once and for all the nature of the God it worshipped:

> ... if the author has painted her enormous canvas with a commixture of stagecraft, history and theology, the greatest of these is theology; and, as it happened, the theology contained the most entertainment value.[26]

What did threaten to side-track her in the run-up to the Colchester Festival was the death in March of Ivy Shrimpton from broncho-pneumonia and measles. But, as she had had minimum contact with her since the adult Anthony had left home, she was happy to leave the handling of Ivy's estate to her son who, at twenty-seven, was doing well with an invest-ment management company in London. She hadn't had that much contact with him, either, and arranging Ivy's funeral and sorting out her belongings probably meant they spent more time together than ever before. Ivy left everything—about four thou-sand pounds—to Sayers, who handed it on to Anthony. And Anthony it was who paid for the grave space in Banbury where Ivy was buried.

After Constantine, it was back to Dante: in fact she wrote a playlet about him for BBC Schools programmes in 1952, unim-portant but for the fact that Richard Burton was in the cast (but failed to turn up for the live broadcast); she also began a novel about Dante and Bice (short for Beatrice) which imagines that Dante discovers, having completed the *Comedy*, that his experi-ence amused rather than impressed his one true love. It could have been fun, but Sayers takes it far too seriously, concentrating on the emotional crisis Dante thereby suffers.

Sayers' *Pantheon Papers*, on the other hand, *are* fun. A satirical series written for *Punch*, the papers gently mock the saints of a secular society—although (and this wouldn't have surprised Sayers) they offended some devout Christians who saw them as an attack on the church. Two examples: the first does her full justice, the second illustrates one of her faults, which was to caricature the opposition, and is included here as a frivolous contrast to a very serious debate she was to have with science.

ST LUKEWARM OF LAODICEA, MARTYR

St Lukewarm was a magistrate in the city of Laodicea under Claudius (Emp. A.D. 41–54). He was so broadminded as to offer asylum and patronage to every kind of religious cult, however unorthodox or repulsive, saying in answer to all remonstrances: 'There is always some truth in everything.' This liberality earned for him the surname of 'The Tolerator'. At length he fell into the hands of a sect of Anthropophagi (for whom he had erected a sacred kitchen and cooking stove at the public expense), and was duly set on to stew with appropriate ceremonies. By miraculous intervention, however, the water continually went off the boil; and when he was finally served up, his flesh was found to be so tough and tasteless that the Chief Anthropophagus spat out the unpalatable morsel, exclaiming: 'Tolerator non tolerandus!' (A garbled Christian version of this legend is preserved in Revelation 3:16.) St Lukewarm is the patron saint of railway caterers and is usually depicted holding a cooking pot.[27]

CREED OF ST EUTHANASIA

I believe in man, maker of himself and inventor of all science. And in myself, his manifestation, and captain of my psyche; and that I should not suffer anything painful or unpleasant.

And in a vague, evolving deity, the future-begotten child of man: conceived by the spirit of progress, born of emergent variants; who shall kick down the ladder by which he rose and tell history to go to hell.

Who shall some day take off from earth and be jet-propelled into the heavens; and sit exalted above all worlds, man the master almighty.

And I believe in the spirit of progress, who spake by Shaw and the Fabians; and in a modern, administrative, ethical, and social organization; in the isolation of saints, the treatment of complexes, joy through health, and destruction of the body by cremation (with music while it burns), and then I've had it.[28]

A decade of overwork, physical and emotional fatigue, and—it has to be said—a devotion to good food, had taken its toll on Sayers. She was fat by the time her husband died; afterwards, she put on weight at an alarming rate. Marshall & Snelgrove's corset department did its best: 'After about nine months' devoted labour on the part of all concerned a wearable garment has at last been achieved,' she wrote, 'and I am quite willing to settle the account.'[29] Her friends watched her physical decline with some concern. She had always been a large woman, but Norah Lambourne remembers how 'marvellously proportioned' she was, and how well she carried herself. She also wore beautifully-cut tailor-made suits and could look 'magnificent'. Now, however, the years were catching up with her, not least the long periods working late into the night or very early in the morning so as not to disturb Fleming. She was so tired, she said, that she let herself go, and Patrick McLaughlin felt that in her latter years she was 'always fighting fatigue'.

Sayers, as we have seen, was one of the great letter-writers, and it is not too fanciful to imagine that as deadlines loomed, emotional pressures intensified and aches and pains became more of an irritant, she would reach for pen and paper, toss off a letter, and feel refreshed and invigorated. This rings true certainly for the literary correspondence, conducted over a decade, between Sayers and C. S. Lewis.

She had known Lewis since the war years. An Oxford man (though later to accept a professorship at Cambridge), Lewis combined theological passion with intellectual rigour, writing popular novels about a mythical land called Narnia and popular theology in books like *The Screwtape Letters* and *The Four Loves*. He was, therefore, a man after Sayers' own heart. He was also one of the Inklings, a group including J. R. R. Tolkien and Charles Williams, who believed they had caught an 'inkling' of the divine plan, and who met over many mugs of beer to argue about the world and read out loud their latest scripts. Sayers would have fitted in well, but, alas, she was not in Oxford and she was not a man.

Lewis, in fact, called her 'one of the great English letter-writers', and no doubt fired by the deserved compliment she wrote long, literary letters at regular intervals. His were cooler, briefer, but they too kept coming.

Sayers often confused what she ought to do with what she felt like doing, and so determined was she to *enjoy* her work that she sailed blithely on without asking herself if she was enjoying her work or simply indulging herself. Lewis spotted this fault very early on in their relationship, following her refusal to contribute to a series of booklets comprising 'a sort of library of Christian knowledge for young people in top forms at school'.[30] She wasn't, she replied, quite sure that this was the right thing for her to do. Lewis pounced:

> I also am haunted at times by the feeling that I oughtn't to be doing this kind of thing. But as the voice, when interrogated, can never give a good reason, I doubt if it comes from above. How is one to decide? . . .[31]

> Of course one mustn't do *dishonest* work. But you seem to take as the criterion of honest work the sensible *desire* to write—the itch. That seems to me precious like making 'being in love' the only reason for going on with a marriage. In my experience the *desire* has no constant ratio to the value of the work done. My own frequent uneasiness

comes from another source—the fact that apologetic work is so dangerous to one's own faith. A doctrine never seems dimmer to me than when I have just successfully defended it.[32]

Sayers apparently worked on her reply for two days 'when I ought to have been working on Dante'.

> When you call this realisation that one must say nothing but what one wants to say an 'itch' you are wide of the mark. With the exception of *The Mind of the Maker*, everything, almost, I have written has been simply a commissioned job . . . I have to ask: Is there any truth, apprehended by me, which the platform, the medium, gives me a suitable opportunity to communicate? If I have no truth asking to be communicated, then neither the money, nor the hope of influencing people, or of giving pleasure, or fulfilling a demand, or anything else might weigh with me . . . I think one of the causes of misunderstanding between us is that the only kind of love I understand at all is the kind that you put the lowest—the love of the artist for the artefact. That means that all my values seem to you to be very low-grade. That may be quite true, but the fact remains that they are the only ones I can use with any sort of honesty and meaning.[33]

Lewis argues no further, except to say that the only difference he sees between them is that he sees nothing but doubts 'where all looks self-evident to you'.[34] Sayers may have counted this as a victory. If so, it was a hollow one, because she never gets to grips with his main argument: it is an example of one of her failings, to erect the bricks of what someone *should* be saying, and then easily demolish them. Her dubious doctrine of 'the proper job' remained intact.

Nearly ten years later it is Sayers' turn to take Lewis to task, though in my judgment he wins this argument, too. Sayers is none too happy with Pauline Baynes' illustrations to Lewis' Narnia books: the 'bad drawings' are 'boneless and shallow';

Aslan (the Christ figure) makes her 'uncomfortable';[35] in short, Miss Baynes is not up to the job and should go. Lewis had already admitted to his own 'serious reservations' about her ...

> ... But she had merits (her botanical forms are lovely), she needed the work (old mother to support, I think), and worst of all she is such a timid creature, so easily put down ... At any *real* reprimand she'd have thrown up the job; not in a huff but in a sheer, downright, unresenting, pusillanimous dejection.[36]

Sayers, clearly thinking Lewis a bit of a softie, retorts that she 'rather thought there might be some charitable motive lurking in the background—and that's fine so long as it doesn't do positive harm'.[37] But she cannot refrain from pressing her point:

> It doesn't really matter that the 'Dawn Treader' is clearly unseaworthy, and that the sorceress in *The Magician's Nephew* wouldn't seduce a sex-starved sailor who had been ten years on a desert island ... But every so often I become acutely embarrassed. Not my business, of course—but I say this because I want to make it plain that my discomfort is not wholly aesthetic ... I entirely agree that it's no good trying to coerce or argue artists into giving what they haven't got. Either they burst into tears, or go sullen, or—if they are hearty extroverts—they cheerfully run out fifteen new versions, each worse than the last.[38]

Finally, an amusing if innocuous letter from Sayers, included here because it introduces us again to a subject, science, and a personality, Kathleen Nott, which together were to create for Sayers the deepest, most lacerating, spiritual crisis of her life:

> It is a sound enough principle that you cannot establish theological truth by falsifying scientific and artistic truth—any more than you can establish scientific truth by falsifying theology. Miss Nott would probably agree with the first part of this, but not the second. The queer thing is that the pan-scientist apologists tend to claim far more for

'scientific method' than the real scientists do themselves, and seem quite unaware that the physicists, at any rate, have completely sold the pass. Except, perhaps, Mr Fred Hoyle, but I regard him with the utmost suspicion, for he has publicly announced that he does not like cats . . .
Dislike of cats nearly always argues a stiff neck and a proud stomach; nobody can persuade himself that he is a hero to his cat . . .[39]

The Passionate Intellect

Kathleen Nott's book *The Emperor's Clothes* was published in 1954.[1] In it she set out to attack, using the scientific method, 'the dogmatic orthodoxy' of writers like Sayers, Williams, Lewis, Eliot and Graham Greene. On one level the style is rumbustiously rude, ascribing vulgarity, fundamentalism and trickiness to Sayers, on another the content is a legitimate expression of an atheist who finds God's perfect goodness and omnipotence incompatible. Also, theology cannot possibly be a genuine branch of knowledge because 'there is no experimental check on theology'.[2] None of the writers under attack rose to the challenge. Sayers didn't even read the book. And that would have been that had not the Honorary Secretary of the Advisory Council of St Anne's, a brilliant student of science who at thirty was Deputy Director of Research at Imperial Chemical Industries, a writer and a broadcaster, taken up and run with Miss Nott's thesis.

To John Wren-Lewis Christianity and science were complementary, and science had given mankind the chance to move from the age of superstition into the age of proven truth. Apply the scientific method to the spiritual world, his argument ran, and man just might become a worthy inheritor of the earth. The essential difference between Wren-Lewis and Sayers was that he thought theology should be subject to science, and she thought science should be subject to theology.

Wren-Lewis ensured that Sayers couldn't ignore him in the way she had ignored Kathleen Nott by pushing the personal application: Sayers, as an arch-exponent of 'dogmatic orthodoxy', was interested only in the dogmatic pattern. Was this,

he wondered, what intelligent agnostics and atheists were looking for when they came to St Anne's? The conflict came to a
climax in the vestry of St Thomas's Church in Regent Street
(the church used by St Anne's personnel) on the night of
Maundy Thursday. We do not know exactly what was said
there, but it was pertinent and probing enough to send Sayers
home on Good Friday to write a seventeen-page letter to Wren-
Lewis. Throughout this biography I have allowed Sayers, as
often as possible, to speak in her own words, and as this letter
is probably the most candidly confessional she ever wrote—
nothing like it exists outside the Cournos letters—I intend to
quote it almost in its entirety. Readers will not be bored: here
is Sayers letting down her defences, justifying what she is doing,
confessing human and spiritual weakness, and springing sur-
prises on those who refuse to accept that the public image and
the private life of any individual are rarely compatible:

> Dear John, I have been thinking about what we were
> saying last night in the vestry. You are, of course, perfectly
> right. It is a thing that I have always known, and is the
> reason why I never speak or write *directly* about Christian
> faith or morals without a violent inner reluctance and a
> strong sense of guilt. I am not sure that every time I open
> my mouth on the subject, I am not falling into mortal sin.
> But I am not *sure*, and therefore I do not like to be
> altogether intransigent about it. The position of people
> like Eliot and Lewis and me is rather more complicated
> than people perhaps quite realise. So, if you can bear it, I
> ought—possibly—to try and explain it a little ... I am not a
> priest. If I were, it would be my profession as well as my
> vocation to subdue every other consideration to that of
> preaching to every sort of person: to study the
> 'contemporary situation' in all its aspects; to learn and
> make contact with every type of person, so as to be able to
> speak to their condition and in their language and to
> present to them the *whole* content of the Faith, and not
> only those bits of it on which I could speak with the special

authority and sincerity which come of personal experience ... I am not by temperament an evangelist. If I were, my thirst for saving souls would overcome all secondary considerations, and my obvious and burning sincerity would at any rate prevent me from appearing smug, whatever else it exposed me to. Charity would cover many mistakes I made. But I have not the passionate love for my fellow-men; I find it very difficult to love them at all, though for the most part I like them and get on with them, and can live with them in kindness if not in charity. This is a defect in me, but it is no use pretending that it does not exist. Evangelism is something to which I do not feel myself called.

I am quite without the thing known as 'inner light' or 'spiritual experience'. I have never undergone conversion. Neither God, nor (for that matter) angel, devil, ghost or anything else speaks to me out of the depths of my psyche. I cannot go to people and say: 'I know the movements of the spirit from within' ...

It follows naturally, perhaps, from this that I am quite incapable of 'religious emotion'. This has its good as well as its bad side. I am not seriously liable to mistake an aesthetic pleasure in ritual or architecture for moral virtue, or to suppose that shedding a few tears over the pathos of the Crucifixion is the same thing as crucifying the old man in myself. Nor can I readily dismiss religion as a 'sublimation of sex', or anything of that kind, because I know perfectly well that it is nothing of the sort. But the lack of religious emotion in me makes me impatient of it in other people, and makes me appear cold and unsympathetic and impersonal. This is true. I am.

I have a moral sense. I am not sure that this derives from religious belief ... I do not enjoy it. If I ever do a disagreeable duty, it is in the spirit of the young man in the parable who said 'I go not', but afterwards (probably in a detestable temper) went grumbling off and did the job. On consideration, I think that the existence and nature of the

Christian God is the only rational sanction for the moral sense. But moral sense by itself is not religion—or at any rate not Christianity.

Of all the presuppositions of Christianity, the only one I really have and can swear to from personal inward conviction is sin. About that I have no doubt whatever and never have had. Neither does any doctrine of determinism or psychological maladjustment convince me in the very least that when I do wrong it is not I who do it and that I could not, by some means or other, do better. The other day I did find myself accounting for not having written a necessary letter to a sick person, thanking her for some rather feeble poems, on the ground that I had a 'thing' about not telling charitable lies in connection with poetry. In a sense it was true—I *have* a 'thing' about that. But the 'inward monitor' said firmly that my behaviour arose from a mixture of sloth and cruelty. It also reminded me, horribly, that on at least two other occasions when I had done exactly the same thing, the sick person had died before my letter went. So (you will be glad to hear) I wrote the letter, which did not take five minutes. But the point is that when anything speaks out of my interior it speaks in the outmoded terms of scholastic theology and faculty psychology, and I do not really know how to establish communication with people who have modern insides.

But since I cannot come at God through intuition, or through my emotions, or through my 'inner light' . . . there is only the intellect left. And that is a very different matter. You said that I, and the rest of us, gave people the impression of caring only for a dogmatic pattern. That is quite true. I remember once saying to Charles Williams: 'I do not know whether I believe in Christ or whether I am only in love with the pattern'. And Charles said, with his usual prompt understanding, that he had exactly the same doubts about himself. But *this* you must try to accept: when we say 'in love with the pattern', we mean *in love*. (Though Charles was different, he did love people, and he

was capable of romantic love and I think of a personal love
for God in a way that I am not . . .) The thing is, however,
that where the intellect is dominant it becomes the channel
of all the other feelings. The 'passionate intellect' is *really*
passionate. It is the only point at which ecstasy can enter. I
do not know whether we can be saved through the
intellect, but I do know that I can be saved by nothing else.
I know that, if there is judgement, I shall have to be able to
say: 'This alone, Lord, in Thee and in me, have I never
betrayed, and may it suffice to know and love and choose
Thee after this manner, for I have no other love, or
knowledge, or choice in me' . . .

Now, if you have borne thus far with this egotistical
preamble, I will try to come to the point.

The above is my equipment, as it were.

By training I am, more or less, a scholar; by vocation I
am a writer of stories and plays. Now, for a persona of that
training and equipment there is only one unforgivable
sin—I mean, literally unforgivable, in that it will end by
rotting away one's sense of right and wrong, and that is the
falsification of one's 'proper truth'. You may murder your
mother and commit adultery five nights a week and still
keep a living conscience. But if once you begin to distort
facts, or to write things for any purpose other than that of
telling such truth as you know, or to affect emotions you do
not possess—then you will begin and slip and slide into
illusion and into a living Hell, because you will be
destroying the only instrument by which you make contact
with reality. But it is very difficult—I cannot tell you how
difficult it is, or how insidiously all the *good* in the world, as
well as all the evil, conspires to push you into betrayal.

Look what happens . . . I wrote detective novels
harmlessly and profitably for about twenty years. They
were all right. I wrote them as well as I know how; and
though some bits and pieces of some kind of philosophy of
life crept into one or two of them, nobody bothered
much . . .

Then, one day, I was asked to write a play for
Canterbury about William of Sens ... I liked the story,
which could be handled as to deal with the 'proper truth' of
the artist—a thing on which I was then particularly keen.
It had to be Christian, of course; and I could see—indeed I
knew well enough—the besetting sin of the artist: to put
himself above the work, which is his special temptation to
'make himself as God'. So I wrote the thing and enjoyed
doing it. I never, so help me God, wanted to get entangled
in religious apologetic, or to bear witness for Christ, or to
proclaim my faith to the world, or anything of that kind. It
was an honest piece of work about something I really
knew. It was All Right. And still nobody bothered.

When the show came to London, I couldn't escape the
normal Press interviews ... And as a result of one of them,
I wrote the article 'The Greatest Drama ever Staged' ...
Well, that was all right too. It merely said that, whether
you believed in Christ or not, it was ridiculous to call the
story of the Incarnation and Redemption *dull*. I didn't say
more: I could scarcely say less ...

That did it. Apparently the spectacle of a middle-aged
female detective-novelist admitting publicly that the
judicial murder of God might compete in interest with the
corpse in the Coal-Hole was the sensation for which the
Christian world was waiting ...

Anyway, from that time ... I suppose that hardly a
week has gone past without at least two demands ... that I
should write or say something on a religious question ...
And life becomes nothing but a desperate struggle to hold
on to the rags of one's integrity ...

If you say that you have no knowledge of the subject,
they say they quite realise how busy you are and may they
ask you again later. If you say that you are a 'creative'
writer, and that the writing of treatises and direct doctrinal
admonitions saps your energy and ruins your sensitivity,
they say that your play did so much good that everybody
wants to hear you make a speech ... They flatter and press

and wheedle and invoke former acquaintance or mutual friends or the needs of the Church and the welfare of society, till to go on saying 'No' is impossible. One writes an article or appears on a platform or answers a letter—and so one becomes involved, and if one is not desperately careful one finds one's self saying or writing things that are out of one's range or false to one's 'proper truth'—or else putting together a series of hasty and second-hand commonplaces—or, unconsciously or even deliberately, exploiting one's own personality. 'What Christ means to me'—'How my faith helps my work'—'The Life of Prayer'—'The Grace of God in Daily Life'—it is obvious that my type must not write that kind of thing . . .

And then there is the terrifying ease by which you may substitute yourself for God, encouraging people to follow you and not Christ. 'They will believe it if *you* tell them'—but they must not—they must believe it only if it is true. 'You can set them a Christian example'—Yes, by living, not by talking—and what do they or you know of me? 'They will listen to you when they would not listen to the priests'—too true: but that is the priest's safeguard and theirs. 'What *you* say is so different from what the Church says'—no, no, no! What I say is what the Church says— only the language is different. Throw my accursed book out of the window: I have nothing to give you but the Creeds. 'But do *you* believe all these petrifying dogmas?'— Listen: it does not matter to you whether I believe or how I believe, because my way of belief is probably not yours. But if you will only leave me in peace till some truth so takes hold of me that I can honestly show it to you through the right use of my own medium, then I will make a picture for you that will be the image of that truth: and that will be not the Creeds but the substance of what is in the Creeds. But unless it is a living truth to me, I cannot make it truth to you: I should be damned, and you would see through it anyhow, bad work cannot be hid . . .

I have written a great deal, and perhaps said nothing.

But I should like somebody to understand the position of the 'intellectual' Christian when ... he gets caught up in the machine of apologetics. It is useless to blame him for being intellectual—all his passion, all his sympathies, all his emotions, all his truth, all *reality* are mediated to him through the intellect, and if you force him out of his contact with reality, he can only deviate into falsehood— the damning falsehood to his 'proper truth'. He is liable, like other men, to succumb to his own propaganda ... but he has the advantage of knowing the danger he stands in. All the same, he is walking a tight-rope the moment you require him to bear a witness that is not absolutely spontaneous, and when he falls, he falls like Lucifer, because he has lost not only Beatrice but Virgil.

It may be that our particular kind of intellectual has had his day. If so, it would be better just to leave us alone— we are too old to change very much—and let us get on quietly with the only things we feel fitted for. We have perhaps done something. The Christian to-day may be feared and hated, but he is no longer despised as a moron and a milk-sop. Some of us have fought with beasts at an intellectual Ephesus. If we are harsh in our manner now it is partly, I think, because we have been the baited bull in the ring, and cannot lose the habit of impaling people on the horns of dogmatic dilemmas ...

Have I anything more to add? Yes, just this. You complain that the books we write are all right for Christians, but not for the heathen—all right for highbrows, but no good for lowbrows. Again, that is largely true. But it is precisely the educated near-Christians or woolly Christians that we write for. *They* are our people and the sheep of our pasture. We are not priests, dedicated to the service of all sorts and conditions of men, nor evangelists, called to labour in the foreign mission-field. Our religious writings have necessarily to be addressed to the same set of people who read our other books. That is all we are trained for. I think it very likely that the time has come when we ought to be superseded. I am not quite sure that we ought to be chastised by our even-Christians for not doing that which we are neither called nor fitted to do. I am not exactly asking for gratitude and appreciation—although . . . I do sometimes wish that the people who clamour for us to open their bazaars, address their ordinands, and allow them to perform our plays at derisory fees, would occasionally rally round when we are under fire. The C of E attitude to the 'lay apostolate' is painfully like that of a government to a slightly disreputable secret agent: 'Do your job, but remember, if you get into difficulties you must extricate yourself; His Majesty's Government cannot appear in the matter.' But it would be nice not to be so chivvied. It would be nice not to be continually summoned from what one is doing to do something different and unsuitable. And it would be nice not to be continually pushed and pulled and coaxed and squeezed (always from the highest motives and in the name of the Incorruptible God) into corruption.

I am so sorry—the cat has trodden on the page!

I think it comes to this: that, however urgently a thing may be needed, it can only be rightly demanded of those who can rightly give it. For the others are bound to falsify and so commit the greatest treason: to do the right thing for the wrong reason. And, by the time you have done it, you know it is no longer the right thing.

Yours with apologies for going on and on about it. D.L.S.[3]

John Wren-Lewis's reply was a good deal briefer: 'Sufficient attention has not been paid to the whole question of what life in the modern world feels like to most people' . . . 'I am not a modernist at all in the sense of finding it hard to believe any of the traditional Christian dogmas, but I do believe that the only way to help people to an understanding of Christianity is to start where they are and lead them to all the meanings of the dogmas in terms of their own experience' . . . 'I can feel sympathetic with the modern man and do not think it is any use just telling him he is wrong, because a whole range of factors have gone into making him feel what he does feel' . . . 'Modern psychology really has shown that a lot of the things we once thought to be voluntary and worthy of punishment are really compulsive and worthy of pity'.[4]

In her next letter Sayers presses him to comment on what she sees as his error in blaming the intellectual for being intellectual. He accepts the challenge:

> I frankly do not believe that anyone approaches reality
> wholly in terms of the intellect—and I really mean this, i.e.
> I do not mean merely that people ought not to try to do it,
> but actually that no-one really does. In approaching
> reality I am quite sure it is the feelings and, at a later stage,
> the will, that are really important.[5]

The correspondence continued. The question remained the same: how to meet with intelligent unbelievers? Were they wholly without hope in this world and the next? Or did they have within them a spark of the divine which simply needed igniting? For Wren-Lewis it was a case of starting where they were. For Sayers it was a case of starting with dogma, or the Creeds. Only one concession was made between them, and it was Sayers who made it: Creeds were the result of revisions, based on experience, of earlier drafts, and 'there is no reason why there should not be other such revisions . . .'[6]

A public debate was now planned, at St Anne's House, with Sayers and C. S. Lewis on one side and Kathleen Nott on the other. Robert Graves and Sir Lewis Namier, very much Nott supporters, also hoped to be there. But on the day itself, none of the opposition showed up and Sayers was able to turn on a solo performance. It was virtuoso Sayers, but it was very much Sayers being Sayers and not Sayers addressing the points pertinently put by Wren-Lewis. By now, however, she *had* read Miss Nott's book, and in this extract from her speech she begins by quoting from it:

'If Miss Sayers blames the scientists . . . for the fact that the pursuit of truth does not directly and inevitably lead to happiness, she should logically also blame the theologians'. But the Church has never pretended to guarantee anybody 'happiness' in this world. On the contrary, in this world she notoriously promises nothing but trial and tribulation and has been bitterly blamed by the Humanists for so doing. It is true that to the individual soul she holds out the promise of inward peace, despite tribulation . . . But even this peace may be subject to rude attacks . . . If I blame the followers of science, it is for holding out delusive hopes of a kind of happiness that is not attainable in this life. But this the Church has never done. What *she* has emphasised is the value of suffering. It is never the pursuit of truth that breaks men's hearts, but the vain pursuit of happiness.[7]

More than twenty-five years later Kathleen Nott was sent a copy of Sayers' address by Barbara Reynolds, and invited to comment. She does so in somewhat dry academic fashion, says that she would have found the debate interesting and provocative, and sensibly concludes that neither of the protagonists would have changed their ideas and beliefs one whit: 'When it is fundamentally an argument about knowledge and faith and particularly about the possibility of assimilating or fusing them, the difficulty appears insuperable.'[8] Sayers and Wren-Lewis, however, did come at least to acknowledge each other for what they were, two very different kinds of Christian who needed, because of the narrow focus of their individual faith, something of the other's perspective.

But what of that seventeen-page letter from Sayers to Wren-Lewis? Out of it emerge two points crucial to our understanding of where Sayers stood in matters of faith. Was she only in love with the dogmatic pattern, and, if so, is that enough? And, as someone who had nothing to give but the Creeds, was it not a fatally damaging admission that these are not statements of unalterable truth but 'the result of revisions, based on experience, of earlier drafts'?

Brabazon, in his biography, argues that this is 'fatal to her argument', for she is 'conceding, in effect, that only a historical accident had prevented the Creeds from being revised and updated . . . What is that but an admission that they no longer have the breath of life in them? And that being the case, what was Dorothy offering to our century after all?'[9] Well, she was offering what the *Bible* teaches as Truth, and however much theologians, councils or synods may revise what they care to call the Creeds, the essential dogma is to be found in the words of Jesus and the apostle Paul.

A Creed is no more than a shorthand version of an original, some would say divinely-inspired, text, and is subservient to it. The issue is whether Sayers believed the unchanging Bible, not whether she believed the changing Creeds, and the evidence is that she did. She may have been wrong, of course, but that's another matter. Sayers also, far from losing confidence in the Creeds, understood precisely their purpose and nature, as she clarified in a letter to Barbara Reynolds three years later:

> . . . the event, the act of God in history, is all-important, because it ties the thing to this world, and to time and place and the flesh. But, given the central interpretation, the event is susceptible of all interpretation in all senses that don't contradict the central truth. Hence, the paramount importance of the central dogma. It doesn't, and it isn't supposed to, exhaust the meaning of the event, but it's more like a set of pegs, hammered in to prevent the whole fabric being wrenched out of shape in one direction or the other, through people getting emphatic about one or other particular aspect of it. Hence heresies and other distortions, which are always due to an oversimplifying emphasis on one truth at the expense of others. The nothing-but system of interpretation which sits down heavily on little bits whereas the whole truth is always walking a razor edge of delicate balance between the lop sided exaggerations. Because being in time and space, it

can't all be seen at once, and therefore always appears to be teetering along a narrow line.

Was Sayers only in love with the dogmatic pattern? She says so. Is that enough? It can be. The Rev. Dr E. L. Mascall, mathematician as well as theologian, argues persuasively in favour in an article entitled 'What happened to Dorothy L. Sayers that Good Friday?':

> [She was] intensely anxious to avoid any kind of apologetic that was not radically rational and intellectual, any offer of Christianity as providing emotional satisfaction, personal fulfilment or any other motive for acceptance than the conviction of its truth . . . Her central concern is clear and it is supported by almost everything that she ever wrote about religion. It is that, when all is said and done, the only really relevant reason for accepting Christianity is that you are convinced that it is *true*; not that it is comfortable or uncomfortable, interesting or uninteresting, profitable or unprofitable, or what-have-you, but simply that it is *true*.[10]

It need not follow that Sayers' private experience of Christianity was detached and remote. Dr Mascall's contention is that Sayers was absolutely right in her insistence that the intellect, too, can be passionate, and that ecstasy can enter as legitimately at that point as at any other: 'This can be true on the purely natural level, as every pure mathematician knows; it can be true on the supernatural level as well.'[11] As Sayers herself had emphasized: 'When we say "in love with the pattern", we mean *in love* . . . The "passionate intellect" is *really* passionate.'[12]

Mascall, incidentally, credits Sayers, as Wren-Lewis did not, with having 'some appreciation of the variety and complexity of the human soul and some sensitivity to its doubts and hesitations'[13]—the range of her knowledge of literature, if nothing else, should have given that—and also with having a respect for 'the intelligence and honesty of the unbeliever':[14]

She would have sympathised with the reactions expressed

by the formidable and intellectual lady Miss Marghanita Laski in 1963 at the time of Dr J. A. T. Robinson's famous little book, *Honest to God*. Miss Laski made it plain that the only Christians for whom she had any use were the orthodox ones; for it was quite clear what they held and she was convinced that it was false. Furthermore, she was indignant when people told her that she was really an unconscious Christian because she wanted to make the earth a better place; she wanted to make the earth a better place, but she was no kind of Christian, but a conscious and professing atheist. Dorothy would have understood.[15]

1 3

The Last Battles

Sayers, grossly overweight and plagued by arthritis in the feet, found it increasingly difficult to stir herself out of Witham. Work demanded daily discipline at her desk, and socializing meant friends coming to her rather than she to them. Norah Lambourne, who after Fleming's death had moved in with Sayers for sixteen months, often stayed for several days at a time; she remembers a house 'full of lovely things', comfortable, with log fires a cosy priority. She remembers a friend who chatted amiably from cats through nonsense rhymes to theology, who adored jigsaw puzzles, and who completed *The Times*' crossword by eleven every morning, often in the bath. There was also a serious purpose to the visits; Sayers' growing collection of rare books was a goldmine for a designer to quarry through. Sayers, though, was never fighting fit again, her decline probably hastened by smoking too much: Barbara Reynolds would place a pack of fifty Senior Service beside her chair, and it would be nearly empty at the end of the day. At that time, of course, people were not warned of the dangers.

Never fighting fit again, perhaps, but the fighting went on, to finish Dante, to translate the eleventh-century poem *Chanson de Roland*, to write for children, to keep St Anne's ticking over, to finance a group of out-of-work professional actors, and inevitably to lambast a newspaper or a correspondent whenever she thought they had got something wrong. Volumes of Dante essays were published in 1955 and 1957,[1] and in between Penguin published her translation of *Purgatory*, which was rated superior to her *Hell*. Only *Paradise* lay ahead, but she knew it was 'by far the toughest nut of the three books'.[2] So she took a breather from

Dante, no doubt partly in her belief that there is always a 'right time' to encounter great works, and instead began to translate *Chanson de Roland*, complete with the wars of Charlemagne and his court:

> It is arguable that all very great works should be strictly protected from young persons; they should at any rate be spared the indignity of having their teeth and claws blunted for the satisfaction of examiners. It is the first shock that matters. Once that has been experienced, no amount of late familiarity will breed contempt; but to become familiar with a thing before one is able to experience it only too often means that one can never experience it at all. This much is certain; it is not age that hardens arteries of the mind; one can experience the same exaltation of first love at fifty as at fifteen—only it will need a greater work to excite it. There is, in fact, an optimum age for encountering every work of art; did we but know, in each man's case, what it was, we might plan our educational schemes accordingly. Since our way of life makes this impossible, we can only pray to be saved from murdering delight before it is born.[3]

It may have been for intellectual relief that Sayers, in the last years of her life, wrote books for children—or, more accurately, a brief text to accompany pull-out portions of illustrated children's calendars. There followed *The Days of Christ's Coming, The Story of Adam and Christ*, and *The Story of Noah's Ark*: 'Yes, to be sure, there were Dragons in the Ark, or there wouldn't have been one for St George to fight with; but they are all dead now.'[4] Back in 1944, Methuen had published her one authentic children's book, *Even the Parrot—Exemplary Conversations for Enlightened Children*, with such chapter headings as 'The Cat or Family Affection', 'The Bee-Hive or the Perfect Society', and 'The Rabbit or Town-Planning'.

One newspaper to feel the lash of her pen was the *Church Times*, which in an article on Sayers in its 'Portraits of Personalities' series, rolled out the clichés and ladled out the

lies. Especially galling was the line: 'At Oxford her prowess led
to hopes of a fellowship. These were not fulfilled—a cruel disappointment.'[5] Sayers snorted:

> Sir.—Allow me to inform you that I never at any time
> either sought or desired an Oxford fellowship. If anybody
> entertained such hopes on my behalf, I am not aware of it,
> and if I disappointed anybody by my distaste for the
> academic life, that person has my sympathy. But I suspect
> that the 'cruel disappointment' exists only in the romantic
> imagination of your columnist . . .[6]

Sayers was by now reasonably well off, with book and play
royalties alone enabling her to live comfortably if not extrava-
gantly. But she was no hoarder and could be extremely generous
to good friends and worthy causes. One of the latter, in her view,
was a group of out-of-work actors who in 1954 put on a performance of *The Man Born to be King*. She went to see it, and
thought the quality of acting superior to that of the BBC produc-
tions. She had no hesitation, therefore, in promising to finance
them for a year.

St Anne's mission to intellectual agnosticism had been ticking over gently and uncontroversially, but early in 1957 Patrick
McLaughlin—the pressure having told on him—handed in his
resignation, and with it much of the flair and passion critical to
the work. His opponents sidled out of the woodwork again, and
clamoured for closure. It fell to Sayers, as both chairman of the
council of St Anne's and a churchwarden of St Thomas's, Regent
Street, to take up the fight on McLaughlin's behalf, and this she
did typically by arguing for an enlarged vision: why not build a
multi-purpose centre complete with chapel, library and theatre?
Bishops were lobbied, circulars sent out, architects consulted,
but all to no avail—and on 26 July 1957 the decision was taken to
close the House. McLaughlin joined the Roman Catholic
Church in 1963, and died at the age of seventy-nine in 1988.

Sayers settled back in *Paradise*, and a relatively quiet period
publicly was broken only by *The Sunday Dispatch*'s clever ruse
of sending her old friend, Val Gielgud, to interview her: one

'reporter' she would be guaranteed not to send away with an empty note-pad. She turned it to her advantage, though, insisting that the half-page spread included a sizeable plug for the recently-published *Song of Roland*.

Friday 13 December was the happy day that she became a godmother—to her friend Barbara Reynolds, who had accepted the Christian faith and decided to be baptized. Sayers, who only recently had supported her friend's application for the Serena Professorship of Italian Studies at Oxford, must have been delighted on all counts. Tired though she looked, she wouldn't be denied the pleasure of buying Christmas presents for Barbara Reynolds' children.

A few days later she returned to London for further Christmas shopping, leaving instructions for the delivery of the gifts. She should have met Patrick McLaughlin that afternoon, but she rang to say shopping had taken longer than expected and she had decided to go straight home. Sayers was met at Witham by Jack Lapwood who drove her to 24, Newland Street, where she went upstairs to deposit her hat and coat on the bed (the light was left on), and came downstairs only to collapse and die instantaneously from a stroke. Her body was found by the cleaner at eight the following morning.

For the newspapers it was a chance to dabble in mystery. How did she die? demanded one intrepid reporter: 'The greatest crime writer since Conan Doyle was found dead in the hallway of her house . . . She was fully clothed—Miss Sayers' routine evening wear: black georgette dress, Chinese mandarin coat, pince-nez hanging on tape, with a huge gold seal hanging from a chain round her throat.' Another reporter dreamt up a sinister discovery of the body: the gardener had stumbled across it in the bedroom.

For Sayers' friends, news of her death came as a terrible and unexpected shock. Barbara Reynolds was 'stricken' by it . . . 'Then the post came with letters from her about the previous weekend, and a little card to my daughter who Dorothy knew was always very much upset if anyone was cruel to animals. She had sent her a card of St Hubert and the stag he had shot out hunting.

Dorothy had written on it the story and added that there was Christ himself crucified between the stag's antlers. Despite her tiredness, she had found time to do *that*.' Her Christmas gifts arrived as the obituaries appeared—all chosen with generosity and thoughtfulness.[7]

Sayers was cremated on 23 December at Golders Green. Remembering her *Pantheon Paper*, 'Creed of St Euthanasia', she would probably have preferred burial. Her ashes were deposited in the little chapel in the base of the tower of St Anne's, and there Sayers rested in anonymity until the Dorothy L. Sayers Literary Society, in 1978, installed a memorial tablet. This reads: 'In memory of Dorothy Leigh Sayers, D.Litt., Scholar and Writer, Churchwarden of this Parish 1952–1957. Born 13th June, 1893. Died 17th December, 1957. Whose ashes lie beneath this tower. "The only Christian work is good work well done."' In January 1958 a memorial service was held at St Margaret's Church, Westminster.

Immediately following the announcement of Sayers' death, Muriel St Clare Byrne hurried to Witham to sort out her friend's affairs. That meant, first of all, the will, and it soon emerged that the only one in existence was dated 1939. This left everything to her husband, and in the event of his death to their 'adopted son', John Anthony. The estate was valued at a little under £35,000. John Anthony was, of course, news to Muriel, but a day or two later the man himself appeared and admitted to the true relationship. Her reaction was simply to say 'Thank God you've come.' She passed on the information to Sayers' intimates, and Norah Lambourne speaks for them all when she says she was 'shocked and hurt' that Sayers hadn't felt able to confide in her closest friends. The will was a bit of a surprise, too: 'There were so many people she would like to have helped to get on with their "proper work". The trouble was that she left it too late. She hated going to the doctor, was scared of knowing things weren't right, so died without premonition and without thinking of updating her will.'[8]

The public, however, remained in the dark about John Anthony. The pretence that he had been adopted at the age of ten continued. Until, that is, one of Sayers' biographers, Janet Hitchman,[9] discovered, during research at Somerset House, that Anthony's birth certificate named Sayers herself as the mother. The space for the father's name was left blank. Hitchman made this information public in 1975, to only a mild public flutter, it has to be said. Anthony Fleming—who after his mother's death had found 'as devastating a collection of "juvenalia" as any established writer could hand down to posterity'[10]—now decided that the record should be put entirely straight, and co-operated with James Brabazon on *Dorothy L. Sayers: The Life of a Courageous Woman*. He himself died in 1984.

In 1987, during a service of thanksgiving for the life and work of Sayers, the Dean of Canterbury, the Very Rev. John Simpson, eulogized 'a woman committed to the pursuit of truth and the highest standards'. It was, he said, this pursuit of truth that linked together all the various strands of her work: 'Not many in this century have made truth and excellence their pursuit. We are only too familiar with the pursuit of self-fulfilment, of power, of compassion, kindness—even of a form of justice. But all these are at best only pale reflections, and at worst perversions, of what in God's plan they are meant to be, unless underpinned by truth and excellence. A person who makes truth and excellence his or her pursuit is indeed a person of deep insight, worthy of honour, worthy of emulation. In this thirtieth year of her death and the fiftieth year of her writing her Canterbury play, *The Zeal of Thy House*, we give thanks to God for Dorothy L. Sayers, a woman of great scholarship, talent, Christian faith, and, above all, commitment to truth.'

Just weeks after her death, C. S. Lewis wrote to Anthony Fleming, concluding the letter: 'For all she did and was—for delight and instruction, for her militant loyalty as a friend, for courage and honesty, for the richly feminine qualities which showed through a part and manner superficially masculine and even gleefully ogreish—let us thank the Author who invented her.'[11]

These tributes, two among many, sum up so much that was special and memorable about Sayers. She devoted her mature years to the pursuit of truth, convinced that to do anything less was somehow a betrayal of the spirit; the laudability of such a quest, in her case passionately unswerving, cannot be questioned, but for Sayers it was forever tied to her very human perception that to pursue what the world pursues—happiness—is to be guaranteed a broken heart. After Cournos, she could never again contemplate that. What perhaps she didn't reckon with is that the pursuit of truth may not break one's heart, but without constant self-awareness it can very easily squeeze it dry of emotion. Lewis got Sayers right at an earthier level: her 'militant loyalty as a friend' is what she remains cherished for among those who were closest to her. They love Wimsey, but they love his creator more. As they never tire of saying, Sayers was, quite simply, hugely entertaining and incomparable company. What made her so was her 'careless rage for life' which revealed itself in the tensions, mostly creative, between combativeness and vulnerability, between a knockabout style and a devout seriousness, between bombast and frailty.

In the later Wimsey novels, Sayers—in the role of Wimsey's uncle—pens a short biography of the great man. 'I should be glad to see Peter happy,' says Uncle Paul, 'but as his mother says, "Peter has always had everything except the things he really wanted," and I suppose he is luckier than most.' Sayers, unwittingly, had constructed the perfect epitaph for herself.

Bibliography

Here is a selective list of Sayers' published and unpublished works: selective in that they are chosen as her most important and, in the writer's view, best work.

Selected Published Works

Poems and articles in the school magazine *Godolphin Gazette*, 1909–11.

Op 1, a book of poems published by Basil Blackwell, 1916.

Catholic Tales and Christian Songs, another book of poems from the same Oxford publisher, 1918.

Poems in *The Oxford Magazine, Oxford Outlook, Oxford Chronicle, Oxford Journal Illustrated, The New Witness*, 1916–20.

'The Tristran of Thomas—A Verse Translation' in *Modern Languages*, 1920.

Poems in *The New Decameron*, Basil Blackwell, 1920–25.

Whose Body?, Sayers' first detective novel, T. Fisher Unwin, London, and Boni and Liveright, New York, 1923.

Clouds of Witness, her second, T. Fisher Unwin, London, 1926 and Lincoln McVeagh, New York, 1927.

Unnatural Death, detective novel, Ernest Benn, London, 1927 and Lincoln McVeagh, New York, 1928.

The Unpleasantness at the Bellona Club, detective novel, Ernest Benn, London, and Payson and Clarke, New York, 1928.

Introduction to *Great Short Stories of Detection, Mystery and Horror*, Gollancz, London, 1928 and Payson and Clarke, New York, 1929.

Lord Peter Views the Body, detective short story collection, Gollancz, London, 1928 and Payson and Clarke, New York, 1929.

Tristan in Brittany, one of Sayers' early translations, Ernest Benn, London, and Payson and Clarke, New York, 1929.

The Documents in the Case, detective novel with help from Robert Eustace, Ernest Benn, London, and Brewer and Warren, New York, 1930.

Strong Poison, detective novel, Gollancz, London, and Brewer and Warren, New York, 1930.

'Behind the Screen', Sayers' contribution to a radio serial penned by members of the Detection Club, published in *The Listener*, 1930.

'The Scoop', a two-part contribution to a similar radio serial, also printed in *The Listener*, 1931.

The Five Red Herrings, detective novel, Gollancz, London, and Brewer, Warren and Putnam, New York, 1931.

Introduction to *Great Short Stories of Detection, Mystery and Horror, Second Series*, Gollancz, London, 1931 and Coward-McCann, New York, 1932.

The Floating Admiral, an introduction and a solution to a detective novel written by members of the Detection Club, Hodder and Stoughton, London, 1931 and Doubleday, Doran, New York, 1932.

Have His Carcase, detective novel, Gollancz, London, and Brewer, Warren and Putnam, New York, 1932.

Murder Must Advertise, detective novel, Gollancz, London, and Harcourt Brace, New York, 1933.

'The Conclusions of Roger Sheringham', a contribution to *Ask A Policeman*, Arthur Barker, London, and William Morrow, New York, 1933.

Hangman's Holiday, detective short story collection, Gollancz, London, and Harcourt Brace, New York, 1933.

The Nine Tailors, detective novel, Gollancz, London, and Harcourt Brace, New York, 1934.

Introduction to *Great Short Stories of Detection, Mystery and Horror, Third Series*, Gollancz, London, 1934 and Coward-McCann, New York, 1935.

Gaudy Night, detective novel, Gollancz, London, 1935 and Harcourt Brace, New York, 1936.

Introduction to *Tales of Detection*, J. M. Dent, Everyman's Library, 1936.

'Aristotle on Detective Fiction', a speech given in Oxford and printed in *English: the Magazine of the English Association*, Volume 1, Number 1, 1936.

'The Murder of Julia Wallace', a contribution to *The Anatomy of Murder*, another book by members of the Detection Club, this time about real-life murders, John Lane, The Bodley Head, London, 1936 and Macmillan, New York, 1938.

Busman's Honeymoon, a play with the help of Muriel St Clare Byrne, Gollancz, London, 1937 and Dramatists' Play Service, New York, 1939.

Busman's Honeymoon, detective novel, Gollancz, London, and Harcourt Brace, New York, 1937.

The Zeal of Thy House, a play for Canterbury Cathedral, Gollancz, London, and Harcourt Brace, New York, 1937.

'The Psychology of Advertising', article in *The Spectator*, 1937.

'The Greatest Drama Ever Staged', article in *The Sunday Times*, later published by Hodder and Stoughton, 1938.

BIBLIOGRAPHY

Double Death, Part 1, a contribution to a detective novel penned by members of the Detection Club, Gollancz, London, 1939.

The Devil to Pay, a play for Canterbury Cathedral, Gollancz, London, and Harcourt Brace, New York, 1939.

In the Teeth of the Evidence, detective short story collection, Gollancz, London, 1939 and Harcourt Brace, New York, 1940.

He That Should Come, nativity play for radio, Gollancz, London 1939.

Begin Here, an essay in time of war, Gollancz, London, 1940, Harcourt Brace, New York, 1941.

'The Church's Responsibility', address given at the Archbishop of York's Conference on 'The Life of the Church and the Order of Society', 1941, later published by Longmans Green, 1942.

The Mind of the Maker, a theological essay, Methuen, London, and Harcourt Brace, New York, 1941.

The Man Born to be King, a series of radio plays on the life of Jesus Christ, published by Gollancz, London, 1942 and Harper, New York, 1949.

The Other Six Deadly Sins, address to the Public Morality Council, published by Methuen, London, 1943.

Even the Parrot—Exemplary Conversations for Enlightened Children, Methuen, London, 1944.

The Just Vengeance, a play for the Lichfield Festival, 1946, published by Gollancz, 1946.

Unpopular Opinions, a collection of articles and addresses, Gollancz, London, 1946 and Harcourt Brace, New York, 1947.

Creed or Chaos, a collection of theological essays, Methuen, London, 1947 and Harcourt Brace, New York, 1949.

The Comedy of Dante Alighieri the Florentine. Cantica I: Hell, translation, Penguin Classics, 1949.

The Emperor Constantine, a play for the Colchester Festival, Gollancz, London, and Harper, New York, 1951.

'Pantheon Papers', theological satire in *Punch*, 1953–54.

Introductory Papers on Dante, a collection of essays, Methuen, London, 1954 and Harper, New York, 1955.

The Comedy of Dante Alighieri the Florentine. Cantica II: Purgatory, translation, Penguin Classics, 1955.

Further Papers on Dante, a collection of essays, Methuen, London and Harper, New York, 1957.

The Song of Roland, translation, Penguin Classics, 1957.

The Comedy of Dante Alighieri the Florentine. Cantica III: Paradise, translation, completed by Barbara Reynolds, Penguin Classics, 1962.

'Talboys', detective short story written in 1942, published by Harper, New York, 1972.

Striding Folly, three Wimsey short stories including 'Talboys', New English Library, 1973.

Wilkie Collins, unfinished biography, published by the Friends of the University of Toledo Libraries, 1977.

Select Unpublished Works

The Matador, a screenplay based on the novel *Blood and Sand*, 1920.

The Mousehole, a Detective Fantasia in Three Flats, part of a play featuring Lord Peter Wimsey.

My Edwardian Childhood, part of an autobiography, 33 pages, 1930s.

Cat o' Mary, part of an autobiographical novel, 209 pages, 1930s.

Thrones, Dominations, part of a detective novel featuring Wimsey and his wife Harriet Vane.

Notes

PREFACE

1 Letter from Sayers to John Cournos, 27 October 1924

2 Letter from Sayers to John Cournos, January 1925

3 James Brabazon, *Dorothy L. Sayers: The Life of a Courageous Woman*, Gollancz, 1981

4 'The Greatest Drama Ever Staged', the *Sunday Times*, 3 April 1938, later published in *Creed or Chaos*

5 Ibid.

6 Ibid.

7 From P. D. James' foreword to James Brabazon's biography

8 *Gaudy Night*

9 Ibid.

10 Letter from Dr James Welch to the Archbishop of Canterbury, William Temple, 18 June 1943

11 Letter from the Archbishop of Canterbury to Dr James Welch, 21 June 1943

12 Letters from Sayers to the Archbishop of Canterbury, 7 September 1943 and 22 September 1943

CHAPTER ONE

1 Letter from Dr James Welch to Sayers, February 1940

2 Letter from Sayers to Derek McCulloch, 11 October 1940

3 Letter from May Jenkin to Sayers, 19 November 1940

4 Ibid.

5 Letter from Sayers to May Jenkin, 22 November 1940

6 Letter from Sayers to Derek McCulloch, 28 November 1940

7 Ibid.

8 Ibid.

9 Letter from Sayers to Dr James Welch, 23 July 1940

10 Letter from Sayers to Dr James Welch, 28 November 1940

11 Letter from Sayers to Dr James Welch, 7 December 1940

12 Letter to Sayers from May Jenkin, 19 December 1940

13 Letter to Sayers from Dr James Welch, 30 December 1940

14 Letter from Sayers to Dr James Welch, 2 January 1941

15 Ibid.

16 Val Gielgud, *British Radio Drama 1922–1956*, Harrap 1957

17 Letter from Sayers to the Rev. Patrick McLaughlin, 4 April 1941

18 'Creed or Chaos', an address delivered in Derby, 4 May 1940, and later published in *Creed or Chaos*

19 Letter from Sayers to Dr James Welch, 23 July 1941

20 From Sayers' introduction to the published version of *The Man Born to be King*

21 The *Daily Mail*, 11 December 1941

22 From Lord's Day Observance Society (LDOS) advertisements, 12 December 1941

23 LDOS protest sent to the BBC, 12 December 1941, and quoted in advertisements

24 Letters from readers to the *Daily Telegraph*, 2 January 1942

25 Question asked in the House of Commons, 19 December 1941

26 Letter from Sayers to Dr James Welch, 7 December 1940

27 From Sayers' introduction to the published version of *The Man Born to be King*

28 Letter from Sayers to the *Daily Telegraph*, 7 January 1942

29 Letter from Sayers to the Rev. B. E. Payne, 11 February 1942

30 Letter from Sayers to F. Aldrington Symons, 1 January 1941

31 From Dr Welch's foreword to the published version of *The Man Born to be King*

32 Ibid.

33 Ibid.

34 Letter to Sayers from Mr B. E. Nichols, 16 October 1942

35 Janet Hitchman quoting the LDOS in 1975 in her biography of Sayers, *Such a Strange Lady: An Introduction to Dorothy L. Sayers*, New English Library, 1975

36 Sayers' comment in 1953, quoted in Janet Hitchman's biography

37 Letter from Sayers to Val Gielgud, January 1942

38 'The Execution of God', the *Radio Times*, 23 March 1945

39 From Sayers' introduction to the published version of *The Man Born to be King*

40 Letter from Sayers to Lady Lees, 29 August 1944

41 Letter from Sayers to her son Anthony Fleming, 2 January 1940

CHAPTER TWO

1 *Cat o' Mary*

2 Letter from Mrs Cross to M. L. Lord, August 1977

3 Letter from Sayers to Ivy Shrimpton, 10 December 1928

4 *My Edwardian Childhood*

5 Ibid.

NOTES

6 Ibid.

7 'Ignorance and Dissatisfaction', *Latin Teaching: The Journal of the Association for the Reform of Latin Teaching*, October 1952

8 'The Fen Floods: Fiction and Fact', *The Spectator*, 2 April 1937

9 *Cat o' Mary*

10 Ibid.

11 *My Edwardian Childhood*

12 Ibid.

13 Ibid.

14 *Cat o' Mary*

15 Ibid.

16 Ibid.

17 *My Edwardian Childhood*

18 *Cat o' Mary*

19 Ibid.

20 Letter from Sayers to Dr James Welch, 21 December 1940

21 Letter from Sayers to Dr James Welch, 7 December 1940

22 Ibid.

23 *Cat o' Mary*

24 Ibid.

25 Ibid.

26 Ibid.

27 Letter from Sayers to Ivy Shrimpton, 28 March 1907

28 Letter from Sayers to Ivy Shrimpton, 7 February 1907

29 By C. S. Lewis

30 Letter from Sayers to Ivy Shrimpton, 15 January 1907

31 Letter from Sayers to her son, Anthony Fleming, December 1940

32 Letter from Sayers to Ivy Shrimpton, 23 February 1908

33 Ibid.

34 Ibid.

35 *The Lost Tools of Learning*, Methuen, 1948

36 Letter from Sayers to Ivy Shrimpton, 28 June 1908

37 Letter from Sayers to Ivy Shrimpton, 6 November 1908

38 *Cat o' Mary*

39 Ibid.

40 Ibid.

41 *Whose Body?*

42 G. K. Chesterton, *Orthodoxy*

43 *Cat o' Mary*

44 Letter from Sayers to Ivy Shrimpton, 15 April 1930

45 Letter from Sayers to her parents, 29 October 1911

46 James Brabazon, *Dorothy L. Sayers: The Life of a Courageous Woman*

47 *Cat o' Mary*

48 Ibid.

49 Ibid.

50 Ibid.

51 'Target Area', *Fortnightly*, March 1944

52 *Cat o' Mary*

CHAPTER THREE

1 'What is right with Oxford', *Oxford*, Summer 1935

2 'Eros in Academe', *Oxford Outlook*, June 1919

3 Vera Farnell, *A Somervillian Looks Back*, privately printed at Oxford University Press, 1948, quoted by permission of the publishers.

4 Quoted in James Brabazon, *Dorothy L. Sayers: The Life of a Courageous Woman*

5 Vera Brittain, *Testament of Youth*, Cedric Chivers, 1971

6 Letter from Sayers to Muriel Jaeger, 30 July 1913

7 Letter from Sayers to her parents, 8 March 1914

8 Letter from Sayers to her parents, 2 March 1913

9 Letter from Sayers to her parents, 6 June 1915

10 Sayers writing to the *Daily News* of 9 February 1927, in response to an article

11 Letter from Sayers to her parents, 6 December 1911

12 Vera Brittain, *Women at Oxford*, Harrap 1960

13 Letter from Sayers to Cyril Bailey, 23 September 1946

14 Letter from Sayers to her parents, May 1914

15 Letter from Sayers to her parents, 24 January 1915

16 Letter from Sayers to her parents, September 1917

17 Letter from Sayers to her parents, 7 February 1915

18 Letter from Sayers to her parents, 30 May 1915

19 Letter from Sayers to her parents, July 1914

20 Letter from Sayers to her parents, 16 May 1915

21 Letter from Sayers to her parents, 23 May 1915

22 Letter from Sayers to her parents, 6 June 1915

23 Vera Brittain, *Women at Oxford*, Harrap, 1960

24 Letter from Sayers to Muriel Jaeger, 27 July 1915

25 Published in Sayers' *Op. 1* under the title 'To M J' (Muriel Jaeger)

26 Letter from Sayers to her parents, 7 June 1913

27 *Song of Roland*, Penguin, 1957. Her first attempt at translation from the French was at Somerville

28 *Op. 1*, Basil Blackwell, Oxford, 1916

29 Ibid.

30 Ibid.

31 Ibid.

CHAPTER FOUR

1 *The Lost Tools of Learning*, Methuen, 1948

2 The *Sunday Times*, 9 September 1934

3 Letter from Sayers to Muriel Jaeger, 14 November 1916

4 Letter from Sayers to her parents, 2 June 1916

5 'Members of the Bach Choir on Active Service', *Oxford Magazine*, February 1916

6 Quoted in Janet Hitchman, *Such a Strange Lady: An Introduction to Dorothy L. Sayers*, New English Library, 1975

7 Letter from Sayers to Muriel Jaeger, 8 March 1917

8 Letter from Sayers to her parents, 19 June 1917

9 Letter from Sayers to her parents, July 1917

10 *Catholic Tales and Christian Songs*, Basil Blackwell, 1918

11 Ibid.

12 Ibid.

13 Ibid.

14 Letter from Sayers to Muriel Jaeger, 2 October 1918

15 Letter from Sayers to Muriel Jaeger, 6 January 1919

16 James Brabazon, *Dorothy L. Sayers: The Life of a Courageous Woman*

17 *Cat o' Mary*

18 *Oxford Poetry*, 1919

19 Eric Whelpton, *The Making of a European*, Johnson

20 Ibid.

21 'Eros in Academe', *Oxford Outlook*, June 1919

22 *Oxford Poetry*, 1919

23 Letter from Sayers to her parents, 25 May 1919

24 Letter from Sayers to her parents, 6 June 1919

25 Letter from Sayers to Muriel Jaeger, 22 July 1919

26 Eric Whelpton, *The Making of a European*

27 Letter from Sayers to Leonard Green, 29 August 1919

28 Letter from Sayers to Ivy Shrimpton, 23 December 1919

29 Eric Whelpton, *The Making of a European*

30 Ibid.

31 Letter from Sayers to Muriel Jaeger, 8 March 1920

32 Letter from Sayers to her parents, 2 November 1919

33 Letter from Sayers to her parents, 23 November 1919

34 Letter from Sayers to her parents, 7 December 1919

35 Letter from Sayers to her parents, 27 February 1920

36 Letter from Sayers to her parents, 1 July 1921

CHAPTER FIVE

1 Vera Brittain, *Women at Oxford*, Harrap 1960

2 Letter from Sayers to her parents, February 1919

3 'Obsequies for Music', *London Mercury*, January 1921

4 'The Poem', *London Mercury*, October 1921

5 Letter from Sayers to her parents, 16 July 1921

6 Letter from Sayers to Ivy Shrimpton, 23 December 1921

7 Letter from Sayers to her parents, 24 November 1921

8 'How I Came to Invent the Character of Lord Peter', an article by Sayers in *Harcourt Brace News*, New York, 15 July 1936

9 Letter from Sayers to Dr James Welch, 5 November 1940

10 Letter from Sayers to John Cournos, 27 October 1924

11 John Cournos, *Autobiography*

12 Letter from Sayers to her parents, 8 November 1921

13 James Brabazon, *Dorothy L. Sayers: The Life of a Courageous Woman*

14 Letter from Sayers to her parents, 18 January 1922

15 Letter from Sayers to John Cournos, 4 December 1924

16 Letter from Sayers to John Cournos, 22 August 1924

17 Ibid.

18 Letter from Sayers to her mother, 18 December 1922

19 Ibid.

20 Letter from Sayers to her parents, November 1923

21 Letter from Sayers to Ivy Shrimpton, 23 February 1908

22 Letter from Sayers to Ivy Shrimpton, 1 January 1924

23 Letter from Sayers to Ivy Shrimpton, 16 January 1924

24 Letter from Sayers to Ivy Shrimpton, 27 January 1924

25 Ibid.

26 Letter from Sayers to Ivy Shrimpton, 6 February 1924

27 Letter from Sayers to Ivy Shrimpton, 2 May 1924

NOTES

28 Letter from Sayers to John Cournos, 22 August 1924

29 Letter from Sayers to John Cournos, 27 October 1924

30 Letter from Sayers to John Cournos, 4 December 1924

31 Letter from Sayers to John Cournos, 5 February 1925

32 Letter from Sayers to John Cournos, 22 February 1925

33 Letter from Sayers to John Cournos, January 1925

34 Letter from Sayers to John Cournos, 13 August 1925

35 Ibid.

36 Letter from Sayers to John Cournos, January 1925

37 'The Other Six Deadly Sins', an address delivered at Westminster, 23 October 1941 and later published in *Creed or Chaos*

38 Ibid.

39 Ibid.

40 Ibid.

41 'Forgiveness', *Unpopular Opinions*

42 Ibid.

43 Ibid.

44 Ibid.

45 Letter from Sayers to John Cournos, January 1925

46 'Strong Meat', *Creed or Chaos*

47 'The Triumph of Easter', *Creed or Chaos*

48 'Why Work?', an address delivered at Eastbourne, 23 April 1942, and later published in *Creed or Chaos*

49 Letter from Sayers to her mother, 14 April 1926

50 Letter from Sayers to Charles Williams, 18 October 1944

51 Lecture given by Sayers on 12 February 1936

CHAPTER SIX

1 *Murder Must Advertise*

2 'The Other Six Deadly Sins', *Creed or Chaos*

3 'The Psychology of Advertising', *The Spectator*, 19 November 1937

4 Ibid.

5 Letter from Sayers to Ivy Shrimpton, 13 May 1927

6 Dr Barbara Reynolds in discussion with the Rev. Patrick McLaughlin and Norah Lambourne on 'Dorothy L. Sayers As We Knew Her' at Canterbury, 3 August 1987, published by the Dorothy L. Sayers Society, March 1989

7 Letter from Sayers to the *Evening Standard*, 19 November 1928

8 Letter from Sayers to Ivy Shrimpton, 24 September 1928

9   Letter from Sayers to Ivy Shrimpton, 10 December 1928

10 The American critic Howard Haycraft

11 *Great Short Stories of Detection, Mystery and Horror*, Gollancz

12 *Behind the Screen*, a radio serial broadcast June/July 1930 and published in *The Listener*, 2 July 1930

13 Norah Lambourne

14 Howard Haycraft (ed.) *The Art of the Mystery Story*, Grosset & Dunlap, 1946

15 Ibid.

16 Ibid.

17 Herbert Brean (ed.) *The Mystery Writer's Handbook*, Harper 1956

18 Ibid.

19 'Eros in Academe', *Oxford Outlook*, June 1919

20 Q. D. Leavis, 'The Case of Miss Dorothy Sayers', *Scrutiny*, December 1937

21 Letter from Sayers to Peter Haddon, 1 November 1935

22 Alzina Stone Dale, 'Wimsey Lost and Found', *The Armchair Detective*, Spring 1990

23 'Dr Watson's Christian Name', *Unpopular Opinions*, Gollancz, 1946

24 'Aristotle on Detective Fiction', a lecture by Sayers at Oxford in 1935, and later published in *Unpopular Opinions*

25 Mary Ellen Chase, 'Five Literary Portraits', *Massachusetts Review*, Spring 1962

26 Ibid.

27 'Would You Like to be 21 Again?—I Wouldn't', the *Daily Express*, 9 February 1937

CHAPTER SEVEN

1   The *Church Times*, 8 April 1938

2   Ibid.

3   Ibid.

4   Ibid.

5   Ibid.

6   Ibid.

7   Ibid.

8   Letter from Sayers to her son, Anthony Fleming, 2 January 1940

9   Ibid.

10 The *Church Times*, 18 June 1937

11 Ibid.

12 The *British Weekly*

13 The *Church Times*, 18 June 1937

14 *Modern Languages, A Journal of Modern Studies*, October 1938

15 James Brabazon, *Dorothy L. Sayers: The Life of a Courageous Woman*

16 'The Greatest Drama Ever Staged is the Official Creed of Christendom', the *Sunday Times*, 3 April 1938

17 Ibid.

18 'The Dogma is the Drama', *St Martin's Review*, later published in *Creed or Chaos*

19 Letter from Sayers to Ivy Shrimpton, 18 May 1938

20 Letter from Sayers to *The Times*, 22 November 1938

21 *The Devil to Pay*, Gollancz, 1939

22 Ibid.

23 James Agate, the *Sunday Times*, 23 July 1939

24 'The Wimsey Papers XI', *The Spectator*, 16 January 1940

25 Letter from Sayers to Ivy Shrimpton, 21 August 1934

26 Letter from Sayers to Muriel St Clare Byrne, 23 November 1939

27 Letter from Sayers to 'Eileen Wincroft', 27 September 1939

28 The *Sunday Times*, 10 September 1939, later published in *Unpopular Opinions*

29 The *World Review*

30 The *World Review*, later published in *Unpopular Opinions*

31 *Begin Here*

32 Ibid.

33 Letter to Sayers from Sir Richard Acland, 4 April 1940

34 Letter to Sayers from Sir Richard Acland, 7 July 1942

35 Ibid.

36 Letter from Sayers to Sir Richard Acland, 9 July 1942

37 *Malvern 1941: The Life of the Church and the Order of Society*, Longmans

38 Ibid.

CHAPTER EIGHT

1 Letter from Sayers to Mr Lambert of the BBC

2 Letter from Sayers to the Archbishop of York, 24 November 1941, written after rejecting an invitation from the BBC to appear on 'The Brains Trust'

3 Sayers quoted in Janet Hitchman, *Such a Strange Lady: An Introduction to Dorothy L. Sayers*, New English Library, 1975

4 Letter from Sayers to the Rev. A. Handel Smith, 1 September 1943

5 Letter from Sayers to *Jack o' London's Weekly*, 7 April 1944

6 *The Mind of the Maker*

7 *The Zeal of Thy House*

8 *The Mind of the Maker*

9 *The Times Literary Supplement*, 9 August 1941

10 *The Mind of the Maker*

11 Ibid.

12 Statement of Aims for the proposed *Bridgehead* series of books

13 Letter from Dr James Welch to the Archbishop of Canterbury, William Temple, 18 June 1943

14 Letter from the Archbishop of Canterbury to Dr Welch, 21 June 1943

15 Letter to Sayers from the Archbishop, 4 September 1943

16 Letter from Sayers to the Archbishop, 7 September 1943

17 Letter to Sayers from the Archbishop, 15 September 1943

18 Letter to Sayers from the Archbishop, 22 September 1943

19 Letter from Sayers to the Archbishop, 24 September 1943

CHAPTER NINE

1 Letter from Sayers to Muriel St Clare Byrne, 2 March 1946

2 'Target Area', *The Fortnightly*, March 1944; *The Atlantic Monthly*, March 1944

3 Letter from Sayers to the Rev. G. H. Crosland, 18 May 1943

4 Letter from Sayers to the Rev. G. H. Crosland, 16 June 1943

5 Letter from Sayers to Miss Amy Davies, 26 November 1941

6 Letter from Sayers to Mrs Mary Stocks, 8 September 1947

7 Letter from Sayers to Captain H. L. Davies, 8 September 1948

8 'Why Work?', an address delivered at Eastbourne, 23 April 1942, later published in *Creed or Chaos*

9 'The Other Six Deadly Sins', an address delivered at Westminster, 23 October 1941, later published in *Creed or Chaos*

10 Letter from Sayers to General Sir Wyndham Deedes, 16 April 1943

11 Letter from Sayers to J. J. Lynx, 28 June 1943

12 Letter from Sayers to Messrs Lindsay Drummond, 5 July 1944

13 James Brabazon, *Dorothy L. Sayers: The Life of a Courageous Woman*

CHAPTER TEN

1 *New York Times Book Review*, 21 August 1949. The novel under review is *Many Dimensions*.

2 Letter from Sayers to Prof. G. L. Bickersteth, 12 June 1957

3 Charles Williams, *The Figure of Beatrice*, Faber and Faber, 1943

4 *Essays Presented to Charles Williams*, Oxford University Press, 1947

5 Letter from Sayers to Charles Williams, 16 August 1944

6 *Essays Presented to Charles Williams*, Oxford University Press, 1947

7 Ibid.

8   Ibid.

9   'Ignorance and Dissatisfaction', *Latin Teaching: The Journal of the Association for the Reform of Latin Teaching*, October 1952

10 Letter from Sayers to E. V. Rieu, 23 March 1945

11 Ralph E. Hone, *Dorothy L. Sayers: A Literary Biography*, The Kent State University Press, 1979

12 'Love was Dante's Salvation'

13 Ibid.

14 Ibid.

15 Letter from Sayers to Charles Williams, 31 August 1944

16 Letter from Sayers to Charles Williams, 26 September 1944

17 Letter from Sayers to Charles Williams, 31 August 1944

18 Ibid.

19 Letter from Sayers to Charles Williams, 26 September 1944

20 Letter from Sayers to Charles Williams, August 1944

21 Letter from Sayers to Charles Williams, 31 August 1944

22 Letter to Sayers from Victor Gollancz, quoting Charles Williams, 29 December 1933

23 Letter to Sayers from Charles Williams, 7 September 1944

24 Letter from Sayers to Charles Williams, 14 September 1944

25 Letter from Sayers to Margaret Douglas, 16 May 1945

26 Letter to Sayers from E. V. Rieu, 8 April 1945

27 Letter to Sayers from Dr Barbara Reynolds, 4 June 1949

28 Letter from Sayers to Norah Lambourne, 27 August 1946

29 Letter to Sayers from Dr Barbara Reynolds, 15 November 1949

30 Letter to Sayers from C. S. Lewis, 11 November 1949

31 Letter from Sayers to C. F. Fahy, 20 October 1950

32 From Sayers' introduction to her translation of *The Divine Comedy I: Hell*

33 Letter from Sayers to Charles Williams, 31 August 1944

CHAPTER ELEVEN

1   Letter from Sayers to the Rev. Patrick McLaughlin, 12 January 1941

2   The Rev. Patrick McLaughlin in discussion with Norah Lambourne and Dr Barbara Reynolds on 'Dorothy L. Sayers As We Knew Her', 3 August 1987, published by the Dorothy L. Sayers Society, March 1989

3   Ibid.

4   Ibid.

5   Letter from Sayers to the *Daily Sketch*, 5 March 1946

6   The *Daily Sketch*, 27 February 1946

7   Letter from Sayers to the *Daily Sketch*, 5 March 1946

8   Letter from Sayers to Canon A. Linwood Wright, 21 March 1946

9   Sayers' introduction to *The Just Vengeance*, Gollancz, 1946

10 *The Just Vengeance*

11 Letter from Sayers to Muriel St Clare Byrne, 2 March 1946

12 'My Belief about Heaven and Hell', the *Sunday Times*, 19 January 1957

13 Letter from Sayers to the *Daily Telegraph*, 1 May 1947

14 'Socialism Means Tyranny', the *Evening Standard*, 1944

15 Letter from Sayers to Dr James Welch, 31 March 1949

16 Letter from Sayers to Norah Lambourne, 26 April 1947

17 Letter to Sayers from Dr J. G. Benjamin, 11 May 1949

18 Letter from Sayers to Norah Lambourne, 20 July 1949

19 Letter from Sayers to Muriel St Clare Byrne, 12 June 1950

20 Letter from Sayers to Una Ellis-Fermor, 12 June 1950

21 Dr Barbara Reynolds in discussion with the Rev. Patrick McLaughlin and Norah Lambourne (see note 2)

22 The Rev. Patrick McLaughlin (see note 2)

23 Norah Lambourne (see note 2)

24 'The New Cosmology', BBC Radio, 26 September 1950

25 Letter from Sayers to Norah Lambourne, 14 May 1949

26 The *Church Times*, 6 July 1951

27 *Punch*, 2 November 1953

28 *Punch*, 13 January 1954

29 Letter from Sayers to Marshall & Snelgrove, 8 March 1954

30 Letter to Sayers from C. S. Lewis, 23 July 1946 *

31 Letter to Sayers from C. S. Lewis, 29 July 1946

32 Letter to Sayers from C. S. Lewis, 8 August 1946

33 Letter from Sayers to C. S. Lewis, August 1946

34 Letter to Sayers from C. S. Lewis, 7 August 1946

35 Letter from Sayers to C. S. Lewis, 8 August 1955

36 Letter to Sayers from C. S. Lewis, 5 August 1955

37 Letter from Sayers to C. S. Lewis, 8 August 1955

38 Ibid.

39 Letter from Sayers to C. S. Lewis, 21 December 1953

CHAPTER TWELVE

1   Kathleen Nott, *The Emperor's Clothes*, Heinemann, 1953; Indiana University Press, 1958

2   Ibid.

3   Letter from Sayers to John Wren-Lewis, 15 April 1954

4   Letter to Sayers from John Wren-Lewis, 20 April 1954

5   Letter to Sayers from John Wren-Lewis, 28 May 1954

6   Letter from Sayers to John Wren-Lewis, 18 June 1954

7   Sayers' speech at St Anne's House, Soho, 27 October 1954

8   Kathleen Nott writing in *Seven*, March 1982. *Seven* is an annual review published by Wheaton College, Illinois. Dr Barbara Reynolds is on its Editorial Board.

9   James Brabazon, *Dorothy L. Sayers: The Life of a Courageous Woman*

10 *Seven*, March 1982 (see note 8)

11 Ibid.

12 Letter from Sayers to John Wren-Lewis, 15 April 1954

13 *Seven*, March 1982

14 Ibid.

15 Ibid.

CHAPTER THIRTEEN

1   *Introductory Papers on Dante*, Methuen 1954, Harper 1955; *Further Papers on Dante*, Methuen 1957, Harper 1957

2   Letter from Sayers to E. V. Rieu, 24 August 1956

3   *Further Papers on Dante*, Methuen 1957, Harper 1957

4   *The Days of Christ's Coming*, Hamish Hamilton, 1953; *The Story of Adam and Christ*, Hamish Hamilton, 1955; *The Story of Noah's Ark*, Hamish Hamilton, 1956

5   The *Church Times*, 19 August 1955

6   The *Church Times*, 26 August 1955

7   Dr Barbara Reynolds in discussion with Norah Lambourne and the Rev. Patrick McLaughlin on 'Dorothy L. Sayers As We Knew Her' at Canterbury, 3 August 1987, published by the Dorothy L. Sayers Society, March 1989

8   Norah Lambourne (see note 7)

9   Janet Hitchman, *Such a Strange Lady: An Introduction to Dorothy L. Sayers*, New English Library, 1975

10 Anthony Fleming in his preface to James Brabazon's authorized biography

11 Letter from C. S. Lewis to Sayers' son, Anthony Fleming, 21 January 1958

Author's Acknowledgments

My principal acknowledgment goes to the Marion E. Wade Center in Wheaton College, Illinois, where I studied both published and unpublished letters and other writings of Dorothy L. Sayers. Without that access to such a wealth of material there would have been no book. Subsequently, the help and encouragement of the Center's Associate Director, Marjorie Lamp Mead, has been invaluable.

Another major acknowledgment goes to other works on Sayers, which provided a stimulus to investigate for myself this remarkable woman with 'a careless rage for life', and of course plentiful initial background information. I must mention James Brabazon's magisterial official biography, *Dorothy L. Sayers, The Life of a Courageous Woman*, Gollancz; Ralph E. Hone's *Dorothy L. Sayers, A Literary Biography*, The Kent State University Press, Kent, Ohio, which has always been a favourite with those who knew Sayers best; Janet Hitchman's *Such a Strange Lady*, New English Library; Barbara Reynolds' *The Passionate Intellect, Dorothy L. Sayers' Encounter with Dante*, The Kent State University Press; Catherine Kenney's *The Remarkable Case of Dorothy L. Sayers*, The Kent State University Press; and *Dorothy L. Sayers*, by Dawson Gaillard, Frederick Ungar Publishing Co, New York.

Further acknowledgments appear in no particular order, certainly not that of importance, but all have helped to make the biography possible:

The Dorothy L. Sayers Society, and in particular Mr Christopher Dean and Col. R.L. Clarke
Miss Norah Lambourne
Dr Barbara Reynolds
Messrs Victor Gollancz Ltd
Lambeth Palace Library
The Kent State University Press, Kent, Ohio

The *Church Times*
The BBC for permission to quote letters written by Dr
James Welch, Mr Derek McCulloch, Mr B.E. Nichols and
Miss May Jenkin
Penguin Books
Oxford University Press
Curtis Brown Group Ltd
The Rev. Aubrey Moody
Lord Runcie.

All extracts from the letters, articles and novels of Dorothy
L. Sayers appear by arrangement with David Higham Associ-
ates. Ms Kate Lyall Grant was unfailingly courteous and helpful
in her dealings with me.

Finally, two well-deserved acknowledgments. First, to my
editor, Pat Alexander of Lion Publishing, who has had to bear
broken promises too numerous to recall, and has somehow managed to do so with a smile. Secondly, to my wife, Anne. Used to
my long absences on BBC work, she has had to put up with
marriage to Sayers when I have been at home. Her encouragement has been unflagging, however, even to the point of typing
up most of the manuscript. It is to Anne that I dedicate the result.

Index